W9-AGV-139

Introduction to
Computational Linguistics

MATHEMATICAL LINGUISTICS
AND AUTOMATIC LANGUAGE PROCESSING

A Group of Monographs and Textbooks

General Editor: David G. Hays, The RAND Corporation

Already Published:

1. David G. Hays (Ed.)
   Readings in Automatic Language Processing, 1966

2. David G. Hays
   Introduction to Computational Linguistics, 1967

In Preparation:

Ferenc Kiefer
Mathematical Linguistics in Eastern Europe

Henry Kucera and George K. Monroe
A Comparative Quantitative Phonology of Russian, Czech, and German

Robert R. Freeman, Alfred Pietrzyk, and A. Hood Roberts (Eds.)
Information in the Language Sciences: Proceedings of the Conference held at Airlie House, March 4–6, 1966, under the Sponsorship of the Center for Applied Linguistics

Introduction to
Computational Linguistics

David G. Hays

The RAND *Corporation*

AMERICAN ELSEVIER PUBLISHING COMPANY, Inc.

NEW YORK

SOLE DISTRIBUTORS FOR THE CONTINENT OF EUROPE
ELSEVIER PUBLISHING COMPANY
335 Jan Van Galenstraat, P.O. Box 211
Amsterdam, The Netherlands

SOLE DISTRIBUTORS FOR GREAT BRITAIN
MACDONALD & CO. (PUBLISHERS) LTD.
Gulf House
2 Portman Street
London, W. 1

Library of Congress Catalog Card Number: 67-17936

PRINTED IN THE UNITED STATES OF AMERICA

PREFACE

Although the purpose of this book is primarily to serve as a basic text in university courses open to students who have no previous experience with computational linguistics, I hope that it may have other uses as well.

I have written the book with the needs of students in mind because I believe that many linguists must soon be trained, at all levels (scientists, engineers, and technicians), to prepare and carry out applications of the computer as a language processor. I believe that the time will soon come when linguists take the computer as much for granted as they do the typewriter and the tape recorder; when social scientists will rely on automatic language processing at least as much as on automatic statistical analysis: when educators will take the computer for granted as a tool of their trade; when the entire publishing industry, not merely the part of it that supports science and scholarship, will use it extensively. Only universities and colleges can provide the trained personnel that all these applications will require, and for that training they need *books*— and not just this one!

Outside of university courses, this book may be useful to linguists, computer specialists, and managers. Anyone who has not had previous contact with computers will probably find that for thorough comprehension he needs more practice in the beginning than he can get from working the problems in the book. He should consult some of the references listed at the end of Chap. 1. In a course, the instructor will want to have problems worked in the languages of the local computing center, and may run a laboratory as part of the course. With varying amounts of laboratory work, supplementary problems, and additional reading, this book can serve for either one or two semesters.

Computer specialists may find that the explanations of the problems their language-processing clients will be bringing are too brief, but perhaps they will find here an appreciation of the growing art of computational linguistics, a body of techniques that make the computer an effective, workable tool for language processing. There is more to numerical data processing than teaching the rudiments of

programming to mathematicians, and there is more to language processing than explaining the fundamentals of programming to linguists.

This book is written on several levels, and the levels are intermixed.
Some readers may want to disentangle them. Managers, who want to
understand the general ideas without being trapped by the details,
should be able to recognize the sections they want to read. Students
who must understand everything will quickly discover that some
passages can be read at once quickly with good comprehension, but that
other sections, in which storage schemes and algorithms are described,
can only be read with pencil in hand. In working through these sections,
the only technique that can succeed is to carry out a concrete example for
each algorithm; to lay out particular input, and to follow the algorithm
step by step as the computer would do, changing what is stored on paper
as the algorithm requires. The student who finds this process most
difficult is the one who has the most to gain by performing it, repeatedly
if necessary, until he understands exactly what happens when each
algorithm is put to work.

The logic of the book is to begin with the computer, then to proceed
from the linguistically most superficial, therefore most completely
studied and most easily understood, topics to those that have been
most refractory and remain most difficult to grasp. Only after the
elements have been treated are the fields of application examined. For
most readers, therefore, the topics of greater interest—those in which
research is needed, on the one hand, and those in which application is
profitable—come late in the book. A good instructor will make up for
this in his introductory lecture; the independent reader who is doubtful
about the book's utility for him can turn to the end of the volume and
examine the later chapters before attacking the beginning seriously.

In the early chapters, when I hope the reader is learning techniques
that are basic to all of computational linguistics, the illustrations are
concerned with details. To continue that strategy through discussions of
transformational grammar, research methods, and translation would
enlarge the book without adding proportionately to its value. There is
substance for many books in the design and testing of schemes for
linguistic research in which the computer plays a leading role; putting
efficient research systems together requires thoughtful, inventive
application of real expertise. The same can be said for other systems.
Nevertheless, the reader can understand what research schemes are
about by filling in the generalities of Chap. 11 with the details of Chaps.
1–7.

Several topics that could have been included are not. Phonology is
scanted, despite the need for computers to reduce the massive data

obtainable in a well instrumented laboratory; programmed control of articulatory mechanisms is a fascinating possibility. Historical and comparative studies, and the geography of dialects can use computers. Outside linguistics, there are applications worth extensive discussion in literary scholarship, history, psychology, sociology, anthropology, and folklore. The techniques and systems discussed in this book will, I think, be useful in those fields. To let one stand for all, psychological studies of interviews and personal documents should have at their disposal all the linguistic levels of a text; words carry emotional connotations, but so do their syntactic interconnections and the ideas they express. Give psychologists the systems described in Chap. 13, and they will use all the facilities provided. Psychology is not a branch of computational linguistics, but it should be a good customer.

The arrangement of references to the literature adopted for this book is not original, but perhaps not very common either. The references necessary to give credit for major contributions, plus those that I think are most likely to be helpful to the student, are collected at the end of each chapter. Some annotations accompany the references; the reader who goes from any problem in the text to the list of references should be able, through the annotations, to discover immediately whether any reference on the point has been listed.

I am grateful for this opportunity to acknowledge how much I have learned from colleagues at The RAND Corporation, especially Martin Kay and Theodore W. Ziehe; from Charles F. Hockett, Sydney M. Lamb, and Eugene D. Pendergraft; from Bernard Vauquois and his associates in the Centre d'Etudes pour la Traduction Automatique at Grenoble; from Yves Lecerf, André Leroy, and others in the Ispra research center of Euratom; and from many others who, like those I have named, have taught me more than I can reveal by referring to their publications. The help of those who have examined drafts of this book deserves mention; among them are students at California State College and the University of California, both in Los Angeles, and participants in a postdoctoral seminar, sponsored by the National Science Foundation, at RAND. Most of the typing was the work of Sally Belford, in whose energy and competence I have delighted.

DAVID G. HAYS

Santa Monica, California
November 1966

TABLE OF CONTENTS

2. The transformational model 210
    2.1. Syntactic translation 210
    2.2. Semantic translation. 213
3. The sememic model 214
4. Engineering 215
    4.1. General considerations 216
    4.2. Use of human operators. 218
    4.3. Linguistic engineering 219
References 221

List of computer instructions   223

Index   225

LIST OF FIGURES

Chapter I

COMPUTERS AND ALGORITHMS

The automatic digital computer is a machine for carrying out instructions. Of course a steam shovel also obeys instructions, but its repertory is limited. It is an effective mechanism for moving earth, but is ill-adapted to other purposes. Computers move no earth, and in fact any physical work they do is incidental to their processing of information. Since they are physical machines, they must perforce do some physical work, but good design requires that they do as little as possible. Computers work with representations of facts, ideas, or what have you; and they are demonstrably capable of carrying out any instruction whatsoever on these representations, no matter how complex, subject to limitations in principle concerning time and the amount of information to be stored during the job. Insofar as anything can be in this world, computers are perfect.

A complex instruction for information processing is called an algorithm. The purpose of the computer is to carry out algorithms; to make them efficacious and convenient, the nature of algorithms has been studied intensively. Each task given a computer has much in common with all the others. It is not necessary to decide in advance what algorithms will be carried out, and then build a computer with a special ability to do each one. Instead, each new algorithm is analyzed into smaller segments, components that have been carried out before. Ultimately, every algorithm is analyzed into *elementary* instructions, and the computer is built with a limited vocabulary of elementary instructions as its repertory. The modern computer was born when John von Neumann conceived the idea, late in the 1940's, of listing small tasks, giving each one a name, and building a machine that would be able to perform any algorithm because it could be shown that any algorithm could be composed of instruction tasks in its repertory.

Algorithms have a second characteristic of fundamental significance. They include conditional instructions. When the steam shovel is told to dig into a hillside, it does so with no ifs, ands, or buts. When the computer is told to add -*s* to the written form of an English word to make a plural, it can be instructed to do so if the word does not end with *-y*, *-x*, *-sh*, and so on; and in those cases to add *-es*, change *-y* to *-i* and add *-es*, and so on. These conditional instructions make it possible for a single algorithm to apply to an indefinitely large number of cases, cases the computer user may not have foreseen in detail, and cases where circumstances may vary considerably. Without conditional instructions, computers would not be universal machines.

The third essential ingredient of computing as it exists today is the treatment of programs as if they were data. Computers can store and process algorithms, just as they can store and process numbers. These three ingredients—a vocabulary of elementary instructions, conditional instructions, and homogeneity of instructions and data—were invented all at once; together they make the computer a useful, even a fascinating, device.

I. STORAGE

When information is stored outside the brain of an animal, it is usually by putting something somewhere. The commonest storage medium in human affairs is paper, and the stuff commonly applied to it is ink or a near relative. On a Chinese checkerboard, information is stored by putting marbles into cup-shaped depressions. Cribbage players keep track of their scores by moving pegs down a sequence of holes drilled in a board.

These different ways of storing information have in common two aspects: an array of positions, and an alphabet of markers. How much work is done by each can vary. The cribbage players have each one peg, and a large number of holes to equal the different scores they can obtain. On a blank sheet of paper, the positions are scarcely defined, and nearly all of the work is done by the alphabet. Computers make about the same division of labor as crossword puzzles or bookkeeper's worksheets do. In a crossword puzzle, there is a very definitely planned arrangement of positions, each allowed to receive exactly one letter of a fixed alphabet. Likewise, the bookkeeper's worksheet, ruled off into rows and columns, is convenient since it provides fixed places for numbers to be written.

But storage is of no help in computing unless it is active. A computer works by examining the information it has stored, carrying out an instruction, and storing new information as a result. When a man does a calculation, he may use pencil and paper, but the information processing goes on inside his head. However much he may write down, it is the representation of the numbers in his brain that he manipulates. Computers are possible only because active storage media were found.

There is nothing mysterious about active storage. A simple relay will illustrate the principle. A latching relay consists of two coils, an armature, and two springs (see Fig. 1). The armature is attracted to

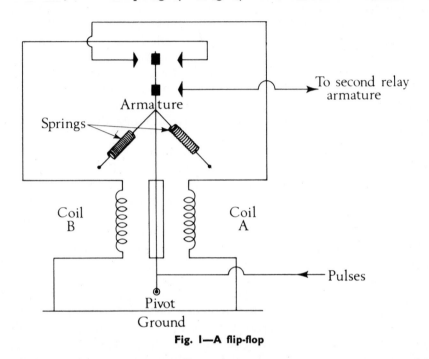

Fig. 1—A flip-flop

either coil when a current passes through. When no current is passing through either coil, the springs hold the armature in position; without the springs, the armature might lie halfway between its two end positions. When current passes through coil A, the armature is pulled over to the right and electrical circuits are completed on that side; when it moves to side B, different circuits are connected. Now suppose the circuits on the armature are connected with those energizing the coils in such a way that if the armature is on side A the current passes through coil B, but if the armature is on side B, the energizing current passes through coil A. Given a source of short pulses of current, say once every second, the armature will flip from side to side, and will be on one side after an even number of pulses, on the other side after an odd number. This is not much computing, but with another relay we can do more. Let the pulse go through the armature circuit to another relay, exactly like the first, if the armature of the first relay is on side A, and not otherwise. Now the second relay will be on one side after a number of pulses divisible by four, on the other side after a number not divisible by four.

Starting with both armatures in position B, we can count the first three pulses in this way: After the first pulse the first armature will move to side A, so the configuration of the two armatures is AB; after two pulses, the first relay will flip back to side B, and the second will move to side A. The third pulse moves the first relay to side A, and the second relay stays on side A. The fourth pulse would return both relays to side B, leaving them in the same condition as if no pulses had been received. If we wish to count up to seven pulses, we can do so by adding a third relay to the system, wired to receive a pulse only when both of the first two relays are on side A.

Each of the relays is a device called a flip-flop; each is capable of storing one bit of information. We can count only odd-even with one bit; we can count up to three with two bits; and in general we can count up to $2^N - 1$ with N relays. In electronic computers, tubes, transistors, or ferrite cores serve as flip-flops. The details need not concern us, but the abstract principle is important.

The principle is not that flip-flops can be used for counting, but that physical devices can be made to react in such a way that information is stored and available when needed. Since the armatures of relays can carry as many circuits as desired, we can use one group of circuits to establish a count and another to sense what it is. Furthermore, with additional wiring, we can arrange to reset the entire counter to its null or 0 condition whenever we please. In general, a system of N flip-flops can be made to take on 2^N different configurations, and each configuration can mean whatever we like.

For example, each configuration of an array of flip-flops can be taken to correspond to a letter of some alphabet. The number of letters in the alphabet is important only because it determines how many flip-flops there shall be. For example, the Roman alphabet has 26 letters. Five flip-flops are enough, since $2^5 = 32$, which is larger than 26. We can assign 26 different configurations, among the 32 possible with five flip-flops, to correspond to the letters of the Roman alphabet, and our digital computer is capable of storing the graphic forms of words.

Talking about flip-flops is cumbersome. We are interested in information, not in electronic design. Let us speak of bits hereafter, one bit being the amount of information a flip-flop can store. We need two symbols to correspond to the two states of a flip-flop; we use 0 and 1. Historically, *bit* is derived from *binary digit*, and the binary digits are indeed 0 and 1. But we are not necessarily referring to number systems and their properties when we speak of bits. Storage in a digital computer generally consists of scores or hundreds of thousands of positions in each of which one bit, either a 0 or a 1, can be stored. If we think of the stored information as numerical, we can do arithmetic with binary numbers. If we think of the stored information as logical, we can consider the 1 state to represent truth and the 0 falsehood. But if we are thinking about language processing, we can take configurations of bits to represent characters from an alphabet, and disregard both logic and arithmetic.

2. PROGRAMS

The instruction that gets a job done does not always specify a procedure for doing it. If a bilingual person is nearby, I may say "Translate this book from Russian into English" and get the effect I want. The instruction is effective under the circumstances, but nothing about the instruction will be of any help if it falls to my lot to produce translators, either human or mechanical. Furthermore, I may be able to specify what I want with great precision, and yet not be able to issue detailed instructions for getting the answer. There is a difference between being able to recognize an answer when one is offered and having a program for getting a solution given the problem. In general, a complicated machine can take a short instruction, whereas a simple machine requires a complicated instruction of the kind we call a program. The complex machine embodies its own programs.

Computers are simple machines. Their instruction repertories are small, and it sometimes requires great ingenuity to discover a sequence of computer instructions that will perform a given job. Let us see what it means for a computer to have the capacity to carry out an instruction, beginning with a simple example.

2.1. Access to stored information

Most of the storage available in a computer is divided into cells. A cell is a sequence of bits, say 36. Most cells are capable of just two operations: assuming a configuration and reporting what it is. Furthermore, there is typically just one cell available for transfers of information to or from all the rest. Let us call this the working register. The machine can carry out two instructions:

Store. When this instruction is performed, the first bit of the working register is used to control the first bit of a storage cell, the second bit to control the second, and so on up to the 36th. To perform this operation,

36 connections must be made and 36 energizing currents either transmitted or not. Each current is transmitted if a certain position of the
main register contains a 1, and causes the corresponding position of
the storage cell to become a 1. The current does not pass if the working
register contains a 0, and the corresponding position of the storage cell
becomes or remains 0 in that case. To obtain the right result, the
machine must be designed so that the storage cell is set to 0 before the
transfer occurs, or becomes 0 during the transfer if the current does not
pass.

Set working register. This operation goes in the opposite direction,
setting each bit position of the working register according to the
contents of the corresponding position of a storage cell.

A computer may have only one working register, but it generally
has thousands of storage cells. In addition to the name of an operation,
either *store* or *set working register,* an instruction must indicate which
storage cell is to be used. Thus an instruction contains at least two
names, one for the operation and one for the operand, and the name
of the operand determines which 36-bit storage cell will be connected
with the working register. Typically, the 36 connections are made
simultaneously.

2.2. Conditional transfer

Another simple operation is the comparison of two configurations.
For example, we might wish to decide which of two words comes
earlier in alphabetical order. For the sake of simplifying this operation—and it will be a common one—we must associate configurations
with letters of the alphabet in a sensible way. A bit is either 0 or 1;
let 0 be associated with coming earlier, and 1 with coming later. We
use six bits to represent a letter; make the first bit 0 for the first half of
the alphabet, and 1 for the latter half. Among the letters with first bit
0, make the second bit 0 for the first half of the letters, and 1 for the
rest, and similarly for letters in the second half of the alphabet. Now
the alphabet is quartered, with 00 in the first two bits indicating the
first quarter, 01 the second, 10 the third and 11 the fourth. We will
have a little freedom at the end, if we continue this process, since there
are only 26 letters but 64 configurations. Since we have a good many
other characters to represent, aside from letters of the alphabet, we
may as well use one bit to distinguish letters from the rest. Say we put
a 0 there for letters, and 1 for everything else. We assign the configuration with six 0's to serve as a blank. Now we can make the comparison.

Compare. When this instruction is performed, the first bit of the working register is compared with the first bit of a storage cell. If they are identical, the comparison moves to the next position. If they are different, then the configuration in the working register is reported earlier in the alphabet, or numerically smaller, if it contains a 0 (the configuration in the storage cell contains a 1 in that position), and later in the alphabet (numerically larger) if the working register contains a 1. If the comparison reaches the 36th position, without finding a difference anywhere, then the configuration in the working register is reported identical to that in the storage cell.

The result of the comparison is one of three conditions, which must be reported. There are many ways to report a result like this, but the most important, and the most remarkable in view of its value in programming, is by modifying the order in which parts of the program are carried out.

Normally, a program is a sequence of instructions for small operations that are to be performed one after another. When a comparison is performed, the result of the comparison determines what instruction will be carried out next. In case of identity, the next instruction in the program will be performed. If the number in the working register is larger than the one in storage, the next instruction performed is determined by an operand of the compare instruction; likewise, if the number in the working register is smaller than the one in storage, another operand specifies what instruction must be carried out next. For instructions like this to work, it must be possible to name instructions in the same way storage cells are named. But we have already asserted that programs and data are treated in the same way in computer storage. When the program is fed into the computer and performed, the instructions will be in storage, and the names of instructions will be the names of the cells in which they are stored.

2.3. Abbreviations

For convenience, we need a simple notation for instructions. Let us do it this way:

STORE(A)

This is the instruction to store the contents of the working register in cell A.

SWR(A)

This instruction sets the working register to the contents of cell A.

TRANS(A, B, C)

This instruction transfers control to place B in the algorithm if the word stored in cell A is smaller than the word stored in the working register, to location C if the stored word is larger than the word in the working register, and to the next instruction in the algorithm in case of identity.

Some of the elements of instructions refer to places in machine storage. It very often happens that the algorithm must be applied over and over to material at different places in storage. For example, to find the alphabetically earliest word in a list would require making a sequence of comparisons, starting with a word in a certain place and going down a list. Computers always have facilities for iteration, and we will assume one that allows us to name the first cell in a sequence of cells, say A, and then count downward from there. Let I be the name of a cell; then A(I) means the cell that can be found by starting at location A and counting down as many cells as the number stored in I. If cell I contains 0, A(I) means A itself.

With these few types of instructions, and one or two others that can be introduced as we go along, we can see by an example how a program is organized.

2.4. A sort program

One of the commonest jobs in linguistic computation is arrangement in alphabetic order. Sorting jobs come in all sizes, giving the computer up to several hours' work. When the amount of material to be arranged is large, it cannot be placed in storage all at once and we are not yet ready to see how input and output are handled. If the amount is small, it can be arranged in alphabetical order by means of a simple program.

The reader who has no previous experience with computer programming may require a word of caution at this point. Before reading the rest of the section, he may want to work some of the examples at the end of this chapter. Then, taking pencil and paper, he will lay out storage as it might be before the sort program is applied, and work through the program, instruction by instruction, as it is explained in the text. The reader with programming experience will know just how much of this he has to do; the novice is best advised to do far more of it than he imagines could be needed, until experience proves that he can understand how a new program works with only a modest effort.

We assume that one word form is stored in each cell and that the comparison described in the preceding section will give correct results.

Our plan is to go through a list of words, looking at each pair in turn. If they are out of order, we will interchange them. When we come to the end of the list, if we have made no interchanges, the words are in alphabetical order. But if we made any changes we may yet need to make more, and must start over again. We assume that the word forms are stored in cells F + 1, F + 2, . . . , F + N. Initially, cell I contains 1, cell J contains 2, a cell that will be called *One* contains 1 also, a cell named *Zero* contains 0, and cell *N* contains N. Cells I and J are used as index registers, marking the place in the list where work is being done.

The sort program is presented in Fig. 2. Each line in the figure contains one instruction. The lines are numbered for convenient

Location	Instruction	Comment
1. Sort:	SWR(F(I))	Compare forms in F + I, F + I + 1
2.	TRANS(F(J), Swap, X)	
3. X:	SWR(J)	Compare J = I + 1, N
4.	TRANS(N, Z, Y)	
5. Z:	SWR(Q)	Is Q set?
6.	TRANS(One, Stop, Stop)	
7.	SWR(Zero)	Set I to 1, J to 2, Q to 0
8.	STORE(Q)	
9.	ADD(One)	
10.	STORE(I)	
11.	ADD(One)	
12.	STORE(J)	
13.	GOTO(Sort)	
14. Y:	STORE(I)	Increase I and J by 1
15.	ADD(One)	
16.	STORE(J)	
17.	GOTO(Sort)	
18. Swap:	STORE(T)	Swap the forms in F + I, F + I + 1
19.	SWR(F(J))	
20.	STORE(F(I))	
21.	SWR(T)	
22.	STORE(F(J))	
23.	SWR(One)	Set Q to 1
24.	STORE(Q)	
25.	GOTO(X)	

Fig. 2—A sort program

reference, but the numbers are not used for transfers in the program. Instead, the symbols *Sort*, *Swap*, X, Y, and Z are used. They refer respectively to lines 1, 18, 3, 14, and 5 (see the figure). Following some of the instructions, there are comments. These are customary, for the sake of those who must read programs, but they have no formal status.

Entering the program at line 1, we are to compare the forms stored in cells F + I and F + I + I. Since I contains 1, these are the first two forms in the original list. The content of the first cell is moved to the working register and a conditional transfer is made to location *Swap* if the word in F(J) is earlier in alphabetical order, or to location X, line 3 otherwise.

But the otherwise in this case means that the two forms being compared are in alphabetical order. We need not interchange them, and so we test whether the end of the list has been reached. The content of cell J is moved to the working register and a conditional transfer is made to location Z if the content of cell J is greater than or equal to the content of cell *N*. As we shall see, the effect of going to location Z is to restart the procedure, hence values of J greater than N will never be considered—the change will be made when J equals N. Transfer is made to location Y if the content of cell N is greater than the content of cell J.

At location Y, line 14 of the program, the values of I and J are both increased by 1. Note that the content of cell J is identical with the content of the working register as we begin this procedure, and one larger than the current content of cell I. By storing that number in cell I, we increase the content of cell I by 1. Now we must add 1 to the content of the working register, using a new instruction:

$$\text{ADD(A)}$$

The effect of this instruction is to increase the numerical value of the content of the working register by the content of the cell identified as A. This is simple arithmetic. Since we assume that cell *One* contains a 1, the instruction on line 15 gives us the new value we need to store in cell J. Again we need a new instruction:

$$\text{GOTO(A)}$$

This is an unconditional transfer. The next line of our program cannot be reached in the usual way through this instruction. On line 13 of Fig. 2, the instruction GOTO(Sort) leads us back to line 1, and we go to work with a new pair of word forms.

At location Z, line 5, we do what is necessary when all adjacent pairs of word forms in our list have been examined. If we went all the way through without setting Q, our job is done. The transfer in line 6 stops the procedure for us. But if Q has been set to 1, we go on to set the content of cell I equal to 1, the content of cell J to 2, and to unset that Q by storing 0 in it. We end this part of the program by going back to line 1 and beginning at the top of our list.

On line 18, location *Swap*, we are doing the real work of the sort program. We have found two adjacent word forms out of alphabetical order; the second should precede the first. One of them has been copied into the working register, and we store it in some cell T, to avoid losing it. Next we store the content of cell F(J) in the working register, in order to move it up to cell F(I). Lines 21 and 22 move the content of T into cell F(J). Line 23 sets Q to 1, so that we will know something has been done during this pass through the list of word forms. Finally, we go to X, line 3 of Fig. 2, and test whether the pair of word forms just exchanged were the last two in the list.

This sort program is in fact used in practice occasionally. But examination of Fig. 2 is likely to suggest to the novice that most instructions in a program like this one contribute only indirectly to the work intended. Instructions are being used to keep the index registers I and J in step, to set and test Q, and so on. These housekeeping tasks may be necessary, but a notation that took them for granted would be welcome. In the next section, we see how an algorithmic language simplifies the programmer's job by hiding the housekeeping.

3. ALGORITHMS

A computer is a collection of hardware; every instruction in its order code, such as SWR(A), causes some part of the hardware to operate. A large computer has more hardware than a small one. If we are to write an instruction in a program, it must be executed somehow, but there is no rule that it must be executed directly by hardware; it can instead be executed by another program. This very important realization led to the development of instructions much larger and more grandiose than those in any real computer.

Hardware necessarily costs money. Heretofore it has not been economical to include hardware for instructions unless most users of the computer would call for their execution fairly often. Instructions that are needed less often can be provided in software.

3.1. Compiling

Suppose, for example, that we often need to sort short lists, each list always consisting of one-cell entries, always in the same alphabet. Then we would like to have an instruction SORT(A, B), which would cause the machine to put into lexicographic order the B cells starting at cell A. But other users of the same machine would rarely call on that instruction, and so the hardware would be wasted. Instead of putting the operation into the machine, let us put it into a library; before or during the execution of our program, the computer has some way of consulting the library and replacing the single instruction with a sequence of instructions, perhaps the sequence shown in Fig. 2. Henceforth, we can write a program using the instruction SORT as if it were executed by the hardware of our computer.

This facility is useful, and so are many others. For example, the program in Fig. 2 represents the cells in the machine by names, not by numbers. When the program is actually executed, numbers must be available. Furthermore, the multiletter designations we use for instructions must be replaced by something more compact, since it would be wasteful of machine memory to store three to five letters to designate an instruction when six to ten bits would be enough.

For these and other reasons, almost every program is interpreted, compiled, or translated by another program which converts it into an expanded, compressed, and specified version. Compilers work before execution, interpreters work at the time of execution; this difference is important, but not for our immediate purposes. What we need to see now is that if we make all we can of the fact that our program is to be compiled, we can define a felicitous and parsimonious language for the writing of programs or algorithms. We must pay a cost; our programs will take more time to execute because the compiler is less capable than a highly skilled programmer of adapting the quirks of the machine to the necessities of our task. What is lost in execution time will probably be made up for manyfold by savings in programming time.

One system of this kind is called Algol. It is used very widely in Europe, and at many American computing centers; it is the only notation permitted for the publication of algorithms in the *Journal* and *Communications* of the Association for Computing Machinery. The reader who wants to use Algol should study one of the books devoted to it, and also acquaint himself with any special features or restrictions used in the computing center where his program will be run. Beginning in Sec. 3.2, we treat some features of the language, but some of its essential characteristics are not discussed at all in this book.

3.2. Iteration

One of the common problems facing a programmer is to perform the same operation repeatedly on all the items in a list or other array. We sorted a list of words by comparing each item in the list with the one following it; whenever the adjacent items were found to be out of order, we interchanged them. A simple way of going through a sequence of data will be a great advantage.

Let us give the array a name; for example, F. We designate a single element in the array by F[i]. Now we want to write an instruction calling for a certain operation to be performed on all of the F[i].

One way to do it is with a statement having two parts. The first part tells where the operation is to be performed, the second tells what is to be done. We mark these two parts by writing **for** ... **do** ... In the first part of the statement we can write something like:

for i := 1 **step** 1 **until** N − 1 **do** ...

which says that values of i beginning with 1, by steps of 1, are to be taken until i has the value N − 1. We stop one short of the last item in the array because—in the sort program—we are comparing each item with the one following. We could go by other steps if necessary, begin at another place, and end where we please. The equal sign is prefixed with a colon in order to make it clear that we want the i to take on the indicated values, not to find an i in storage which already has a certain value. Following the word **do** we will insert an instruction.

3.3. Conditional statements

In the sort program, we want to carry out an interchange only where necessary. In many other instances, we need conditional statements. A simple version of the conditional is **if** ... **then** ... In the **if**-clause, we want to state a condition; for example, a relation:

if F[i] > F[i + 1] **then** ...

Here we are referring to the items stored as the i-th and (i + 1)-th components of the array F.

Sometimes when the condition is unsatisfied we want to do nothing; at other times we may have something specific in mind that must be done when the condition fails. Hence we need a slightly more complex version of the conditional: **if** ... **then** ... **else** .... For example, if SORT marks the beginning of the program that runs through F, and OUT is the location to which control passes when the sort is completed, we can write:

if Q = 1 **then goto** SORT **else goto** OUT

This instruction decides whether another pass through the array is needed or the sort is complete.

3.4. Nested programs

In Algol, a program consists of statements. An **if**-statement or a **for**-statement has a conditioning part and a conditioned part saying what is to be done. However, it may take more than one statement to express that. For example, interchanging two elements of an array requires several operations.

We can form a composite statement by writing **begin** at the beginning and **end** at the end. The individual statements between these markers are separated by semicolons:

$$
\begin{array}{ll}
\textbf{begin} & X := F[i]; \\
& F[i] := F[i + 1]; \\
& F[i + 1] := X; \\
& Q := 1 \\
\textbf{end};
\end{array}
$$

The four elementary statements carry out an interchange by setting some arbitrary X to have the value of the i-th item in the array, then assigning the value of the $(i + 1)$-th item to the i-th component of the array, then assigning the value of X to the $(i + 1)$-th component. Note that each equal sign is preceded by a colon, showing that it is an assignment of a new value.

3.5. The sort program in Algol

The algorithm for sorting realized by a computer program in Fig. 2 is restated in Algol in Fig. 3. It is shorter than before, but that is probably not the main point. Because the notational system is more

$$
\begin{array}{ll}
\text{Sort:} & Q := 0; \\
& \textbf{for } i := 1 \textbf{ step } 1 \textbf{ until } N - 1 \textbf{ do} \\
& \quad \textbf{if } F[i] > F[i + 1] \textbf{ then} \\
& \quad \textbf{begin} \quad X := F[i]; \\
& \qquad\qquad F[i] := F[i + 1]; \\
& \qquad\qquad F[i + 1] := X; \\
& \qquad\qquad Q := 1 \\
& \quad \textbf{end}; \\
& \textbf{if } Q = 1 \textbf{ then goto } \text{Sort} \textbf{ else goto } \text{Out}
\end{array}
$$

Fig. 3—An Algol sort algorithm

powerful, the program needs less description. Comments in such a simple program would be useless. In fact, it may be superfluous to comment even on this introduction to Algol programming. Nevertheless, at the risk of superfluity, let us note that the program first sets the control variable Q to its inactive value 0, then, beginning with the word **for**, runs through the array. At each place in the array, one entry is compared with its following neighbor. If necessary, they are interchanged, and if an interchange is performed Q is set to its active value. The statement beginning with the word **for** closes with the word **end** and a semicolon; then, in a final statement, a new start is made if necessary.

EXERCISES

1. Draw a counter with three flip-flops, as it would be after receiving three pulses; what will the fourth pulse do, and how?

Write the following programs in computer instructions.

2. Find the first occurrence of a word in a sequence. The word to be found is stored as the content of *Word;* the sequence is in S + 1, S + 2, . . . , S + N.

3. Copy a sequence of words in reverse order; they are stored in S + 1, . . . , S + N. Put the last in T + 1, the first in T + N.

4. Delete all occurrences of a word from a sequence, moving the rest of the sequence up. The original length of the sequence is stored in N; put the final length in N(*One*).

5. Count the occurrences of a word in a sequence.

6. Delete all occurrences but one of every word in a sequence.

Use Algol for the following problems.

7. Alter the sort program (Fig. 3) so that it puts the first N components of an array into order, then the first N + 1, beginning with N = 2 and continuing until the whole array is in order. (Note: **for** i : = A **step** − 1 **until** B is allowed.)

8. Take two arrays, S and T, of n and m components respectively, and concatenate them by assigning the values of the components of S to the first n components of U and those of T to the remaining m components of U.

REFERENCES

Readings in Automatic Language Processing (David G. Hays, ed.; American Elsevier Publishing Company, Inc., New York, 1966) is intended for the same audience as the present *Introduction*. References to it will have the form of the one following.

"Specification Languages for Mechanical Languages and their Processors—A Baker's Dozen" (Saul Gorn; *Communications of the Association for Computing Machinery,* Vol. 4, No. 12, December 1961, pp. 532–542; *also* RALP pp. 9–32) explains, somewhat technically, some ways of describing computers and languages.

Natural Language and the Computer (Paul L. Garvin, ed., McGraw-Hill Book Co., New York, 1963) covers much of the field treated here, but from a different point of view.

Thinking Machines (Irving Adler; Signet, New York, 1961) is inexpensive and easy to read.

A Primer of Algol-60 Programming (E. W. Dijkstra; Academic Press, 1960) is widely used and not difficult.

Algorithms and Automatic Computing Machines (B. A. Trakhtenbrot; D. C. Heath, Boston, 1963) takes a more theoretical approach to explanation of computing, but leads the reader carefully step by step.

The Use of Computers in Anthropology (Dell Hymes, ed., Mouton and Co., The Hague, 1965) covers a much wider area than the present volume, but includes several papers on linguistics.

Scientific American devoted all of its issue for September 1966 to "Information", many of the articles published there are useful to a student beginning to study computer applications.

Computational Linguistics: Bibliography, 1964 (David G. Hays and Roxana Ma, RM-4523-PR, The RAND Corporation, March 1965) and *1965* (David G. Hays, Bozena Henisz-Dostert, and Marjorie L. Rapp, RM-4986-PR, April 1966) cover much of the literature for those years.

Computer Literature Bibliography 1946 to 1963 (W. W. Youden; Miscellaneous Publication 266, National Bureau of Standards, March 1965) is another useful source.

Chapter 2

STORAGE STRUCTURES

A list of word forms, each occupying one cell of machine storage, and those cells located consecutively, is easy to deal with. With some index registers, an algorithm can move forward and back through the list, in a way that is convenient for many simple purposes. But linguists have to deal with more complicated materials, and deserve better tools than simple index registers for keeping track of them.

I. STORAGE PROBLEMS

In real life, even a list of word forms needs variable length storage. The commonest word forms in many languages are short, having representations from 1 to 5 or 6 characters in length. But there are also much longer word forms, with representations as long as 20 or even 30 characters. If every word form were stored in a cell or sequence of cells long enough to store the longest, a large part of storage would be wasted. Computer memories grow larger from year to year, but linguists are capable of finding uses for large stores without using tricks like fixed-length cells. For many applications, a good scheme is one that allows a small space for a short word and a long space for a long one. Since it is not likely to be convenient to select the short items in one list and the long ones in another, but rather preferable to intermingle them in some fashion, what is needed is a technique for deciding where the part of storage allocated to one word form ends and the next begins.

We have been dealing with only one relation among stored units; the relation was expressed by the order of the cells in storage. We saw how word forms stored in arbitrary order could be rearranged into alphabetical order, but often several relationships among stored units need to be expressed simultaneously. For example:

In a *dictionary*, the entry words are related to one another by alphabetical order. For each entry word there may be several grammatical descriptions, all related to it in the same way, that is, as grammatical interpretations. Several definitions, semantical interpretations, or translations may be associated with each word also. The definitions of the word may be associated with different grammatical interpretations, or independent of them.

Text might seem simple, but can equally well be made to seem complicated. For example, some linguists choose to deal with interlinear translations, where two texts—each composed of words strung one after the other—are correlated, word by word or sentence by sentence, as original and translation. Or perhaps the secondary text is not a translation but a key to metrical structure, a grammatical analysis, an etymological commentary, or what have you.

A very simple example is the *paradigm*. The paradigm of a Latin noun is typically presented in two columns, one for singular and one for plural, with let us say six rows, one for each case. An entry in the first column is related to preceding and following case entries in the same column, and to the plural—second column—entry for the same case. This is an example of a two-dimensional array; to understand what a three-dimensional array is, imagine the declension of an adjective with different forms for (1) singular and plural, (2) the different cases, and (3) two or three genders.

We shall see many examples of *trees* in linguistic computation, but a strikingly simple example comes from library classification. To find a book, in principle, we first decide which major category it belongs to; there may be ten or 100 of these. Next we look at the secondary divisions of our chosen main subject, and choose one of them. Then we go on to a third level of classification, a fourth, and so on. If we say that we choose a category of rank one, then another of rank two, and so on, then the relationship among subject categories is simply that every category of rank n is a subcategory of one of rank n − 1.

These are some of the applications we will need to deal with; in this chapter we examine a few storage structures that facilitate the processing of such complex materials in high-speed storage. In the next chapter, we turn to external storage.

2. VARIABLE LENGTH STORAGE

In our hypothetical computer, every storage cell has 36 bit positions. We are using 6 bits for each character, hence we can store a word form of from 1 to 6 characters in each cell. Let us now undertake to deal with word forms of greater length.

2.1. Boundary markers

If two or more consecutive storage cells are sometimes used for a single word form, we must somehow be able to recognize the end of a word form. We can do this by using one extra cell, in which we set every bit to 1. Let us represent a cell filled with 1's by ######. The word *prestidigitation*, stored this way, would look like this:

$$
\begin{array}{l}
\text{P R E S T I} \\
\text{D I G I T A} \\
\text{T I O N} \\
\text{\# \# \# \# \# \#}
\end{array}
$$

Special routines will now be needed to work on a list of word forms stored in this way. For reasons explained in Sec. 2.3, linguists using the computer can generally avoid writing these special routines for themselves. Nevertheless, some examples are given here and in Sec. 2.2; by working through them, the reader can learn how variable-length storage is managed in machines with fixed cell size, and dispel more of the magical aura surrounding the computer.

In Fig. 2, lines 1 and 2 test whether the word forms stored in F(I) and F(J) are in alphabetical order. If the word forms can occupy more than one cell each, the test must continue cell by cell until it reaches a boundary marker. The program in Fig. 4 assumes that cells I and J

Location	Instruction	Comment
1.	SWR(I)	Copy I, J
2.	STORE(U)	
3.	SWR(J)	
4.	STORE(V)	
5. Test:	SWR(F(U))	Compare forms beginning
6.	TRANS(F(V), Swap, Seek)	at F + I, F + J
7.	TRANS(Bnd, Step, Step)	Is this a boundary?
8.	GOTO(Endtest)	Yes
9. Step:	SWR(U)	Continue comparison of
10.	ADD(One)	same forms
11.	STORE(U)	
12.	SWR(V)	
13.	ADD(One)	
14.	STORE(V)	
15.	GOTO(Test)	

Fig. 4—A comparison program with boundary markers

index the initial cells of two consecutive entries. Those locations will be needed later; if the two words must be swapped, the exchange procedure must begin with F(I) and F(J), and if no swap is needed the next comparison will match the entry that started in F(J) with another entry whose initial cell must be found.

To protect the contents of I and J, we copy their contents into cells U and V. Starting at line 5, we put the first cell of one entry into the working register and perform a conditional transfer. If the earlier entry in the list has a first cell that precedes the first cell of the later entry in alphabetical order, no further comparison is needed; at location *Seek*, the program will find the boundary cell marking the end of the second entry and proceed to a new comparison. If the high-order cells of the two entries show a reversal, control transfers to *Swap* where an exchange is performed. In the case of equality, either the program has found boundary cells and the two entries are identical, or else the comparison must continue to the next cells of the two entries in order to obtain a definitive result. On line 7, a conditional transfer is made; cell Bnd contains the boundary marker for the comparison. If equality is found, control transfers unconditionally to *Endtest*, corresponding to location X in Fig. 2, a test to determine whether the end of the list has been reached. On line 9, location *Step*, the index registers U and V are advanced and control returns to line 5.

Using a 36-bit cell as a boundary marker is wasteful. Most computers have some way of dividing full cells into subparts, and we will introduce some instructions that illustrate how this can be done.

For simple procedures, all we need do is add instructions that will store one character in a cell and set the working register with one selected character from a cell. We define them in this way:

STORE(A/I). This instruction causes the character stored in the righthand 6 bits of the working register to be transferred to the I-th 6-bit segment of cell A. The content of I can be 1, 2, 3, 4, 5, or 6. The remainder of cell A is unaltered by this operation, and the other 30 bits of the working register do not influence the result.

SWR(A/I). This instruction transfers the characters stored in the I-th position of cell A into the righthand 6-bit segment of the working register. The rest of cell A does not influence the result, and the rest of the working register is unaffected.

Note that unless the working register is known to be empty, it must be cleared before a character is loaded for comparison. If the working register is not cleared, the other positions could influence the comparison.

With these instructions available, we can store the word *prestidigitation* in one cell less than before:

$$
\begin{array}{llll}
\text{P R E S T I} \\
\text{D I G I T A} \\
\text{T I O N } \#
\end{array}
$$

Note that one blank character intervenes between the last character in the word form and the boundary symbol. We have been assuming that short words precede long ones in alphabetical order; thus, *a* is earlier than *and*. Unless the blank character follows the last character in the word form, long forms will precede short ones. The boundary character is represented by six 1's, and comes last in the alphabet.

To compare two word forms, we can use the program in Fig. 4 with small modifications. In determining whether a cell is the last of those used to store a single form in the list, the programmer need examine only the last character of the cell. After line 6 in Fig. 4, we insert an instruction to set the working register to 0, then SWR(F(U)/Six) is used to bring in one character. Line 7 of Fig. 4 contains a suitable conditional transfer, if we assume that cell *Bnd* contains 30 zeros followed by six ones.

2.2. Control numbers

There is another way to use a variable number of cells for the storage of word forms. The plan is to record, before each word form, the number of cells it occupies. The first character position of the first cell used for storing a word form can contain a number from 0 to 63. Let that number denote the number of consecutive cells, including the first, in which the word form is stored. With this plan, we store the word *prestidigitation* thus:

3 P R E S T
I D I G I T
A T I O N

We save almost no space, but we speed up the job of scanning a list.

Comparing two word forms will sometimes give the wrong result if the control numbers are not eliminated. Thus

1 T U B

is alphabetically later than

2 A N O N Y
M O U S

yet 1 is smaller than two. We introduce new instructions:

SRC(A). This instruction shifts the content of the working register to the right A characters. Information at the right end of the working register drops out and zeros are introduced at the left. If A contains 1, everything shifts one character position to the right; if A contains 2, two positions; and so on.

SLC(A). This is the same shift instruction, but in the opposite direction.

Let us consider the program to compare two word forms whose lengths are given by control numbers. In the fragment of a program

presented in Fig. 5, it is assumed that previous operations have left
the initial cell address of the first of the two words to be compared
indexed in J. That is now the correct index to be in cell I, so the content

Location	Instruction	Comment
1.	SWR(J)	Update I
2.	STORE(I)	
3.	STORE(U)	Copy I
4.	SWR(LV)	Update length of first word
5.	STORE(LU)	
6.	ADD(I)	Update J
7.	STORE(J)	
8.	STORE(V)	Copy J
9.	SWR(F(V))	Update length of second word
10.	SRC(Five)	
11.	STORE(LV)	
12.	SWR(F(V))	Eliminate controls
13.	SLC(One)	
14.	STORE(T)	
15.	SWR(F(U))	
16.	SLC(One)	
17.	TRANS(T, Swap, Endtest)	Compare first cells
18. Utest:	SWR(U)	First word done?
19.	ADD(One)	
20.	TRANS(J, Step, Vtest)	
21.	GOTO(Endtest)	Yes
22. Vtest:	STORE(U)	No; second word done?
23.	SWR(V)	
24.	ADD(One)	
25.	STORE(V)	
26.	SWR(J)	
27.	ADD(LV)	
28.	TRANS(V, Step, Step)	
29.	GOTO(Endtest)	Yes
30. Step:	SWR(F(U))	No; test next cells
31.	TRANS(F(V), Swap, Endtest)	Compare
32.	GOTO(Utest)	

Fig. 5—A comparison program with control numbers

of cell J is transferred to I and copied in cell U. Two cells, called LV
and LU, are used to store the lengths of the two words currently being
compared; the content of LV is moved to LU on lines 4 and 5. The
initial location of the first word to be compared, I, plus its length LV,
gives the initial position of the second word, which can be stored in J,
and copied in V.

To determine the length of the second word, the program brings in
its first cell, shifts right five characters, bringing the control number

into the righthand six bits of the working register, and stores the results in LV.

The initial cells of the two words being compared still have control characters, which must be eliminated before comparison is made. Bringing one of them in, and shifting one character to the left, puts the 5 letters in the left hand part of the working register; this much is stored in T. The other word is handled in the same way, except that when it is in position a conditional transfer can be commanded, on line 17. If the words are out of order, control goes to *Swap*. If they are in order but not identical in their first cells, control can go directly to *Endtest*, since there is no problem about finding the starting point of the next word. If the first cells are identical, the program must determine whether there are additional cells to test. Testing, on line 18, whether the first word includes additional cells, we add 1 to U, which will make it equal to J if the last cell of the word has been examined. In that case the program transfers control to *Endtest*. If U + 1 is greater than J, a mistake has occurred. Otherwise, the length of the other word must be tested, beginning on line 22. Storing a new value for U, we go on to take V, the current index of the second word, and add one to it. We store the new value for possible future use, put the initial-cell index of the second word into the working register, add its length, and test whether the updated value of V is equal to or greater than that number. If it is greater, a mistake has been made, and if it is less, we can go on to test the next pair of cells. If equal, we have finished the test for this pair of words and can go to *Endtest* to see if we are through with the list. Starting with the second cells for the two words, there are no control numbers and the comparison can be made as in lines 30–32. Lines 18–29 are repeated after every pair of cells has been tested.

In sorting with variable-length storage, it is necessary to remember that the sortable units are not single cells. If the sort program calls for exchanging two consecutive word forms, the first may occupy two cells and the next three. If they are stored, for example, in cells 38 and 39, and 40, 41, and 42, respectively, the interchange moves one form up to cells 38, 39, and 40, and the other one down to cells 41 and 42. The interchange can be carried out by moving the first word form to a temporary storage area, where enough cells are available to store all of it, moving the second into its new location, and then moving the first from its temporary location into its intended place.

Programs for handling information of variable length are more difficult to write and take more time to run than programs with fixed-length storage, but even today, with storage much less expensive than it was even a short time ago, it is one of the programmer's most valuable commodities. Time is money in computation, but so is space. It is often necessary to use tricks like this, converting time into space, to get a job done at all.

2.3. Variable-length storage in algorithmic languages

It is obvious that programs like those presented in Figs. 4 and 5 would be easier to write in an algorithmic language. The situation can be even more advantageous than that, however, since the designers of compilers or interpreters can handle all the details of variable length storage, allowing the user to write programs as if the cells of the computer were indefinitely extensible.

The official version of Algol has only limited provisions for processing nonnumerical data. It requires the user to state, at the beginning of each program, whether the variables he mentions are logical, integers, real numbers, or floating-point numbers. The purpose of these declarations is to allow the compiler to construct as simple as possible a program that will handle variables of the type he has given.

For language processing, a user would wish to declare that some of his variables refer to strings. Thus, F is a list of strings, each F[i] being one string, that is, a word form. However, having only one kind of string would be like having only variable-length storage. It would be wasteful to assume in every instance that the strings to be processed are individually too long to go into single cells of the computer. A good algorithmic language for treatment of linguistic material would therefore allow at least for declaration of strings and long strings. The associated compiler would treat short strings as capable of being stored in single cells, making no provision for boundary markers or control numbers. Long strings would be noted as typically too large for single-cell storage, and therefore boundary markers would be introduced by the compiler. Throughout this book, it is assumed that the algorithmic language has these provisions, and therefore that further discussion of variable-length internal storage is not necessary when the algorithmic language is in use.

3. ARRAYS

Strictly speaking, any collection of data with an index variable is an array. With one index variable, an array is called a vector. With two, it is a matrix; with N indices, the array is an N-dimensional matrix.

An index variable has a starting point, its origin, usually 0 or 1; in this book we customarily start at 1. The ordinary thing is to use integers, so that if the origin is at 1, and the last value is N, the array is of order N. It is customary to talk of a matrix as having rows and columns; the first index variable mentioned is the row index, the other the column index. Thus, whereas a vector is said to have N components if it is of order N, a matrix is said to have R × C elements if it is of order R by C.

3.1. Arrays in storage

Whatever the true appearance of the hardware may be, the storage of the computer is functionally equivalent to a sequence of cells, numbered consecutively from 1 to the total size of storage. If each datum in an array can go in a single cell, a natural way to store a vector is in consecutive cells, beginning at an origin and continuing cell by cell to the end of the vector. To put a rectangular array into sequentially organized storage requires a convention.

Let us call a rectangular array F; we will put its first element at F(1). We store the elements of the first row in the first C cells, then the elements of the second row, the third row, and so on. To find the element in row I, column J, we can use a program like the one in Fig. 6a. Row I follows I − 1 completed rows, each of C entries; the first three lines of the program determine how many cells must be passed over, using MULT, a multiplication, and SUB, a subtraction. The column

Location	Instruction	Comment
1. Find:	SWR(I)	Allow for I-1 rows
2.	SUB(One)	
3.	MULT(C)	
4.	ADD(J)	Allow for J-1 elements
5.	STORE(M)	in row I
6.	SWR(F(M))	Take I, J element
7.	STORE(X)	
8.	GOTO(Job)	
	(a) Find the (i, j)-th element of F	
1.	SWR(One)	Initialize now
2.	STORE(I)	
3. Enter:	SWR(F(J))	Take an element of F
4.	STORE(G(I))	Put it in G
5.	SWR(J)	Advance one row
6.	ADD(C)	
7.	TRANS(M, Out, Next)	Finished?
8. Next:	STORE(J)	
9.	SWR(I)	Advance one place
10.	ADD(One)	
11.	STORE(I)	
12.	GOTO(Enter)	
	(b) Copy a column of a rectangular array as a vector	

Fig. 6—Simple operations on rectangular arrays

index is merely added on, and the result, M, indexes the desired cell in the array F. The result is stored in a cell X, where it can be found by a program entered at *Job*.

Some arrays are used for arithmetic purposes, others for more strictly linguistic operations. For example, a rectangular array might have in consecutive columns the word forms occurring in a text, grammatical descriptions, semantical descriptions, and so on. If the grammatical descriptions are to be used intensively, it might be wise to get them out for easier access, as the program in Fig. 6b would do.

Rember that the J-th column of a rectangular array consists of the J-th entry in the first row, the J-th entry in the second row (these elements are not adjacent), and so on. The program starts by setting the row index to 1; J is given in advance, since it tells which column is to be taken. Lines 3 and 4 select one element of the rectangular array and put it in the vector array, G. To get to the J-th element in the second row of the matrix, we add C, the number of columns in the matrix. If M is greater than or equal to the current value of J, we replace the old value of J with the new one and increase the index I by 1. When the program stops, the J-th column of the matrix F has been copied into the vector G.

3.2. Algol arrays

In Algol, arrays always have integer variables as indexes. An array can have any number of dimensions. The square brackets used for subscripting an index can contain any number of indexes, separated by commas.

If two matrices have the same order and if their elements are numbers, it makes sense to define the addition of two matrices, as in Fig. 7a. The row index is i, the column index is j, and the matrices of order R by C. Matrix S will be the sum of matrices M and N.

A similar definition of matrix multiplication would be useful for some purposes, but matrix multiplication is ordinarily used to denote the operation defined in Fig. 7b. The two matrices to be multiplied are of order R by J and J by C. The product matrix will be of order R by C. The first two **for**-statements run through the rows of the first matrix, and pair each with the columns of the second matrix in turn. Pairing one row of the first matrix with one column of the second will yield one element of the product matrix, as follows: multiply the j-th element in the given row of the first matrix with the j-th element in the given column of the second matrix; adding the products together creates the sum which is put into the product matrix.

A different kind of problem, and one that will arise with many types

for i := 1 **step** 1 **until** R **do**
  for j := 1 **step** 1 **until** C **do**
    S[i, j] := M[i, j] + N[i, j]
      (a) Addition

for i := 1 **step** 1 **until** R **do**
  for k := 1 **step** 1 **until** C **do**
    for j := 1 **step** 1 **until** J **do**
      P[i, k] := P[i, k] + M[i, j] × N[j, k]
        (b) Multiplication

for i := 1 **step** 1 **until** R **do**
  for j := 1 **step** 1 **until** K **do**
    M[i, C + j] := N[i, j]
      (c) Adjunction

Fig. 7—Algorithms for some matrix operations

of structures in storage, is to form a new array by combining two old ones. For example, we may wish to take two matrices, each having R rows, and attach the K columns of the second on the right of the C columns of the first. The new matrix will be of order R by C + K. The Algol program in Fig. 7c does this. It operates row by row, setting the value of each element in column C + j of matrix M equal to the corresponding element in the j-th column of matrix N.

These are typical operations on stored arrays. Sometimes a new array is formed by performing elementary operations on combinations of selected elements from two or more original arrays, and sometimes whole arrays are reassembled. Not every collection of data is handled effectively as a linear or rectangular array; list structures give the programmer more freedom.

4. LIST STRUCTURES

The invention of list structures had the effect of releasing programmers from the restrictions imposed by simple ordering of cells in machine memory. In building up an alphabetical list of word forms, if the items are received in random order, one technique would be to find the location on the previously developed list of each new item as it arrives, move all the rest down one place, and put the new item into the gap thus produced. Or if a text, a string of word forms, is to be edited by insertion, deletion, or interchange of word forms or strings, one way to carry out the editing is to make all the movements called for. That is, if a word is to be removed, remove it—and shift everything from there to the end of the text up to fill the gap. If a word is to be inserted, create a gap by pushing everything down. If an interchange is to be made, move one segment to temporary storage, move the other segment into its place, adjust what comes between the two interchanged segments if necessary, and transfer the first segment out of temporary storage back into its new position.

With list storage, implicit movements replace actual ones. Even inside a computer, implicit motion is likely to be faster than real movement.

4.1. Simple lists

In a list, every item of information is accompanied by a link. A link is a cell, or part of a cell, in memory. It contains the identification of a new cell, the one in which the next element of the list is stored. Thus, if each word form is stored in one cell, and each link in another, every word-form cell is accompanied by the identification of the cell in which the next word form, in alphabetical order, is to be found. Or, if the word forms that make up a text are stored in individual cells, each with a link, the link accompanying a word form identifies the cell in which the next word form occurring in the text will be found.

To run through an array, we take successive values of an index. The secret of list structures is to give up that simple technique. Instead, we must always start at the beginning of the list and move from item to item by means of the links. If we wish to add an item in the middle of a list, we do it by altering the links, as shown in Fig. 8. According to

Address	Content	Address	Content
$L + \pi$	(old item)	$L + \pi$	(old item)
$L + \pi + 1$	α	$L + \pi + 1$	σ
$L + \sigma$	(vacant)	$L + \sigma$	(new item)
		$L + \sigma + 1$	α
P	π	P	
S	σ	S	$\sigma + 2$
(a) Before		(b) After	

Fig. 8—Linking a new item

Fig. 8a, cell $L + \pi$ contains an item and the next cell a link. The block of storage beginning at $L + \sigma$ is vacant. A pointer P contains π, so that we can get at the old item or its link. Another pointer S contains σ so that we can get at the origin of the vacant block. After adding a new item, the link from the old item will go to σ, the link from the new item will go back to α, and S will contain σ + 2, allowing for the loss of 2 cells to take care of the new item. The new item follows the old one in the list because of the way the links are rearranged.

Suppose for example that we have a list L in alphabetical order. A new item, stored in cell A, is to be added to the list. The program shown in Fig. 9 finds the right place and then makes the insertion. The first

Location	Instruction	Comment
1.	SWR(One)	Initialize pointer
2.	STORE(P)	
3. Find:	SWR(A)	Load new item
4.	TRANS(L(P), W, Insert)	Compare with current entry
5.	GOTO(Out)	New item is on list
6. W:	SWR(P)	Get next list index
7.	ADD(One)	
8.	STORE(P)	
9.	SWR(L(P))	
10.	STORE(P)	
11.	GOTO(Find)	
12. Insert:	STORE(L(S)	Store new item
13.	SWR(P)	Point to link
14.	ADD(One)	
15.	STORE(P)	
16.	SWR(S)	
17.	STORE(T)	Link for new item
18.	ADD(One)	
19.	STORE(U)	Pointer to new link
20.	ADD(One)	
21.	STORE(S)	New available cell
22.	SWR(L(P))	Old link
23.	STORE(L(U))	In new place
24.	SWR(T)	New link
25.	STORE(L(P))	In old place

Fig. 9—A program to add a list entry in alphabetical order

two instructions initialize P. The new item, contained in A, is compared with the first item on the list, stored in L(P). If equality is found, the new item need not be added to the list. If the new item is smaller than the current list entry, we must get the next item on the list; otherwise we make the insertion. To get the next item, we begin by adding 1 to P; now it points to a link. At line 9, we bring the link into the working register and store it as the new value of the pointer P; now P points to the next entry on the list, and we can iterate.

To make the insertion, we store the new item in the first available cell. Bringing P into the working register, we add one to make it point to a link, and store it for later use. Bringing in the address of the cell used to store the new item, we save a copy in a temporary cell T, to provide a link for the new item; add 1 to get a pointer to the new link and put that in temporary storage at U; and add one again to update the pointer to available space. Bringing in the old link, we put it with the new item; bringing in the new link, we put it with the old item. Comparison with Fig. 8 will clarify the operation of this program.

To delete an item from the list, we need only replace the link of the preceding item with its own link. That removes the item from the list, but probably the cell no longer included in the list will be added to a list of available space, since otherwise the two cells would be lost.

4.2. Some complexities

There is no reason to give exactly two cells to every entry in a list. For example, variable length storage is easy to provide. In the block of storage set aside for the list, let the first cell be a link; the first entry can continue with as many cells as necessary for the item to be stored. In a list like this, links always point to links. The end of an item can be marked in any of the ways discussed in Sec. 2 above.

Rectangular arrays are convenient when every cell is filled and the kinds of quantities to be stored are known in advance. In building a dictionary, we may face more difficult problems. We may want grammatical, semantical, and other kinds of information about every item but we may not have all the information we want at the beginning. Furthermore, we may not even know what kinds of information we will need to store. With list structures, it is possible to identify what kind of information is given in each place, without setting aside valuable cells for nonexistent information. We might allow three cells for each entry; one is for the link, one is for the name of an attribute, and one is for a value. Imagine a dictionary stored as a collection of lists, one for each word. If we have grammatical information, one entry in the list contains it. In the attribute cell, we store any abbreviation up to six letters long that will identify the information as grammatical; the actual grammatical description is stored in the associated value cell. The separate items of information for that one word need not be stored in any particular order; to find the grammatical description of a word we go to its list and, using links, look at the attributes until we find the one we want. Going to the corresponding value cell, we get the desired information.

There is a special and important class of lists called pushdown storage. This list has a top, just like any other, and also a bottom. But the rules of the pushdown game permit addition of new items only at the top. The top is also the only place deletions are allowed. Thus, to delete the second item from a pushdown list, one must first eliminate the top item.

The importance of pushdown storage lies in the fact that it has exactly enough power to deal with context-free languages. With pushdown storage, nesting can be accommodated. Work on the outermost layer of a nested structure can be interrupted with the information obtained thus far at the bottom of a push-down store; work proceeds on a nested construction, with new material going on top of what had already been stored. When the nested structure has been completely processed, the pushdown store will contain exactly what is left from the outermost layer. The correspondence between context-free grammars and push-down storage is explored further in Chap. 6.

If each item in a list is accompanied by one link, it is only possible to work through the list in one direction, that is, from the top down. If links to both the previous and following items are included it is possible to work in both directions. Ordinarily, it is more convenient to save the storage space and accept the limitation of going in just one direction.

Lists of lists are also used. The items of the master list are linked together in the ordinary way; each entry on the master list therefore consists of a master link, a minor list name, and a link to the first entry of the named minor list. A minor list consists of linked items. For example, a dictionary could be stored in this manner. The master list links words together; each word is accompanied by a link to a list of attributes with values.

If we think of all the entries on one list as sisters, and regard them all as daughters of some entry on a higher-level list, we can think of a multilevel storage structure as a family tree. Any entry anywhere can have a list of daughters; thus a structure can comprise a list of lists of lists . . . to any depth.

5. TREE STORAGE

In a multilevel list structure, or tree, each entry is the head or origin of a subtree. If the number of daughters of each entry or node is freely variable, they must be stored in a list; on the other hand, if every node has the same number of daughters, say 2, a much simpler scheme is possible.

5.1. Tree sorting

Let us examine the problems of constructing alphabetical lists. A famous technique, using tree storage, takes the first item presented—the presentation is in random order—and puts it in the first position of the list. But there are two links: One that we will call left, and one right. The second word arrives and is compared with the first. If it is earlier in alphabetical order, it is stored in the location designated by the left link, and two new links are created for the new entry. Similarly, if the second word to arrive is later in alphabetical order than the first, it is stored in the cell designated by the right link of the first word, and new links are created for it. The third word is treated in the same way; to reach its cell, we may find ourselves going through one or two links. Suppose that the second word is stored in the left-linked position from the first, and that the third word to arrive falls in alphabetical order between the first and second words. Then the initial comparison for the third item will show that it is earlier than the first in alphabetical order, and lead us to compare the new item with the one stored in the left-link cell of the first item. But now the comparison with the second word shows that the new item is later in alphabetical order, and we go through the right link to store the new item. Figures 10 and 11 show how such a tree might look after 20 or 30 words have been received and stored. Now the advantage of this plan is obvious. If the words were stored in alphabetical order, using a link with each cell to signify the location of the next word in alphabetical order, each item would be placed only after about N/2 comparisons had been made, when N different items had been put on the list. But with the new plan, only about as many comparisons as the base-2 logarithm of the number of entries already on the list will be required on the average. In other words, the alphabetical position of a new item can be determined much more rapidly with this somewhat more complex form of storage.

5.2. Linearizing a Tree

Linear storage being the only kind available in computers, the problem of putting a tree into linear order may seem vacuous. Nevertheless, if a tree is developed by arbitrary additions, with its structure maintained through links, its linear order in storage is haphazard, and for various purposes a more sensible order may be wanted.

One famous arrangement puts the origin node first, followed by the node for the entry reached through its leftmost link, followed by the item reached through that leftmost link, and so on until a terminus is reached; when necessary, a right branch is taken. The lowest available right branch is always used. Applying this plan to Fig. 10 yields the following order: for, and, ago, a (reached through left branches); all, fathers, brought, are, continent, conceived, dedicated, created, equal, forth, score, our, on, new, nation, liberty, men, proposition, seven, years, this, the, that, to.

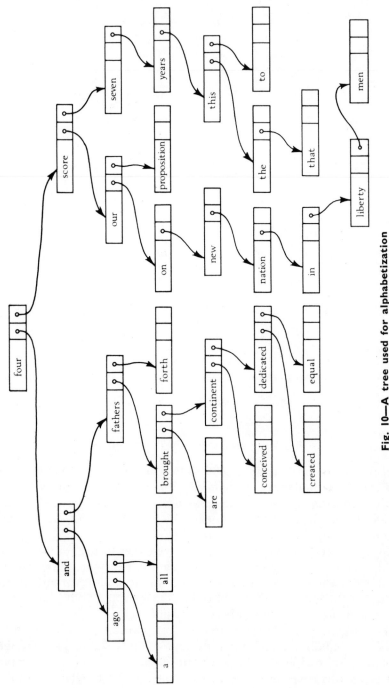

Fig. 10—A tree used for alphabetization

		Links	
Cell	*Word Form*	*Left*	*Right*
1	four	3	2
2	score	7	4
3	and	6	8
4	seven	0	5
5	years	12	0
6	ago	14	25
7	our	11	23
8	fathers	9	10
9	brought	27	13
10	forth	0	0
11	on	15	0
12	this	22	21
13	continent	17	20
14	a	0	0
15	new	16	0
16	nation	18	0
17	conceived	0	0
18	in	0	19
19	liberty	0	26
20	dedicated	28	29
21	to	0	0
22	the	24	0
23	proposition	0	0
24	that	0	0
25	all	0	0
26	men	0	0
27	are	0	0
28	created	0	0
29	equal	0	0

Fig. 11—A tree stored in 29 list entries

If the entries are simply copied in this manner, the structure of the tree is lost. A simple way of preserving it is by making all the zero links in the tree point to pseudo-entries, each containing a special symbol, say X. Then when the tree is linearized, the positions of the X's show unambiguously the shape of the tree.

In logic, every symbol is known to have either 0, 1, 2, or some other fixed number of dependents. An expression in logic can be represented by a tree, and this linearization then yields Polish parenthesis-free notation. Parentheses are needed in general only if the number of dependents from a node is otherwise unknown.

Since the purpose of the sort tree was to create an alphabetical order, it is somewhat disappointing that the famous linearization just described fails to yield an alphabetical list. Naturally, the reason is that the plan just given was never intended to have such an effect when applied to a sort tree. Martin Kay produced an algorithm for that purpose, which is presented here with minor variations. The plan is to start at the origin of the tree and descend through right branches until some node with a left branch is reached; call that node X. Starting at X, descend to the left as far as possible, until a node with no left branch is reached. Call that node Y. Descending from Y to the right, stop when a node with no right branch is reached; call it Z. Now we make three changes in the tree: (1) Set the left link of the node previously pointing to Y at 0. (2) Set the right link of the node previously pointing at X so that it points at Y. (3) Set the right hand link of Z so that it points at X, unless Z = X.

If we imagine a sort tree as having a main line in alphabetic order starting at the origin and descending always to the right with some unfortunate accidents pointing off to the left, we eliminate one accident each time we go through the steps described above. We insert a block along the main, true path; when we have finished the tree will contain no left branches at all, and the right branches will yield alphabetic order.

5.3. Alphabetic linearization in Algol

A tree can be stored for consultation by an Algol program in several different ways. One plan is to use several arrays, one of entries, one of left links, one of right links, and perhaps others. For example, let us call the array of entries Word[i], the array of left links L[i], and the array of right links R[i]. The arrays are coordinated through their indices; for a given value of i, we can find an entry or a left or right link.

An algorithm for putting the entries of a sort tree into alphabetic order is presented in Fig. 12. It follows the plan set forth in the preceding section, but before we examine it we must get acquainted with some other features of Algol.

We have seen one technique for iteration. A **for**-instruction takes the form **for** . . . **do** . . . Following **do**, an instruction is inserted. Between **for** and **do**, a variable and a set of values must be provided. We have already seen how to step the variable by constant addends between lower and upper limits. In Algol, it is also possible to mention all the values required; thus, **for** i := 1, 2, 3 **do** . . . is a valid **for**-instruction. With use of commas, specifications of different kinds can be mixed: **for** i := 1, 2 **step** 2 **until** 6 **do** . . . provides that the instruction will be performed for i = 1, 2, 4, and 6.

Another form is **for** i := E **while** F **do** . . . Here E is an expression that gives a value to i, and F is a proposition that is true or false. Ordinarily, what happens is that the instruction has a chance of

```
         X := 0;
cycle: for i := X while L[i] = 0 do
         begin if R[i] = 0 then goto Out;
            G[R[i]] := i;
            X := R[i]
         end;
         for i := X, L[i] while L[i] ≠ 0 do
            begin G[L[i]] := i;
               Y := L[i]
            end;
         Z := Y;
         for i := Z while R[i] ≠ 0 do Z := R[i];
         L[G[Y]] := 0;
         R[G[X]] := Y;
         R[Z] := X;
         X := Y;
         goto cycle
```

Fig. I2—Algorithm to put a sort tree in linear order

altering F. Perhaps F uses a new value of i, and E is changed each time the instruction is carried out. As soon as F is false, the iteration stops.

In the algorithm, Fig. 12, an array G[i] is used. Each element of this array is the index of an element through which the current one can be reached on a left or right link. For the algorithm, there is assumed to be no *Word*[0]; a dummy origin is provided for the tree, with a right link pointing to the true origin. If R[0] = a, *Word*[a] is the entry at the origin of the tree.

The algorithm starts by setting X = 0, pointing to the dummy node. The word *cycle* in the figure labels the place for re-entry; we will come back to it later. Now we wish to find a node with a left branch. We set the dummy variable i = X, and if L[i] = 0, that is if there is no left branch for node X, we step down to the right. Now if R[i] = 0, i.e., if there is no right branch from the current node, the algorithm has gone all the way through the sort tree without finding a left branch; the right links form a path through the tree in alphabetic order. The job is done when there are no left links. In the first iteration, we go on to use the content of the right link of the current node as index to the array G. This array, initially empty, is filled in as necessary; the letter G stands for governor. The governor of the node pointed to by the right link of i is of course i. Now we give X a new value, namely R[i], thus moving down a right branch. What happens next is that the new value of X is assigned to i, and if it is still true for the new value that L[i] = 0, the iteration is continued; the first iteration ends when X points to a node with a left branch.

The next stage of the program is performed for i = X, using the value of X left by the previous part of the program. Then, as long as there is a left link from the current entry, we replace the current value of i with a left link and go forward. We fill in one element of the G array and put in a new value for Y. When the relation in the **for**-statement becomes false, Y will index a left descendent of X that has no left dependent.

Now we set a new variable, Z, to that value of Y. As long as the current entry has a right link, we go down it and move Z with us. When we find an entry with no right link, we have the values of X, Y, and Z needed for the following three operations. We change one left link and two right links as shown, and give X the best possible value before restarting. We need not go all the way to the top of the sort tree each time; we can begin with the highest element in the chain just added to the main one leading from the origin downward to the right. Now we transfer control back to the point labeled *cycle* and try again.

It is instructive to trace out, using both arrays and graphs, the operation of this algorithm when the tree shown in Figs. 10 and 11 is submitted to it.

5.4. Cross Links

As we have seen, if there is only one link with each item in a standard list, only one direction of scanning through the list is possible. In a tree stored as a list of lists, only top-to-bottom scanning is possible. Starting at the origin of the tree, any items directly connected to it can be found, and with *them* links to those directly connected to them. But other ways of scanning a tree are convenient, and more elegant storage plans permit them.

To begin with, it may be desirable to scan a tree from bottom to top. The lowest items in a tree can be stored in one list, or at least indications of where they are located can be kept in a list, with links from one to the next across the tree. But one additional link for each item will permit moving upward in the tree; that is, a link can show where an item's governor is located. With these additional links, bottom-to-top scanning becomes possible.

Another kind of scanning that may be wanted is scanning across the descendants of a single node, that is, items—whether end items or not—that are directly connected all to the same governor. To scan in this manner, circular lists are convenient. In the simple kind of list, scanning starts at one end and goes straight through until an indication is found that the other end has been reached. Scanning may go back and forth, but the list has two definite ends. By putting a link from the last item on the list to the first, we can make any list circular. Then scanning never stops, but goes round and round until some special stop condition is reached.

Naturally, with all these kinds of links, an elegantly stored tree becomes a monstrosity to maintain. The number of links to be altered when an item is added or deleted is large. We shall see applications that justify such effort, but they involve many consultations of a stored tree and few additions and deletions.

EXERCISES

Write the following programs in computer instructions.

1. Interchange two word forms. The first begins at $F(I)$; it ends at the first cell containing # as its last character. The second begins in the following cell, and is bounded in the same manner.

2. Revise the solution to Ex. 1 to allow the second word to begin in any cell $F(J)$ following the location of the first.

3. A text is stored in cells $S + 1, \ldots, S + N$; word forms are separated by blanks, but in general a word form need not start in the first position of a new cell. Copy the text into cells $T + 1, \ldots, T + M$, starting each word form flush left in a cell; fill the last cell for each word form with blanks (at least one blank after each word) and insert boundary markers. Put the length of the new sequence in M.

4. Revise the solutions to Exs. 1, 2, and 3 to use control numbers instead of boundary markers.

5. Dictionary information about a word is stored in a list; cell $L + 1$ contains a link, $L + 2$ contains an attribute name, and $L + 2$ contains a value. If the content of $L + 1$ is ϕ, then cells $L + \phi$, $L + \phi + 1$, and $L + \phi + 2$ also contain link, attribute, and value. Cell *Attr* contains the name of an attribute for which the value is wanted; find it if possible and put its value in *Val*.

6. Add an item to a pushdown store.

7. Delete an item from a pushdown store.

Use Algol for the following problems.

8. Each component of *Text*[i] is a word form. Create arrays *Word*[i], L[i], and R[i] such that all the distinct word forms in the text occur, once each, in *Word* and each L[i] is a link to an alphabetically earlier, R[i] to a later, word form.

9. Recast the solution to Ex. 5 (using Algol), assuming that a list of words is in storage, with a list of attributes and values for each. Find the value of a specified attribute for a specified word.

10. Given a circular list—the last item links to the first—with no item marked in any way, scan once through all entries and stop. Note: the first item inspected is not necessarily first on the list, and the number of entries is not known in advance.

11. A tree is stored with two links for each node, one to a sister and one to the parent. With it is stored a list of links, one to some representative of each set of sisters having no daughters (if any node in a set of sisters has a daughter, that set is unrepresented). Find the daughters of a specified node; e.g., if each node has a distinct label, giving a label specifies a node.

Chapter 3

EXTERNAL STORAGE

The difference between internal and external storage is an accident, caused by the fact that computers are in the end physical machines. A computer user would be happiest if he could forego knowing whether his information was stored inside the computer or out at any given time. That degree of happiness may well be attained in the future, but as yet the user who wants effective information processing, with a relatively small computer and a relatively large volume of information, had best know a good deal about the media in which his information is stored.

I. FORMS OF EXTERNAL STORAGE

Rectangular slips of cardboard with holes punched in fixed positions, rolls of paper tape with holes punched in them, and rolls of paper or plastic tape surfaced with some compound that can be magnetized in small spots—these are the three common forms of external storage. The disc pack is another: it is a stack of magnetically sensitized discs that can be plugged into a computer or carried away to a storage shelf. In fact, this is the definition of external storage: a deck of cards, a reel of magnetic tape, a roll of punched paper tape, or a disc pack can be brought to the computer and taken away again; there is no limit to the quantity of information that can be brought in for processing in this manner.

The Hollerith card (Fig. 13) was invented half a century ago, when electronic gear was not being offered for information processing. The 960 positions on the card—80 columns by 12 rows—are located by physical measurement from the edges. Each position is either punched or not. For numerical work, 10 of the 12 positions in a column are identified with the decimal digits, and the other two with any categories the user defines. Often the x (11) position is used to mark negative numbers. For alphabetic work, 26 pairs of holes, each pair including either x or y (12) are identified with letters, and the 10 single positions, 0 through 9, are identified with numbers. Gradually, additional combinations of punches have been given standard interpretations. Three-hole punching is used for various mathematical symbols and punctuation

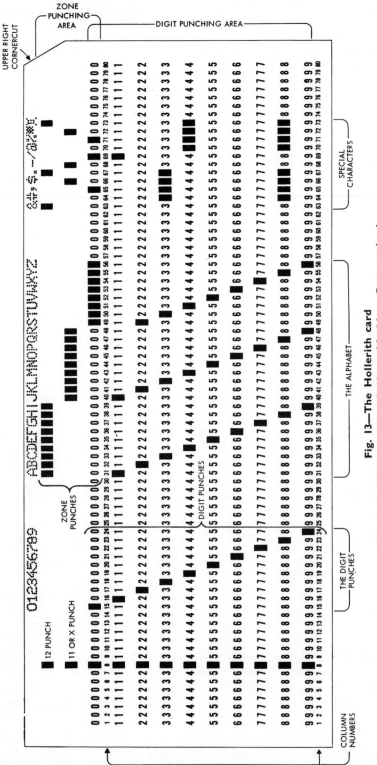

Fig. 13—The Hollerith card

(Courtesy of International Business Machines Corporation.)

marks. When cards are used in the vicinity of the computer, they are sometimes punched not in the Hollerith code just described, but in binary code. Each of the 960 positions is taken independently as one bit, and the information capacity of the card is increased enormously.

Punched paper tape (Fig. 14) can be purchased in 1000-foot spools. Its width ranges up to an inch, and 5, 6, 7, or 8 positions across the tape can be punched. One frame of paper tape is a group of punchable positions arranged side by side across the short dimension of the tape. Binary encoding has always been customary with punched paper tape. Until recently, there was no general standard that all could adhere to, and each manufacturer of a machine for punching paper tape or for printing information on paper under the control of punched paper tape established his own code. But now the American Standard Code for Information Interchange (ASCII) has been established, and perhaps manufacturers will begin using it. It is outlined in Fig. 15.

Like paper tape, magnetic tape has a series of frames, and the places where magnetization is significant are determined by physical measurement across the tape, which ranges from one-half inch to one inch in width. The common way of reading magnetic tape is to watch for the first magnetized spot and predict another at a definite distance along the tape. When magnetized spots cease to turn up, the magnetic-tape reader shuts off, and when restarted begins looking for the first magnetized position once more. Hence there must be "record gaps" of adequate length whenever there is any break in the recording. This is the American scheme; some European machines are different. Magnetic tape usually allows for 7 or 9 parallel sequences of recording positions, and takes one of them for control of its own accuracy. Hence either 6 or 8-bit characters are recorded on tape.

A typical reel of magnetic tape is 2400 feet long. Recording densities vary, but 800 characters per inch is a good figure; at that rate, a record gap occupies as much space as 600 characters. Records of 1200 characters are easy to manage; with a gap, such a record is about 2.25 inches long. Hence about 12,000 of them can be recorded on a reel, making 14,400,000 characters.

External storage serves three different functions. Information stored outside the computer can be brought from a device operated by a person into the computer proper; or from the computer to an output device, such as a printer, that prepares information for a human reader; or external storage can be used for information coming from the computer and ultimately going back in. All forms of external storage can be used for all three purposes. There are devices with keyboards for the human operator that make punched cards, punched

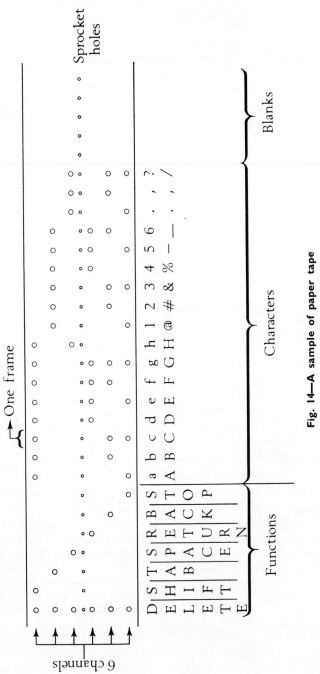

Fig. 14—A sample of paper tape

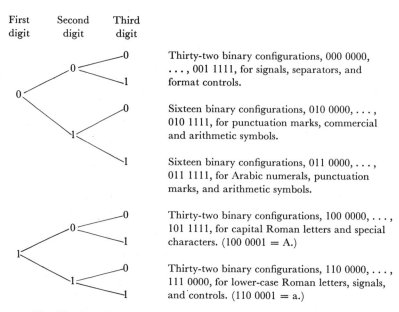

First   Second   Third
digit   digit   digit

Thirty-two binary configurations, 000 0000, ..., 001 1111, for signals, separators, and format controls.

Sixteen binary configurations, 010 0000, ..., 010 1111, for punctuation marks, commercial and arithmetic symbols.

Sixteen binary configurations, 011 0000, ..., 011 1111, for Arabic numerals, punctuation marks, and arithmetic symbols.

Thirty-two binary configurations, 100 0000, ..., 101 1111, for capital Roman letters and special characters. (100 0001 = A.)

Thirty-two binary configurations, 110 0000, ..., 111 0000, for lower-case Roman letters, signals, and controls. (110 0001 = a.)

Fig. 15—American Standard Code for Information Interchange

Note: When 000 0111 is transmitted, a bell is supposed to ring as a signal to the operator of the receiving device; typical format controls are carriage return (000 1101) and horizontal tabulator (000 1001).

paper tape, and magnetic tape; and there are printers, separate from large computers, that can be controlled with cards or either kind of tape. But speed of reading and preparing externally stored information differ from one form to the other. Cards and punched paper tape are read and punched rather slowly, in comparison with the speeds attainable with magnetic tape. Therefore when information is moved to external storage but is intended for later use in the computer, only magnetic tape or a disc pack is truly suitable. The remainder of this chapter is about magnetic-tape storage. What is said could be adapted to the circumstances of the person using only punched cards or only paper tape, but most users will have magnetic tape and their special problems are of greatest interest.

2. BASIC TECHNIQUES

The information stored between two consecutive record gaps on a magnetic tape is a physical record. When a reel of tape has been mounted on a computer's tape mechanism and properly positioned, an instruction to read one physical record can be given. The instruction must tell where the information is to go in internal storage. Even magnetic-tape transfers are slow in comparison with internal working speed, and therefore the usual practice is to start tape reading and go on to something else while the transfer takes place.

2.1. Buffers

The area available to receive information from tape, which must not be violated until reading stops, is a buffer. The size of the buffer must be as large as the largest physical record on the tape, but the physical record must not be so large as to take away too much internal space with buffers. It is not possible to give a command that results in reading the first part of a physical record, and then another command to bring in the remainder. If the tape mechanism stops, the information that passes under the reading head during the mechanical braking action is lost, as is the following information that passes during mechanical acceleration of the tape. The record gaps are made large enough to allow for braking and acceleration, which is why physical records must be taken as whole units.

Each frame on magnetic tape is a 6-bit character. Each cell in storage takes 36 bits. In general, computer design brings the first 6 characters of the record into the first cell of the buffer provided, the next 6 into the next cell, and so on.

With two buffers, tape movement can be made continuous. A command to fill the first buffer is given, and work proceeds elsewhere until the first physical record has been read. A signal comes in at that time, and the program issues an instruction to read another record into the second buffer area. The command can be issued so promptly that braking does not occur. While the second buffer is being filled from tape, the information in the first buffer is processed, and when the second buffer is filled, the first buffer is ready to receive information from the third physical record.

2.2. Input and output programs

A complete program for reading or writing information on magnetic tape must make provisions for several different kinds of control and error conditions. If the information on tape is recorded badly, some of it may not be readable. Even if it is recorded accurately, a mistake can occur in the mechanism that responds to the moving magnetized spots; since the tape has gone past, it is not possible to reread the same data. A program can go back by ordering the mechanism to stop, reposition at the beginning of the current physical record, and read all of it again. Such a complicated and time-consuming operation is not generally performed automatically. In this section we do not consider programs to handle errors, partly because they are complex, partly because they differ from one machine to another, and partly because they are likely to be provided in the standard programs accompanying any computer.

Location	Instruction	Comment
1.	READ(Unit, Buffer, Size)	Start input
2.	SWR(Zero)	Initialize controls
3.	STORE(Next)	
4.	SWR(Size)	
5.	STORE(Input)	
6. Dwell:	SWR(Channel)	Wait for input
7.	TRANS(Quiet, Dwell, Dwell)	
8.	SWR(Buffer(Next))	Test for end of input
9.	TRANS(Filend, Switch, Switch)	
10.	GOTO(Out)	
11. Switch:	SWR(Input)	Swap buffers
12.	STORE(T)	
13.	SWR(Next)	
14.	STORE(Input)	
15.	SWR(T)	
16.	STORE(Next)	
17.	READ(Unit, Buffer(Next), Size)	Start input in next buffer
18.	GOTO(Job)	Start work on previous buffer

Fig. 16—A one-tape, two-buffer reading program

To illustrate the use of buffers and programming for certain controls, we have the program in Fig. 16. This program takes information from one magnetic-tape unit, storing it alternately in two buffers. It delays internal operations until each logical record in turn has been read completely, and watches for the end of material on the tape.

When this program starts operation, a cell called *Unit* contains a number designating one of the magnetic-tape units on the machine. Another cell called *Size* contains a number corresponding to length of each buffer. A block of cells beginning at *Buffer*, and twice as long as the number called *Size*, is reserved for input. The first half of this region constitutes the first buffer, the second half the second buffer. A cell called *Channel* contains one number while the tape unit is in operation, another when it is out of action. By convention, the last logical record on a tape contains six characters, chosen specifically to mark the end of a file. For example, 36 binary ones might be recorded.

The program in Fig. 16 starts by turning on the tape unit. The instruction READ(A, B, C) requires three arguments. The first is the name of a cell containing identification of the tape unit, the second is the first cell to which input is to be directed, and the third is the name of a cell telling how much storage can be used for a logical record. If the size of a logical record is greater than that, the end of the record is lost and control transfers to a location not shown in this figure, where the program has a chance to deal with the mistake.

While the first buffer is filling for the first time, the program initializes two controls: *Next* and *Input*. Lines 6 and 7 contain two instructions which are repeated as long as the input channel is active; in the cell called *Quiet*, a number is stored which will match the contents of *Channel* after one logical record has been read. When the first buffer is filled, the content of its first cell is brought into the working register and compared with the number stored in *Filend*. If there is a match, this record is the last one on the tape. Otherwise, in lines 11–16, the program interchanges the contents of cells *Next* and *Input*. Now, on line 17, reading starts again in a new buffer. The first time through, input goes to the top half of the double buffer, during execution of line 1; when line 17 is first executed, input goes to the lower half of the region. The next time line 17 is executed, input will go to the top once more. While one of the buffers is being loaded, other work can be done; line 18 transfers control to a program that can operate on the block of cells beginning at *Buffer(Input)*. When the other program has completed its work, it returns control to *Dwell*. Thus, input operations cannot resume until work on one buffer is completed and input to the other buffer is also finished. If the time taken to perform the *Job* program is shorter than reading time, the few instructions between lines 7 and 17 will not, in most machines, be long enough for the input to slow down. The tape will move continuously; a program like this is said to be tape-limited.

An output program might be very similar to the one in Fig. 16. Another command WRITE(A, B, C), would be used. The program *Job* would fill buffers instead of using their contents. It would have to fill one buffer before the regular alternation could begin. Instead of testing for a record marking the end of the file on tape, it would of course be necessary—when the output file had been written—to produce such a mark.

2.3. Multi-unit operations

Many operations involving input or output require several reels of tape be handled simultaneously. When a large file is to be sorted, the most convenient procedures use multiple tapes. Perhaps two files of similar information, each already sorted, have to be merged into one. Or perhaps information is taken from one tape, processed, and the results of processing recorded on a second tape.

As an example, let us consider first merging. We need three tape units, which we designate by *Alpha, Beta, Gamma*. Perhaps our two input files are partial dictionaries, concordances of different texts to be combined, a bibliography complete as of the end of last year and a bibliography of this year's work, or a developing file and a set of corrections of newly discovered errors. Each input file, stored on a separate tape reel, occupies one unit; we take *Alpha* and *Beta* as input units. The result of the merge will be written on a new reel of tape, mounted on unit *Gamma*.

For convenience, we need six buffers. When the merging program empties one of its *Alpha* buffers, it calls a reading program to swap *Alpha* buffers and read a new logical record. Similarly, it calls for switches of the two *Beta* buffers. When the merge routine finishes filling an output buffer, it calls a writing program to switch *Gamma* buffers and start writing a new logical record.

Our hypothetical computer has only one working register. Every operation except input and output involves coupling that register to a storage cell; only one such coupling can be made at a time. Reading and writing operations do not use the working register, but occupy a channel. We now face the crucial question whether the machine has only one channel, so that an instruction to read from *Alpha* into storage occupies the machine's input-output system until a logical record is complete. Some machines have two channels or even more, so that it might be possible to read from two channels simultaneously and write at the same time through a third. Naturally, each tape unit must be connected to a specific channel. Machines can differ in this respect even if they bear the same type designation; the purchaser of a machine may be able to specify whether the one delivered to him shall have one or more channels. When computing is simple, the time required to carry out a program may depend on the number of channels available. In any case, a good input–output program for multiunit operations uses all available channels and therefore cannot be transferred from one machine to another unless they have the same number of channels. This kind of detail is generally taken care of by standard programs available to all users of a given machine.

Internally, a merge program must break up its two input streams into appropriate segments. Perhaps each physical record is an indivisible unit, but not necessarily so; it is often appropriate to use buffers of 200 to 1000 cells each. One line of a concordance might occupy 20 to 25 cells; thus up to 40 lines of a concordance might be included in one physical record, but the merge program must intersperse two concordances line by line. Each line is marked in some way as an independent segment within the physical record.

We thus imagine the merge program working actively on an *Alpha* buffer and a *Beta* buffer. Having identified the next segment in each, it compares the two segments. Depending on the purpose of the merge, it may be appropriate to transfer one, the other, or both of two identical segments to output. If the two segments differ, the one that comes earlier is transferred to output and the next segment from the same buffer extracted. The program must also test order within each file. If one file is out of order, the two files cannot successfully be merged.

Sorting is attacked in a different way. We have seen how to sort inside a computer; if a file is too large to be stored internally, it must be taken one section at a time. Beginning in random order, we can fill core, sort internally, and write a block which is in order, but followed by other blocks with which it must be combined. For this stage, we use unit *Alpha* for input and write output on *Beta* and *Gamma* alternately. The next stage, and all following stages, are merges of a special kind.

Input tapes are loaded on units *Alpha* and *Beta* and output is written on units *Gamma* and *Delta*. There is no need to deal with blocks independently; if by happy accident one block consists exclusively of material later in order than anything in the preceding block, the two can be treated as one. In fact, the merge goes like this: Merge input from *Alpha* and *Beta*, writing output on *Gamma* until an item is found out of order. Now start on unit *Delta*. Thereafter, write on either *Gamma* or *Delta*, subject to three conditions. (1) If the next element to be written follows the previous record on both *Gamma* and *Delta*, place it so as to minimize the interval. (2) If the next unit follows the last on one output tape but not the last on the other, write it so as to maintain sequence. (3) If the next unit precedes those on both outputs, choose between *Gamma* and *Delta* in such a fashion as to maximize the reverse interval.

When all of *Alpha* and *Beta* have been processed, the tapes on *Gamma* and *Delta* are taken as input and the process is repeated. If the input can be handled in two coreloads, a single merge pass yields an ordered file. If four coreloads are needed, one merge pass can be expected to produce two ordered files, which must then be merged. The number of passes can thus be predicted from the number of coreloads to be sorted.

3. THE RAND CATALOG SYSTEM

Text can be stored on magnetic tape with each 6-bit frame representing one printed character. Perhaps each sentence is arranged so that it can go into internal memory in an integral number of cells. The number of characters in each sentence must therefore be divisible by 6, a result which is obtainable if characters of some sort, either blanks or something else, are added to fill out each sentence to the proper length. But now suppose that the sentences are taken from an encyclopedia. Each article in the encyclopedia is a collection of sentences, preceded by a heading. For some purposes, headings are different from text; for example, a user may want to search the tape for specific headings and collect the sentences grouped under them.

In the example of the encyclopedia, the headings and text sentences belong to two different data classes. We are about to deal once more with trees: The encyclopedia can be stored on tape as a sequence of trees, each with just two levels. On the upper level, each tree has one node, corresponding to the heading of an article. On the lower level, each tree has one or more nodes, corresponding to the sentences within the article (see Fig. 17).

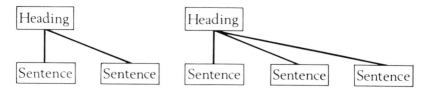

Fig. 17—An encyclopedia stored as a two-level catalog

As we saw in the previous chapter, more complicated situations are not hard to find. Instead of two data classes, a library catalog may have 40 or 50. Instead of two levels, the 40 or 50 classes may be arranged on 2, 10, or a score of levels. The length of each sentence in a text can vary, and so can the amount of material to be put into one datum of almost any class in a real catalog. The RAND catalog system, conceived by Martin Kay and Theodore W. Ziehe, and elaborated by them and colleagues at RAND and other research centers, is intended to provide adequate organizational possibilities for complex files. The object is to settle on a format that can accommodate new structures and to write file-management programs that depend solely on the format. These standard programs obviate the work of writing new ones for a file with a new structure, new data classes, and also new problems.

3.1. Catalog structure

A catalog is a file of information on magnetic tape. In a catalog, there are data, each containing a variable amount of information. The data are assigned to classes, and the classes to levels. The highest level of data recorded in a catalog is called level 1; data directly connected to level 1 data are on level 2, and so on. Data on level 1 are conceived as descending from a fictitious node on level 0 which is never recorded.

There can be only one class of data on level 1. On the second level, there can be as many different classes of data in a catalog as the user requires. Furthermore, any number of data of one class can descend from a level 1 node. For example, in the two-level encyclopedia, each article heading is in a level 1 datum, and only one class of data descend from level 1, namely sentences. But there are as many sentences descending from each heading as the authors of the encyclopedia chose to put in.

If there are two classes on the second level, they are ordered. One of them precedes the other, and all data of the first class descending from a given level 1 node are recorded on tape after the node from which they descend and before data of the other class. With three or more classes, the same rule applies but with the natural extension. For example, a very simple dictionary (Fig. 18) might have entry words on

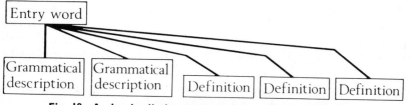

Fig. 18—A simple dictionary stored as a two-level catalog

level 1, and two classes on the second level: grammatical descriptions and definitions. But then all the grammatical descriptions of a given entry word must come before the definitions. If there is some connection between the grammatical descriptions and the definitions—if each definition is applicable only for a certain grammatical description—a different organization of the catalog is required. With three levels (Fig. 19) the entry words can be on level 1, the grammatical descriptions on level 2, and the definitions on level 3. Then an entry word can have one or more grammatical descriptions; each grammatical description in its turn can have one or more definitions associated with it.

A datum consists of two parts: A control element and a content element. In the control element, the catalog system indicates the level

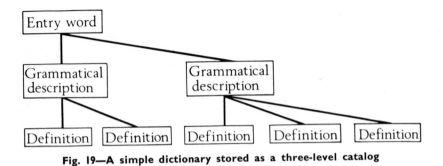

Fig. 19—A simple dictionary stored as a three-level catalog

on which the datum resides, the data class to which it belongs, and the length of the content element. (Some additional information is needed, but need not concern us for the moment.) In the content element of a datum, the system puts whatever information, in whatever encoding, the user provides. It might be a sentence of text, or a whole page. It might be in binary code, Hollerith or something more complex. The user specifies what he wants, and the catalog system handles it—but the catalog system never goes inside the content element of a datum. The price of not knowing what you are handling is that you must always keep it in sealed containers.

3.2. Maps

Since every user is to be allowed to design his own catalog, with as many levels, data classes, and so on as he needs, every file will be different. The safest way to keep track of the structure of a given file, when it may be unique, is to attach a description of the structure to the file itself. Then a program designed to read the file will first read the description and then use that as a guide in reading further. It is somewhat like reading the table of contents of a book, or looking over a map before starting on a trip. Every trip is different, but if a good map is provided, a new driver can make whatever journeys he pleases. The term map has been adopted for the description placed at the head of every catalog.

A map is nothing more than a miniature of the catalog with every data class represented exactly once. Catalogs are large because they contain many data of each class. The map is small since it contains only one of each. The order of data in the map is just like that of data in the catalog. First the single data class on the top level is stated, then the first class on level 2, then the first class on level 3 descending from the data class just named on level 2, and so on. A diagram (Fig. 20) is clearer than words can be in expressing this ordering.

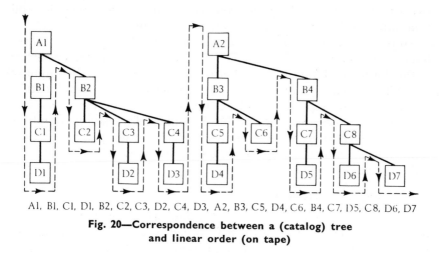

Al, Bl, Cl, Dl, B2, C2, C3, D2, C4, D3, A2, B3, C5, D4, C6, B4, C7, D5, C8, D6, D7

**Fig. 20—Correspondence between a (catalog) tree
and linear order (on tape)**

Thanks to the map, and provided certain control information is given within the catalog, the requirement that at least one datum of every class be present in every position where that class ought to be represented can be dropped. There can be empty data, which occupy no space on the tape. Suppose for example that a text file allows for annotation of every sentence. A data class is established for annotations, and placed in the map as a descendent of the sentence class. But the user may choose to annotate only one sentence in a hundred. It would be exceedingly wasteful to write the controls for an annotation datum just after every sentence datum, if 99 percent of them give no information. Yet the program reading a catalog must know what position to give the next datum it reads. After reading a sentence datum, it expects an annotation datum. If the map of the text file (Fig. 21) shows headings, with sentences descending from them, and with annotations descending from sentences, it is sufficient to show the data class of each datum in the control element. Then an empty annotation will be recognized whenever two sentences follow each other. But what if a heading is missing? Then

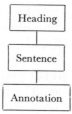

Fig. 21—Map of a catalog with three levels

two sentences follow each other, yet the intention is that they descend from different headings, one present, the other null.

To solve this problem, preceding implicit level numbers are introduced. The control portion of every datum now includes the data class of the datum itself and the number of the level closest to the origin of the map that has been passed over as null since the last non-null datum was recorded on tape. If a null heading is skipped over between two sentences, the preceding implicit level number of the second datum is 1. If two sentences are recorded under the same heading, the preceding implicit level number is 2, that of sentences themselves. With this device, null data are entirely controllable.

3.3. Reading and writing catalogs

The user of a catalog is interested in data. He wants to furnish data one after another and have them recorded, with control information provided by the programs of the catalog system. If he is reading a tape, he wants data to be furnished him one after another, and he wants a 0 or blank datum whenever the "next" datum is null. The catalog input–output system does the work called for by these desires.

To write a catalog, a user must furnish a map. Then, knowing his map he furnishes a datum on level 1. If it is blank, the catalog system writes nothing on tape but prepares to write a datum with appropriate control characters when information is supplied it. If the datum is not blank, control signals are generated and the datum is recorded.

In reading, the map is on the tape, and the program gets it as its first input from the tape. Then, reading the control characters in the first datum, it decides whether any null data have to be given the user's program before the contents of the first recorded datum.

For later use, it is best to have a way of reading and writing catalogs that can be incorporated in Algol programs. The scheme to be presented is hypothetical; it could be made to work, however, by changing an Algol compiler. In fact, each Algol compiler must contain special provisions—the general formulation of Algol has none—for transferring information to and from external storage.

We assume two Algol terms: **putd** and **getd** (d for datum). A complete Algol statement begins with either of them and continues with four variables. The value of the first determines the unit from (or onto) which the transfer takes place. The second is assigned the value of the next datum in the catalog by **putd**; **getd** assigns its value to the next datum of the catalog it is writing. The third variable has as value the class of the datum. The value of the fourth is an indication of any special condition, such as reaching the end of a catalog.

The program in Fig. 22 reads the encyclopedia illustrated in Fig. 17; it writes the headings in an output catalog, and goes to a program called *Segment* for each sentence. That program is assumed to cut sentences into

```
Read:   getd Input, Datum, Class, Error;
        if Error = End of Catalog then goto Close
        else if Class = Heading then
            begin putd Output, Datum, Hdg, Okay;
                goto Read
            end
        else begin putd Output, Null, Sentence, Okay;
                goto Segment
            end;
Write:  if Occurrence = 0 then goto Read
        else begin putd Output, Occurrence, Occ, Okay;
                goto Segment
            end
```

Fig. 22—Algol program to rewrite a catalog

word-form occurrences; it returns zero when the sentence is finished. Each occurrence goes out as a separate datum; sentence boundaries are marked by null data. The output catalog has three data classes, headings, sentence boundaries, and occurrences.

In the first statement, *Input* has a value specifying a unit; the next datum from it furnishes a value for *Datum*, and the class of that datum becomes the value of *Class*. The second statement begins with a check on *Error*; if the end of the input catalog has been reached, a program entered at *Close* must put an end to the output catalog. Otherwise, if the input datum is a heading it is copied into the output catalog as a datum of the class which is the value of *Hdg*; for one reason or another, *Hdg* and *Heading* might have to have different values.

If the datum obtained is not a heading, it must be a sentence. First a null datum is written; that is, the program that actually writes the catalog is warned to set the preceding implicit level number of the next datum to show that a null datum of class *Sentence* has been passed over. Control goes to *Segment*, which cuts off the first part of the sentence, assigns it as the value of *Occurrence*, and returns control to *Write*. There, a datum of class *Occ* is written unless *Occurrence* has zero value—a signal that the current sentence is exhausted and a new one must be obtained.

This discussion of way to read and write catalogs is both hypothetical and incomplete. Nothing is said here about starting a new catalog or ending one, for example. As with every topic treated in this book, full coverage of details would require too much space. Moreover, the reader who wants to use a standard version of Algol to work with information stored in catalogs will not wait for **putd** and **getd** to be installed; Algol allows procedures, coded in the instruction repertoire of the computer itself, to be inserted by any user.

3.4. Other operations with catalogs

The catalog system might be useful if it could do no more than read and write catalogs, taking into account variability in the length of data, variability in the number of data of any class descending from a single datum, and the possibility that some data are null. But it would not be as useful as it ought to be. The user of a catalog should be able to instruct the system to arrange the contents of his file in a certain order, to combine two of his files into one, or to select from his files information that he wants specifically, without leaving him the task of winnowing through the entire content.

The problem of sorting a catalog can be solved if the user will furnish two kinds of information. For one thing, he must prescribe the order to be established among classes of data, all on the same level, and all descending from one superordinate class. With this much information, the map of the catalog can be sorted. Now the data of a single class, all descending from a single node, must be ordered internally. What the user provides the catalog system for this purpose is a program that can decide, given the contents of any two data, which comes first. If the given class always contains numerical information, the program may simply decide which datum has the smaller numerical value. If the contents are words, it may choose the one earlier in alphabetical order. As far as the catalog system is concerned, the user's rule is entirely arbitrary, and he can apply a different rule to every different data class, if he will only furnish the necessary number of programs.

When information to be put into a catalog is furnished in random order, and then must be sorted, duplicate data must be suppressed. The system provides for this, in the following manner. Sorting will eventually bring any two identical data on level 1 together, separated only by descendents of one of them. The two data on level 1 are reduced to a single datum; now the descendents of the two level 1 data must be sorted together, so that all those of the earliest data class, whether originally descendants of the first or the second of the data found to be identical, are collected. Within each class of level 2 data, a sort is made by content, and now identical data on level 2 may be discovered. The entire process is repeated, until the lowest level is reached. In some files, a substantial reduction of space occupied on tape is achieved by elimination of duplicates, but the major purpose served is that of avoiding complexities in finding material. If a datum having the desired content can be identified, it is the only one in the file that would meet the specifications. If duplicates were allowed, it would be necessary to go on searching.

There are many ways to select a part of the contents of a file. Here we can examine only a few possibilities. A catalog, with its map, is recorded on tape; the user wants a portion of it. To obtain it, he writes a new catalog, this one having the same map, but in its data he can write down different information.

If he writes information that could be contained in a datum of that class, he intends to match data in his file with exactly the same content.

If he indicates no restriction, he means to take any datum of that class.

If he writes *first, second, last,* et cetera, he means to take the datum in that position, within the class specified, among descendants of a common datum.

A catalog search system can now compare what we will call the request catalog with the target catalog. We assume that the two catalogs are ordered appropriately. Take the first level 1 datum in the request catalog. If it imposes no restriction, go to the first level 1 datum in the target catalog and proceed; if it specifies contents, go to the level 1 node that matches it, and proceed. If it gives a number, count level 1 data to that position and proceed. In any case, do not go as far into the target catalog as the location where the next requested datum on level 1 would be found.

Once the system has made an identification on level 1, it goes on to make an identification on level 2 in exactly the same manner. When it has successfully made identifications on all levels to the bottom of the catalog, it has some information on every level; on some levels, the information was provided by the user, and on other levels it was obtained from the catalog and unknown to the user. All this information is now reported out, in whatever form the user has specified, and the system goes on to seek another identification on the lowest level. If none is found, it moves up one level and proceeds. An especially reasonable way to report to the user is by writing an output catalog with the common map of the request and target files, but expanded by inclusion of specific contents where the requestor supplied no restrictions.

As an example, consider a text file with three levels. The first level has heading data, the second has sentences, and the third has annotations. Let the request leave headings and sentences unrestricted, but specify that the annotation shall be "question". Alternative annotations might be "declarative" and "imperative". The system, in response to this request, will examine every heading datum, go down to each sentence datum in turn, examine its annotation data and if any one of them contains "question" transfer the heading, the sentence, and the annotation to a new catalog. The user thus obtains a catalog of question sentences, which he can manipulate as he pleases. It is presumably very much smaller than the target catalog, but perhaps much larger than the request, which consisted of exactly three data.

Two catalogs can be merged, whether they have the same map or not. If they have different data on level 1, the user can only have one catalog written behind the other. If they have the same class on level 1, the user specifies an order for all of the different classes on level 2, including those in both catalogs, but always keeping the relative order of the classes from one catalog unchanged. If the two catalogs have one or more common classes on the second level, the user specifies the arrangement of descendant classes on the third level, and so on.

The merge program looks at the first level 1 data in the two catalogs and decides which comes first in the merged catalog. If they are different, it deals with the descendants of the earlier one first; if they are identical, it deals with the descendants jointly. On the second level, it either takes all the descendants of the earlier level 1 datum, or decides which level 2 descendant is earlier. Its whole job is to take things in order, eliminate duplicates, and produce an ordered catalog with the specified map.

EXERCISES

1. Write a program to handle output, on the model of Fig. 16.

2. A text is stored on tape; each word occurrence begins flush left in a 36-bit cell (when the tape is read normally) and ends with the character # (binary 111 111) flush right. Organize a program to read the text, make a sort tree (dropping duplicates), linearize the tree alphabetically, and write the result on a new tape. (Note: organize the program; do not write detailed code.)

3. What would you do if the sort tree in Ex. 1 filled all available space before all the input text had been read?

4. On two tapes, information is stored in 108-bit segments. In each segment, the first 36 bits contains the spelling of a word, and the remainder contains information about it. On each tape, the segments are in alphabetical order by word. Write a program to merge the two tapes.

5. Write one word each on 50 slips of paper, shuffle them, and divide them into two equal stacks; call these Alpha and Beta. Take the top slips from the two packs and put them face down in a new pack, Gamma. Now take a new slip from each of Alpha and Beta, and follow the instructions at the end of Sec. 2.3, creating a Delta

pile as necessary. (Note that it is always necessary to know the last word put in Gamma and in Delta.) When Alpha and Beta are empty, count the breaks of alphabetical order in Gamma and Delta. Reshuffle the slips and start over with new Alpha and Beta, but this time keep four slips in central storage. Take slips alternately from Alpha and Beta, but put one slip on Gamma or Delta each time, maintaining a sequence if possible. How many sequence breaks are there this time? Why the difference?

6. Draw a map for a simple bibliography.

7. If a bibliography is organized by subject classes, and an author index is wanted, what catalog manipulations must be performed?

8. Write an Algol program to read a dictionary of the kind illustrated in Fig. 18. Put the entry words into an array EW[i]; put the grammatical descriptions into an array G[j]. Make each P[i] a pointer to the first component of G[j] that belongs to EW[i]. Of course, an entry word can have any number of grammatical descriptions. Do not store definitions.

REFERENCES

Natural Language in Computer Form (Martin Kay and Theodore W. Ziehe; RM-4390-PR, The RAND Corporation, February 1965; *also* RALP pp. 33–49) explains the use of alphabet flags and also introduces catalog structure.

"The Catalog: A Flexible Data Structure for Magnetic Tape" (Martin Kay and Theodore W. Ziehe; *AFIPS Conference Proceedings*, Vol. 27, Part I (1965), pp. 283–291) explains how recursive catalogs, containing other catalogs as data, are built, and surveys addressing problems.

The Catalog Input/Output System (Martin Kay, Frederick D. Valadez, and Theodore W. Ziehe; RM-4540-PR, The RAND Corporation, March 1966) treats the movement of catalogs between core storage and magnetic tape.

Contribution à la Théorie des Catalogues (Michel Trehel; thesis presented to the Faculty of Sciences of the University of Grenoble, November 1965) develops a formal setting for problems of transformation and other manipulations of catalogs.

Chapter 4

ACQUISITION, STORAGE, AND PRESENTATION
OF TEXTUAL DATA

Computer programmers use the words input and output ambiguously. Transfers between core storage and magnetic tape are called
input and output operations, even if the magnetic tape in question is
being used merely to store data between successive main frame
operations. When a typist sits at a keyboard typing manuscript into a
machine readable form, that is also called input; and when a high-
speed printer produces pages for inspection by a linguist, that is
output. The present chapter is concerned with the acquisition of data
from sources external to the computer complex, and presentation of
data to a human audience.

Every linguist who uses a computer must be touchy about acquisition
and presentation of data. His informants, his colleagues, his assistants,
editors, and he himself are accustomed to thinking of certain graphic
shapes as belonging to their language. In his own work, the linguist is
hampered if he does not have an adequate range of basic characters,
variants on them such as italics and bold face, special symbols of the
kind used for phonetic transcription, diacritics, and facilities for
positioning characters relative to one another as need be. Such problems
arise both in transcription of source documents and presentation of
intermediate or final results. When he works for someone else, the
linguist's techniques may be worthless if he cannot provide reproducible
pages of "graphic arts" quality. Some publishers may occasionally
accept book indexes that resemble nothing so much as "cryptic tele-
grams from a mechanical god," but in general they will not look past
the presentation to see the advantages of automatic indexing or other
processing.

Aside from his demands for quality, entailing large fonts and flexible
arrangement schemes, the linguist's problems of acquisition and
presentation are compounded by the human operator's inadequacy as
translator of graphic shapes into key strokes, the simplicity of keyboard
devices and printers, and the internal restriction to six or eight-bit
characters. To deal with such an array of horns on his dilemma, the

linguist must have many ways of encoding the same information. At acquisition, he must have encoding schemes adapted to the limitations of the operator and recording device; for internal operations he must have encoding schemes suitable to uniform treatment of indefinite variety; and for presentation of his results he must have a variety of schemes, graded by cost and output quality, so that he can meet the requirements of a specific task without wasting funds.

No linguist should be expected to design complete facilities for acquisition and presentation of data, starting with general principles and standard hardware. Fortunately, the tendency to standardization of encoding schemes and dissemination of programs for handling them is well established. The purpose of the present chapter is to set forth basic ideas and indicate the general lines of packaged systems that every computing linguist can eventually have as his birthright.

I. DEVICES AND CHARACTER SETS

A complete rig, including acquisition and presentation systems, can be put together on one table and wired directly to a computer. We call the rig a *console*. Heretofore, consoles were rare and devices could be classified as suitable for either acquisition or presentation of data. An acquisition device consists of a keyboard and a mechanism for recording key strokes sequentially in a medium that can be sensed at low cost by a machine: Magnetic tape, punched paper tape, or Hollerith cards. A third and optional element makes a graphic transcription of key strokes for immediate inspection—for example, on a sheet of paper or along the top edge of a Hollerith card; hardly anyone prints along the edge of punched paper tape. Data presentation devices accept encoded information, by wire or on cards or tape. Some of the encoded information is used to position the paper stock, the printing mechanism, and other parts of the machine; the rest straightforwardly causes printing of characters. Many physical processes have been used for the formation of characters, but three predominate. One causes mechanical contact of a raised character, an ink source, and paper. Another passes a beam of light through a negative of the character onto photosensitive stock. The third moves an electron beam back and forth, around and about, to shape selected characters.

I.I. Keyboards

The standard typewriter keyboard (Fig. 23) is familiar to everyone Some of the buttons are labeled with letters of the alphabet; thanks to *shift* and *shift-lock* keys, each letter key causes printing of the typist's choice of two versions of each character. If only two versions are common, it is because typewriter manufacturers fit their equipment to the needs and financial ability of the customers. It would be possible to build typewriters with three, four, or more versions of each letter. Numbers do not ordinarily have upper-case and lower-case variants.

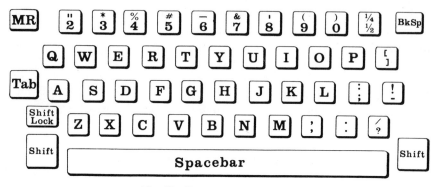

Fig. 23—Typewriter keyboard

Some clever inventor took advantage of the shift mechanism to increase the character set of the standard typewriter by putting symbols into the upper-case positions on the number keys. Obviously, the upper-case symbols are not related to the lower case numbers as the upper and lower-case letters are related pairwise. Besides the keys for graphic marks, typewriters have function keys: *shift, shift-lock, tab, carriage return*, and possibly others.

A paper-tape typewriter uses the same keyboard as a standard electric typewriter; even the function keys punch frames of tape, since otherwise the meaning of a given key stroke would be indeterminate. For example, the punching produced by a letter key stands for the upper-case version of the letter when the typewriter is in upper case, and the lower-case version otherwise. The meaning of a character is also determined in part by its position on the page, and without signals for carriage return and tabulation, positioning would be undecidable. Of course, the locations of the tab stops must be known independently. Paper-tape typewriters are not all identical; one significant difference has to do with line feed, which can be independent of carriage return or combined with it. When they are independent, a carriage return alone moves the typing mechanism to the left margin without advancing to a new line. Some typewriters have backspace and others do not. Some devices, used in the printing industry, have double shifting; with them, upper and lower-case versions of both standard and italic letters are possible.

The typical keyboard of a cardpunch has less variety. Only upper-case characters (in point of fact, caseless characters) are available. Besides the 48 graphic characters, there are just a few function keys, and they do not punch holes in the card. Whereas tabbing on a paper tape typewriter must be recorded, tabbing on a keypunch has the effect of putting the next perforation in a different column. Whereas line advance must be recorded on paper tape, card advance simply puts the following information into a new card.

Paper-tape typewriters have long been used in the communications industry. A tape is typed at the operator's speed, corrected, then transmitted by radio or wire at full speed. They are used for computer input, for some general office work, and in the printing industry. Most paper-tape typewriters provide hard copy; that is, their "buttons" actuate punches and keys that print on paper. Those used by the printing industry often force the operator to work blind. The card-punch is available in versions that print one letter per card column, along the top edge.

1.2. Shifts

Consider the case of the linguist who is about to acquire a block of natural language text for computer processing. He chooses the text; let us say a collection of printed documents. He chooses the best device available to him, perhaps a paper-tape typewriter or a card punch. Surveying the characters and arrangements of the text, he discovers that the printer has outdone him. He has several alternatives, which he can mix to suit his purposes.

He can flatfootedly disregard some distinctions. For example, he can instruct his typist to punch boldface type as if it were the standard lightface variety. He can group together symbols and strings of symbols that are more or less irrelevant to his purposes; thus, he can instruct his typist to punch a single, special character whenever there is a chemical formula, no matter how complex. He can precode some data. For example, he can classify lines set in different type styles, such as chapter headings, section headings, footnotes, and the like, and punch not typographic features such as face, size, and position but instead functional categories. This policy may be more economical than any other, where it is appropriate.

For the rest, he can establish conventional encodings. Thus, the letter string *alf* can be defined to mean the Greek letter *alpha*. Such letter strings must be chosen to have two properties: They must be extremely unlikely in the input text, and they must be easy to re-member, since the typist has to use them. Often combinations such as *period-comma* are used on cardpunches to signify *semicolon*. A sequence like *period-comma* will not often occur in normal printed input, and the typist can quickly remember how to encode a semicolon. To be absolutely certain of unambiguous codes, the linguist must assign one symbol to mean that the following string has a special, not a standard interpretation. A symbol used for that purpose is like a shift, and can in fact be used with a much-simplified encoding convention.

Let us examine first the situation that obtains with a typewriter having interchangeable type and an attached paper-tape punch. The IBM Selectric typewriter mechanism, with type on the surface of a sphere that can be removed and replaced quickly, is one example. Paper-tape punches of this sort are manufactured by Dura Business Machines. If the input mixes two alphabets, such as Greek and Roman or Roman and Cyrillic, a typing sphere can be obtained for each alphabet. The buttons on the keyboard can be labeled each with a character from each sphere. When the typist is following Roman-alphabet copy, with the Roman sphere in the machine, and comes to Greek letters, she stops the machine, takes out one sphere, puts in the other, and continues. The keyboard is easy to use, the paper copy contains the correct information, and the paper tape contains all the information needed to follow the original material except signals to show when the sphere is going to change. For that purpose, one character must be reserved in each alphabet. This character signals a switch to the other sphere, and can be interpreted by a computer without difficulty.

If the typewriter does not have interchangeable type, the same plan can nevertheless be adopted, but with some inconvenience. Let each button have its two labels, say Roman and Greek; the Roman char-acters on the buttons match those printed on paper when the buttons are struck. The Greek characters are arranged in any convenient manner. When the typist comes to Greek letters, she strikes the button signalling a change of alphabet; the computer that receives this input recognizes it and treats the following punches as standing for Greek letters. The printing element of the acquisition device continues to print Roman letters, however, and the inconvenience arises if proof-reading is attempted. If the Greek letters are arranged on the buttons as they would be on a Greek typewriter, the Roman letters printed constitute a strange transliteration; even if the Greek letters are placed to give the best possible transliteration, the result is not good.

Problems of this order have no good solutions; they have diverse partial solutions, appropriate under different circumstances. If the typist is unaccustomed to any alphabet but the Roman, a good plan is to use a nonstandard Cyrillic or Greek keyboard, rearranging the letters to put them on the key tops with the counterparts under whatever translation scheme the typist considers natural. The punching for each character is entirely arbitrary, in any case, and can be decoded by a computer that knows what conventions are in use. If the typist knows the Cyrillic and Greek alphabets, it is perhaps best to retain the standard keyboard and disregard the hard copy except occasionally, when the use of a decoding chart will be required. If the amount of Greek or Cyrillic to be processed is large enough to justify the expense, which can be high, any data acquisition device can be modified to have as its standard hard-copy alphabet the characters on the keyboard in a standard Cyrillic or Greek arrangement.

Many data acquisition problems are less clearly defined but also less grave than those that come with multiple alphabets. The source documents may consist of Roman-alphabet characters with boldface, italics, accents, and a few other symbols that do not appear on the regular keyboard of the device available. The linguist's design job is then to choose conventions that will be convenient to the input typist. One basic principle is to choose the commonest characters of the source document and get them in easy locations on the keyboard, each encodable with a single stroke. The French *e acute* can be put on the keyboard at the cost of one standard, but rarely used, character such as the *circled a* meaning "at." It may be wisest to keep some rare diacritics separate from base letters, instructing the typist to strike a certain key for the diacritic before (or after) the normal key for the base character. In a system of this kind, the French *a* with grave accent might be typed as the two-character sequence *#a*.

To represent the distinction between upper and lower-case letters in Hollerith cards, or to represent the difference between normal letters and italics in most data-acquisition systems, or to enlarge the character set to encompass bold-face characters, special shifts are needed. They work just like the alphabet-change symbols already described. In standard paper-tape machines, a single capital letter is represented by three frames of tape, one for *upshift*, one for the character, and one for *downshift*. The same plan can be used in punching Hollerith cards, if one of the Hollerith characters is reserved to mean shift—*upshift* when the preceding characters are in lower case, *downshift* when the preceding characters are in upper case. To save labor for the typist, it may be appropriate to define a one-character shift that applies only to the single following character. If a word of the source document is in capital letters, the one-character shift can be punched before each character of the word. As on a standard typewriter, so in specially defined systems, "upper case" numbers and punctuation can be given whatever significance is most useful.

Any special features of the acquisition device should be used to the fullest advantage. For example, typists are accustomed to underscoring as a representation for italicized material. If the input device can backspace and underscore, so much the better—the time needed to move backward may well be made up by savings in proofreading and correction thanks to familiarity with the convention. With backspace, overstriking becomes possible. Overstriking can have the effect of eliminating the first character in the position, or it can combine two characters in one place to make a new one, as when a dollar sign is formed by overstriking a slant line with a capital *s*. Since the special features of each device are chosen by each manufacturer from an unlimited set of possible features, there is little of a general nature to be said about their use; the point for the linguist is not to overlook them.

1.3. Presentation problems

When the computer was invented, a complicated device called the lineprinter was in widespread use. It is being replaced by other, entirely different machines for data presentation, but it is likely that linguists will have to deal with lineprinters if they deal with computers at all.

A lineprinter is a mechanical device which positions paper stock, imprints one line of characters across it, then advances the paper and prints a new line. Any electric typewriter does the same thing, but the lineprinter does not print character positions one by one across the line. In its older embodiment, the lineprinter has one complete printing mechanism for each horizontal position on the page. If the sheet is to have 70 or 120 positions from left to right, the lineprinter has 70 or 120 sets of characters. As the paper is being advanced, the independent printing mechanisms are adjusted separately but simultaneously, then put simultaneously into contact with the paper. A later version, first offered by IBM, has one or more sets of characters moving continuously across the page. As soon as any character passes the place on the page where it is wanted, it is struck. Thus several characters may be striking simultaneously; hence the character positions across the page will be filled in an unorderly manner. Devices of the first kind have often had only 48 characters per position; devices of the second kind can easily be modified to print, for example, 80, 120, or 240 characters instead of 48.

Depending on details of their construction, lineprinters are gloriously capable or incapable of such special operations as double striking to obtain characters of greater body, overstriking to obtain composite characters, underscoring, and so on.

A lineprinter with 120 characters, with half-line advance, with multistrike ability and diacritics among its characters, and with the possibility of several kinds of underscoring can produce hard copy slightly more elegant than most typewriters. It still does not have the typist's ability to squeeze letters together, making 3 fit into the space of 2. And it certainly does not have the range of a typewriter with interchangeable keys, or of standard typesetting equipment.

If the text to be presented is encoded with boldface, multiple alphabets, several sizes of each, and other complexities such as tall and short integral signs, the graphic capabilities of the lineprinter must be supplemented with conventions. Thus, transliterations of the non-standard alphabets are needed. It is also necessary to indicate unambiguously when a segment of the text being presented is transliterated from its stored form. Transliterations are needed, of course, for alphabets of mathematical symbols, printer's marks, or any other characters that have to be presented and are not in the repertoire of the device. One way to mark transliterations is by reserving characters to bound them; these characters can be printed on a separate line above the main line of text or raised by half a line. Linguists who are accustomed to phonetic, morphemic, and other transcriptions and techniques for marking them explicitly in text will find such conventions familiar.

1.4. Elegant presentation devices

Electromechanical systems are expensive to build, difficult to make operate fast, and hard to build with large character sets. Clean impressions are not easy to obtain. For all these reasons, both numerical computer applications and automatic language processing have motivated development of other kinds of data-presentation devices. In particular, use of computers in the printing industry calls for very high speed and very high quality.

Early photocomposition devices, such as the first versions of Photon and Linofilm, used photosensitive stock and stored negative images of characters. In general, such systems work in this way. A light beam passes through the image of the character to be printed. Either the light beam is deflected by a mirror to pass through the desired character, or the set of characters is moved physically to bring the desired one into the fixed path of the beam. Then the beam passes through lens systems to obtain the desired degree of magnification. Several different lenses may be available, and moved into position automatically. Thus, several sizes of type may be obtainable from one set of stored images. Another mirror is used to position the beam at the desired place on the photosensitive stock. A standard technique is to fill one line of characters, then advance the material and start again at the left margin. Such a device can be controlled by encoded information from a computer. The incoming codes determine mirror positions, lens selection, and so on.

If the stock can be held steady, and if the beam can be deflected accurately at large angles in horizontal and vertical dimensions, a whole page can be created at one time. Page production simplifies the problems involved in output preparation, since everything in the left-hand column of a two-column page can be transmitted from the computer before material for the righthand column is sent. If each line is being filled separately, it is necessary to process all of one column before transmitting any of it, then to transmit one line of the first column, one line of the second column, and so on.

Instead of the light beam, a stream of electrons can be used; in most systems of this type, the electron beam is not aimed at photosensitive stock but at a screen like that used in a television tube. Where the beam strikes, the screen emits light. The screen can be made flat, and the paper kept in contact with it. Characters are produced in three different ways. One, used in Stromberg-Carlson devices among others, is to pass the electron beam through a negative image of the character. The beam is shaped just as a light beam would be. The second technique, also used by Stromberg-Carlson, is to move the beam through a sequence of short strokes. The letter E would be made with 4 strokes, one for the vertical part and one for each of the horizontal parts. The letter C would be made with a number of short strokes, so that the curve would not be smooth, but the irregularities would be almost imperceptible. A third technique, demanding extremely fine resolution on the screen, is to divide each character into many small regions with outlines that can be described by simple mathematical functions. The beam is run back and forth over each such area, so as to completely fill it in. In the first system, the beam is larger in diameter than any character; in the second, it is about as wide as the strokes that are to be made; in the third, the beam must be much narrower than the stroke of the character. Where the beam strikes the tube, it must not cause luminescence over an area much larger than its own diameter. The third system, developed by M. V. Mathews and associates at Bell

Laboratories, was announced in 1965, when electronic tubes of the required quality were just being offered for the first time.

One other system mixes optical and electronic elements. CBS Laboratories and Mergenthaler developed a device in which the character to be printed is stored as a negative image, through which light passes to a television camera; the character is reformed in the proper location and size on the face of a television-type tube.

Some of these systems were to have speeds of about 10,000 characters per second. At such speeds, it is even reasonable to think of forming halftone images with fonts of dots of various diameters. Thus, text and illustrations could be produced on a page simultaneously.

2. FROM CHARACTER TO PAGE

A good complete system for automatic language processing can accept text from many sources. It operates in a shop equipped with one or more data-acquisition devices, adapted by sets of conventions to the special requirements of many different jobs. The proud possessors of the system can accept text from publishers of books and magazines, from the Library of Congress and other producers of index entries and abstracts, and from other places. Any external source that can submit data in standard, archival format and encoding is to be thanked; but those who use other schemes must be thanked too, and to avoid irony the receiving linguist must have programs available permitting him to read tapes in arbitrary format, and standardized ones, without excess difficulty. Since he wants to simplify the work of his typists, he will use his data-acquisition system on their work also.

We simplify only a little if we assume that every input scheme is divided into pages, that is, independent units; and that every page consists of lines and character positions. Taken together, the i-th character positions of all the lines on the page comprise the i-th column. Each character position is either blank or occupied by a character, which may be composite. To put a composite character in one position, depending on the device in use, the typist may be able to backspace and overstrike, use dead keys for all but one of the characters in the space, or return to the left margin without advancing to a new line and either space or strike across some or all characters on the line.

2.1. Line arrays

For many different operations, and in particular for normalization of text acquired in arbitrary encoding, a thoroughly elaborate representation of the characters on a line—or, more generally, in any text string—is desirable. A line array is a sequence of character positions. In core storage, it is appropriate to think of each character position as occupying one cell. Each position is described by a set of features. The character occupying the position can be determined by inspecting all features at that place; taken separately, the features represent linguistically significant independent properties of the character.

Some features are binary, but not all features need be. Thus, each feature occupies one or more bits in a storage cell. The value of a 1-bit feature is either 0 or 1; the possible values of any feature are the possible configurations of the bits allowed it. Thinking of Algol, the line array is a group of feature arrays; taking the elements of each of the arrays with a common subscript, the whole character can be determined.

In the case of text acquired through a paper-tape typewriter, it might be appropriate to define one feature for underscoring, one for each accent, one to indicate whether the character is a letter or not, perhaps another to indicate whether the character is a number or not, and one to identify the individual character among those of the same class; thus, if the character is a number, this feature identifies it as a certain number, or if the character is a letter, it identifies it as a certain letter. If the input text is transcribed phonetically, a different plan may be more appropriate; features such as vowel-consonant, voiced-unvoiced, and the like may be wanted, thus obviating the need for an arbitrary identifying feature.

If several alphabets are mixed in the input, one feature will be reserved for alphabet identification.

An array of this type permits different kinds of processing. If capitalization is a feature, finding the first capitalized character in the array is done by examining the array of capitalization features. It is of course possible to find the first capitalized character in an array whenever capitalization is unambiguously indicated. It is more convenient, for obvious reasons, to do so in an array of the kind introduced here.

2.2. Acquisition of a line

We are given a paper tape from an acquisition device; in accordance with its content, we wish to fill in a line array. Let us examine some of the conditions we will meet.

When we read a shift code, we must remember what shift we are in until receiving another. On going into upper-case shift, we must start putting in the feature *upper case* (capitalization), whenever we store a letter in the array, but if special marks are the upper-case companions to numbers in lower-case, we will have to store altogether different configurations of features on reading a number-key code. The best we can do is probably store a table of feature combinations for each possible shift of the source device; knowing what shift we are in, we read a frame of input and use its content as an index to a line of the proper shift table.

Frames of input do not correspond to character positions in the array, at least not in a simple way. Some input codes advance us from position to position—these are the ordinary graphic marks, and the spacebar code. Others leave us unmoved; these are dead keys, shifts, and line advance without carriage return. The backspace code moves us backward one position. The tabulator code advances us to the next tab stop forward from our current position. Carriage return without line feed returns us to the first position of the array.

Let us recapitulate. We are working on a line array, we know what shift we are in, and we have a pointer to a certain position in the array. Reading the next frame of the source tape, we look it up in the current shift table, store the features it indicates in the current position of the array, move along the array as it dictates, change shifts if it requires that, and start a new line array if it tells us to.

Only one point in all this requires further discussion. If overstriking is possible we can store features in the same place twice. What we really want is the combination of features previously stored with those added by new input frame. A convenient way to do this is to make sure that no features are stored in the line array before we begin, then to take the union of features present with features added whenever we put anything into the array at all. At the end, a position in the array will be blank if no features were ever attributed to it, but if one or more keystrokes did attribute features to the position they will all be there.

2.3. Presentation of a line

Suppose now that we have a line of text stored in some archival format. We can readily convert that source string into a line array as described in the preceding section. If the line is to be presented by a line printer, it is easy to work from the line array and obtain control signals as necessary for further operation.

The base characters are recoded by paying attention to the features *letter*, *number*, and *identifier*. Now, scan the line array for diacritics. If none are present, go on. If diacritics are found, the paper must be held in place for restriking and the character codes for diacritics can be determined. Next scan for underscore. If there is any, the paper must be held in place for more restriking.

Before the paper is moved up for a new line of printing, the next line array has to be examined. Superscripts in the text itself, which would presumably be indicated by a feature *superscript*, will cause the paper to be advanced a little less than for printing the body line. Superscripts might also be needed to mark the strings within the line that are transliterated from a special alphabet. If these nontextual superscripts occupy print positions across the line, which thereby become unavailable for printing text characters, adjustment of the character positions in the array is necessary.

If the line length specified for presentation does not correspond to the line length of stored material, character counting is necessary. Perhaps a paragraph stored as a few long lines is to be printed as a deeper paragraph of short lines. Taking the first stored line, and forming an array, one printer line is filled. When the next stored line is added to the array, another line can be taken off, and so on.

2.4. Blocks and pages

For the librarian processing a card catalog, one page of input may be a three-by-five inch unit. For the bibliographer, the proper definition of page may be just the amount of material required to describe one publication—perhaps only two or three lines. For a linguist, a page may well be the amount of text that can be printed or typed on an ordinary sheet of paper. The term is taken here to mean an independent unit, acquired or presented by itself. For many jobs, acquisition pages and presentation pages differ; the bibliographer may define the page at acquisition as one entry, but take the presentation page to be what he can put on a sheet of paper.

Typically, a page must be developed in storage as a set of line arrays before any of it can be released for further processing. At input, paper tape may be read line by line until a page boundary is located, then the set of line arrays turned over to other programs for further analysis. When a stored file is to be presented, the material is taken and loaded into line arrays until the capacity of a physical page is reached or until some internal boundary, requiring a fresh start, is identified.

The RAND acquisition system includes a program that develops the page by alternately reading one line of source material and checking whether that line, in combination with preceding lines, establishes a page boundary. It allows fairly sophisticated page-boundary definitions; a program is written in a special language adapted to the purpose, describing what sequence of line types makes a boundary. Conditional expressions can be used; thus, a page boundary might be marked by a line of type A, followed by a line of type B or C, and if type B then type D, or if C then A again. The characteristic line can mark either the end of one page, or the beginning of another. Naturally, if the beginning of a new page is put into storage before the end of an old page is recognized, the fresh beginning must be saved as part of the next page to be developed after the previous page has been processed.

When a program defining page boundaries calls for a line of a certain type, it refers to another program, which defines that type of line as a certain character string. For example, it might be required that a line be blank, or that it contain some nonblank characters, or that it contain exactly five blanks followed by nonblanks, or that it contain a centered, one or two-digit number. Obviously, the features that are assigned the positions in the line array are the ones that can most easily be used in such line-type prescriptions. In fact, the RAND system only allows for selection of certain features and specification of whether they contain ones or zeros. If underscoring is a feature, the system masks out all features but that one and requires that this single bit have the value *one*. A program for determining whether a line is of a certain type can include conditional expressions so that, for example, one program suffices to determine whether a line is blank except for a number flush left or flush right.

A part of a page is a block. In both acquisition and presentation, a block is defined by its left-most and right-most character positions, and by its starting and ending points within those boundaries. A typical two-column page might consist of one block extending across the top of the page from side to side, with two more blocks beneath it, namely the left and righthand columns. Some sort of title might be in the top block, with text in the two columns. The acquisition system takes a page and looks for rows or columns of characters of specified types. Once a block is defined, it can be cut into sub-blocks, and those can be cut again. The acquisition system is thus capable of finding many small, intricately interwoven blocks on a page. The presentation system establishes the blocks and fills them with material given to it. To allow for such combinations as body text and footnotes, the presentation system even provides for boxes with boundaries fixed according to the relative amounts of different kinds of material to be presented. A page can be filled with body text, subject to the requirement that all footnotes referenced within that material be included at the foot of the same page.

2.5. Sophisticated systems

Experimental systems already constructed give some clues about the future. Devices combining photoelectric elements, analogue computing, and digital logic will make it possible to acquire text and illustrations starting from printed pages. Early commercial systems, for reasons of economy, could handle only small character sets and fixed arrangements on the page. A publisher might find use for an automatic page reader, even if he had to equip his manuscript type-writers with special type faces and put all copy on preformatted sheets. Some of the problems of correction might be simplified if the hard copy could serve for proofreading and also as input material; with hard copy and paper tape, matching corrections to errors can be a hard job. For many purposes, automatic printreading is not worth while unless the device is capable of handling large character sets, free arrangements, and changes in character sets from job to job.

Even when reading devices of adequate power are available, they will present a new kind of problem to the user. He will no longer have the pre-editing option or the typist's interpretations that he counts on with keyboard operated input devices. He will scarcely have any alternative but to discriminate chapter headings by size and position. Sentence boundaries may not be determinable except by full-scale analysis of a large portion of the text—in some rare instances, it may be impossible, even after semantical tests are made, to say whether the author intended to end a sentence. In short, once the hardware is ready, there will be software development to do.

Simultaneous parallel acquisition of illustrations and equations along with straight text is already possible, and possesses great advantages. The typewriter has never been a mathematician's tool. Chemists and mathematicians may be able to use specially adapted typewriters for their purposes, but the best way to lay out a structural formula is with the equivalent of pencil and paper. The software problems may be difficult, but they are not insoluble.

A good internal representation of mathematical formulae taking into account their two-dimensional nature—whether by position descrip-tions or by functional relationships—is needed. An integral can be described as a function with four arguments: the lower and upper limits, the integrand, and the variable of integration. It can also be described as occupying a certain place on the page, relative to the graphic marks constituting its arguments. Either or both techniques may be needed, but as yet neither has been worked out adequately and linked with any of the input devices that permits sketches to go directly into computer storage. The grammar of mathematical expres-sions and chemical formulae is much simpler than that of arbitrary pictures. Picture input is possible, but goes little further than direct representation of black, white, and a few shades of grey.

Future acquisition and presentation systems will probably include consoles for input and correction of text, insertion of formulae and illustrations. There will probably be devices capable of producing, at low cost, master sheets from which plates can be made, from which text and illustrations of all kinds are composed in a single run.

3. TEXT STORAGE

A data-acquisition device has three mechanical parts: a keyboard, a printing element, and an encoding element. A data-presentation device has decoding and printing elements. These parts are physical objects, capable of doing certain tasks in certain ways; their capacities define sets of character codes. Different devices have different capabilities, to which acquisition and presentation schemes must be adapted. Internal storage plans must fit the limitations of storage devices, but need not be matched with either acquisition or presentation plans.

3.1. An expandable code

The 6-bit unit can serve for an encoding of text that allows for indefinitely many letters and symbols; indeed, several techniques would work. The one presented here is due to Martin Kay, Theodore W. Ziehe, and collaborators at the RAND Corporation, the University of California, Berkeley, and elsewhere.

Each of the 64 configurations of 6 bits is permanently defined as a flag or an alphabetic character, except one that is set aside to fill unused positions. A flag denotes a certain alphabet; in a sequence of characters, the flags determine how following characters are to be interpreted. One flag denotes the Roman alphabet; the 6-bit configurations following it are treated as Roman characters until another flag appears. There are flags for the Greek, Cyrillic, and other alphabets, and if necessary there can be a flag indicating that the next character is a flag—so that the number of alphabets can grow without limit.

By design, each alphabet consists of 48 characters. In the Roman alphabet, 26 are letters and 10 are diacritics; these, together with the apostrophe, are the graphic characters. One is a blank. But there are also 8 shift characters, that influence the style or position of following graphic characters, and a shift terminator. Some of the shifts are *capitalization, boldface, superscript,* and *large.* Most alphabets require shifts and diacritics. Hence punctuation must be encoded in an alphabet all its own, and symbols (commercial, mathematical, etc.) in another.

A separate alphabet is provided for boundaries, if the linguist chooses to identify and record them. For example, sentence boundaries can be marked.

3.2. Some storage modes

When the catalog system is used for storage of text on magnetic tape, data of certain classes have text strings as values. That is to say, such a datum is a string of 36N bits, or 6N units. The first unit is a flag, and there can be other flags within the datum. The length of the datum is brought up to 6N by means of the filler configuration; if 92 units are needed, 4 fillers are added to make 96, so that the value of the datum just fills 16 cells.

Internally, text storage can be continuous. A line or sentence—even a small book—is stored in consecutive cells with filler only at the end. This mode of storage is natural only in transferring to or from external storage. Most operations on text are more convenient with other storage modes.

A second mode of internal storage is segmental. What the segments are can be decided by the linguist when he plans an operation; they may be morphs for one purpose, word-form occurrences for another, or syllables for a third. Each segment occupies an integral number of cells, with filler at the end if necessary. The filler can serve as a boundary marker, but of course in that case at least one filler character must be recorded at the end of every segment.

Segmental mode has two extreme versions, with many possible intermediates. Let us call one textual; the first character of every segment is an alphabet flag, and all shifts and diacritics are retained in order. If a whole sentence is in italics, the italic-shift character occurs just once in continuous mode, with a shift terminator at the end. When the same sentence is recorded in the textual-segmental mode, an italic-shift character is stored with every segment. Hence each segment can be read in isolation.

The other extreme is to eliminate all flags and shifts. Let us call this version lexical. When a text is reduced to this form, each segment can be expected to match identically an entry in a lexicon. For some purposes, a good plan is to store text in this manner, but to accompany each segment with a cell of information about applicable shifts.

A third storage mode puts just one character in each cell. The line arrays of Sec. 2.1 illustrate use of this mode; there, the whole cell may be filled with features of a character. At the other extreme, each cell can be filled with zeros except for the rightmost six (or even five) bit positions; there one character is stored. It can be a flag, shift, diacritic, or base letter; or all characters except base letters can be eliminated.

In Algol, a reasonable way to store text is in an array. Since the 64 binary patterns of six bits correspond naturally to the integers $0, \ldots, 63$, the components of the array can have integer values. Each component can be used to store one character, or several characters can be stored in one component (as they can in one cell).

3.3. Interconversions

Since the various modes of storage are more convenient for different purposes, it is often necessary to convert a text from one mode into another. Let us consider some of these interconversions.

First, let us suppose that a text is stored in continuous mode, beginning in cell $T(One)$ and ending with at least one filler character. We can read it, character by character, using a double iteration. The instruction $SWR(T(I)/J)$ is executed for $I = 1$ and $J = 1, \ldots, 6$; then I is raised to 2, and the iteration on J begins again.

When each character is to be put into a separate cell, an independent iteration is needed. Let cells $S(One)$, $S(Two)$, etc., be reserved for the text in character-per-cell mode. Then $STORE(S(K))$, with K increased each time, puts the characters away. If storage in segmental mode is wanted, double iteration on this side is necessary.

Tests must intervene. One is to recognize filler, so that the process can be stopped when the text has been exhausted. For conversion to segmental storage, a test for blanks or other segment boundaries is needed. If flags and shifts are to be removed, tests for them come in.

A special indexing instruction can shorten these programs substantially. In many computers, such instructions are primitive; they can also be provided in software. The programmer writes an instruction which the compiler expands somehow into a sequence of instructions that the computer can carry out.

If no indexing instruction is available, iteration must be programmed as it was in several earlier examples. Let I be an index variable for which values from 1 to 6 are wanted. It is given its initial value, used, and then advanced:

```
SWR(I)
ADD(One)
STORE(I)
TRANS(Six, X, Y)
GOTO(Y)
```

If the new value of I is less than or equal to the limiting value 6, control goes to Y, where the new value is used for an additional iteration. When the new value is greater than the limit, control goes to X; the iteration is finished and something else should be done.

Now consider the instruction

$$INDEX(A, B, C, D)$$

where A, B, and C are cell names and D is a program location. Cell A is used for indexing, B contains the increment, and C contains the limit.

Control goes to D if A + B ≤ C, and to the next instruction otherwise. Thus, INDEX(I, *One*, *Six*, Y) has the same effect as the sequence of instructions given above, provided X is understood to be the line following the INDEX instruction.

Now we can return to the problem of converting text from continuous mode into character-per-cell mode. The program in Fig. 24 begins, in lines 1–4, by initializing the three index cells, I, J, and K. At line 5, it takes the next source character and tests (line 6) whether it is a filler;

Location	Instruction	Comment
1.	SWR(One)	Initialize I, J, K
2.	STORE(I)	
3.	STORE(J)	
4.	STORE(K)	
5. Take:	SWR(T(I)/J)	Source character
6.	TRANS(Fill, Error, Put)	Is it filler?
7.	GOTO(Done)	Yes
8. Put:	STORE(S(K))	No; put it away
9.	INDEX(J, One, Six, Kay)	Advance J
10.	INDEX(I, One, N, J-set)	Advance I after J = 6
11.	GOTO(Nofill)	Source exhausted
12. J-set	SWR(One)	Reset J for new cell
13.	STORE(J)	
14. Kay:	INDEX(K, One, M, Take)	Advance K
15.	SWR(T(I)/J)	Output full
16.	TRANS(Fill, Error, Overflow)	Is next source character filler?
17. Done	SWR(K)	Yes
18.	SUB(One)	Set length of output
19.	STORE(Length)	
20.	GOTO(Out)	

**Fig. 24—Conversion of text from continuous mode
to character-per-cell mode**

since the filler character is binary 111 111, no text character can have a greater value, and an error has occurred if one appears to. If the source character is a filler, the text has all been converted (line 7); otherwise, the character is stored in the new sequence (line 8). Now index variable J is advanced (line 14), but if J is too large, I must be advanced to get a new cell of source text (line 10), and J must be put back to its initial value (lines 12–13) before K is dealt with.

On line 11, the situation is that the source text has been exhausted and no filler encountered. Location *Nofill* is to deal with this error. On line 15, the space allotted to the text in character-per-cell mode has been exhausted. If the next source character is a filler (line 16), all is well; if not, an overflow must be announced.

When control reaches line 17, the job is done; the content of K points to the first unused cell. Subtracting 1 yields the length of the character string, which is now ready for further operations.

Conversion into segmental mode is more complex, because flags and shifts must be controlled, filler must be added, and indexing by characters is necessary on both sides. For the sake of a simple example, let us assume that the text contains no shifts and only two flags; let us cut at blanks. The binary configurations involved in comparisons are 001 101, the punctuation flag; 011 101, the Roman flag; 110 000, the blank; and 111 111, the filler.

The program displayed in Fig. 25 would have to be embedded in

Location	Instruction	Comment
1.	SWR(T(I)/J)	Source character
2.	TRANS(Roman, B-test, P-test)	Is it Roman flag?
3. F-save	STORE(Flag)	Save flag
4.	GOTO(Put)	Write output
5. P-test	TRANS(Punct, Put, Put)	Is it punctuation flag?
6.	GOTO(F-save)	Save flag
7. B-test:	TRANS(Blank, Endtest, Put)	Is it blank?
8.	STORE(S(K)/H)	Write output
9.	GOTO(Index)	
10. Return:	TRANS(Blank, Ch-save, Ch-save)	Is next blank also?
11.	GOTO(Index)	Yes; iterate
12. Ch-save:	STORE(Temp)	Save first nonblank
13.	SWR(Fill)	Fill a cell
14. Fillout:	STORE(S(K)/H)	Write output
15.	INDEX(H, One, Six, Fillout)	Next position
16.	INDEX(K, One, M, H-one)	Next cell
17.	GOTO(Overflow)	No next cell
18. H-one:	SWR(One)	Initialize position
19.	STORE(H)	
20.	SWR(Temp)	Get first nonblank
21.	TRANS(Roman, Tempfill, Tempunc)	Is it Roman flag?
22.	GOTO(F-save)	Save flag
23. Tempfill:	TRANS(Fill, Error, Putflag)	Is it filler?
24.	GOTO(Done)	
25. Tempunc:	TRANS(Punct, Putflag, Putflag)	Is it punctuation flag?
26.	GOTO(F-save)	Save flag
27. Putflag:	SWR(Flag)	Old flag for new segment
28.	STORE(S(K)/H)	
29.	SWR(Two)	Next position
30.	STORE(H)	
31.	SWR(Temp)	First nonblank
32.	GOTO(Put)	
33. Endtest:	TRANS(Fill, Error, Put)	
34.	GOTO(Done)	

**Fig. 25—Section of a program to convert text
from continuous to segmental mode**

one similar to that of Fig. 24; it replaces lines 5–7 of Fig. 24, which would also have to be modified to index characters within the cells of S(K). In Fig. 25, lines 2, 5, 7, and 33 test the successive characters of the text; a flag (line 2 or 5) is saved in a cell called *Flag* before being put into its new place. A filler (line 33) marks the end of input.

A blank (line 7) marks the boundary of a segment. Any following blanks must be copied, the remainder of the current cell filled, and a new cell started with a flag. On line 8, the blank is stored. From line 9, control goes to a sequence of instructions not shown in the figure; there, I, J, K, and H are advanced, with the necessary tests for end of input and for overflow. Normally, control returns to line 10. Lines 10 and 11 go through any blanks that follow the first; when a nonblank character is reached, it is saved in cell *Temp* (line 12). The next position receives a filler (lines 13 and 14), and H is advanced. Filler characters are stored until H reaches its limit; then K is advanced (lines 16 and 17), and H is reset (lines 18 and 19).

If the first nonblank character is a flag (line 21 or 25), the situation is the same as if there had been no preceding blank; control returns to line 3. If it is a filler (line 23), the input is exhausted. Otherwise, the last flag received is copied (lines 27 and 28) and H is raised from 1 to 2. The first nonblank character is brought into the working register, and put into its new place.

3.4. Feature arrays

The interconversions of Sec. 3.3 retain the encoding of source text; flags and shifts remain after the conversion programs are applied. When the processing to be performed is most clearly formulated in terms of base characters, with occasional references to shifts and diacritics, the arrays introduced in Sec. 2.1 are convenient.

In programs for character recoding, an instruction form not previously introduced is useful. Heretofore, only cell names have been indexed, not locations. Since instructions are stored in the same cells used for data, indexing locations is not particularly difficult, whether it be carried out with hardware or expanded by a compiler. Suppose a location, say *Enter*, is fixed in a sequence of instructions. Then upon execution of GOTO(*Enter*) control passes to that location. We now introduce the notation GOTO(*Enter*(A)); upon execution of this instruction, control passes to the location found by counting downward from location *Enter* as many lines as the number stored in Cell A.

If cell A contains the binary pattern representing a character, then of course the pattern is interpreted as a number and the transfer of control takes place. There are 64 patterns of 6 bits. If the 64 lines beginning with *Table* contain appropriate instructions, GOTO(*Table*(A)) can speed recoding.

For our purposes, every character is a flag, a shift, a shift terminator, a diacritic, a base character, or a blank. Each type requires its own kind of processing.

A cell in the array is reserved for each base character or blank; the righthand 6 bits are used to identify base characters. The lefthand 6 bits always store a flag. In between, 24 bits are used for shifts and diacritics. For example, the first of those bits might be 1 if the character is capitalized, the second if it is in italics, and so on. Some other bit, e.g., the thirteenth, might be 1 if the character carries an acute accent, etc.

When a base character appears, it goes in a new cell with all current shifts, and the current flag. When shifts and flags appear, they are stored outside the array. When a diacritic appears—always earlier than the associated base—it is held. When a shift terminator appears, it clears the current shifts.

Combining bits to form the desired content of a cell is best done with a new operation:

$$OR(A)$$

This instruction changes the content of the working register by putting 1's in it wherever cell A contains 1's; the positions where cell A contains 0's are unaffected. A similar operation is:

$$AND(A)$$

This instruction puts 0's in the positions of the working register where cell A contain 0's, without changing those where A contains 1's.

The program in Fig. 26 relies on a sequence of 64 instructions with initial location *Table*; it indexes into that sequence from line 3. Each instruction in the *Table* sequence is a GOTO; if the indexing character is a flag, the instruction is GOTO(*Flag*), and so on. Control always returns to line 4, 8, 14, 17, 23, or 30 of Fig. 26, unless there are undefined characters that lead to an error routine.

A flag (line 4) is stored in the first character position of cell *Flg*, where it remains as the current flag until another replaces it. It is also used as index in a sequence of cells originating at *Codelist*; each of those cells contains a number. The one associated with the current flag is stored in F.

Another sequence of cells, originating at *Code*, is used to convert shifts, diacritics, and base characters. To enter it, we add the current content of F (line 8; this gets us into the part of the *Code* sequence appropriate to the current flag) to the current character, already in the working register. The sum, stored in P, is used as an index (line 10).

Location	Instruction	Comment
1.	SWR(T(I)/J)	Take a character
2.	STORE(Char)	
3.	GOTO(Table(Char))	What kind is it?
4. Flag:	STORE(Flg(One))	A flag; save it
5.	SWR(Codelist(Char))	And get new pointer
6.	STORE(F)	
7.	GOTO(Get)	
8. Shift:	ADD(F)	A shift; decode it
9.	STORE(P)	
10.	SWR(Code(P))	And combine it with
11.	OR(Inshift)	other current shifts
12.	STORE(Inshift)	
13.	GOTO(Get)	
14. Unshift:	SWR(Zero)	A terminator
15.	STORE(Inshift)	Clear current shifts
16.	GOTO(Get)	
17. Accent:	ADD(F)	A diacritic; decode it
18.	STORE(P)	
19.	SWR(Code(P))	And combine it with
20.	OR(Diac)	other current diacritics
21.	STORE(Diac)	
22.	GOTO(Get)	
23. Char:	ADD(F)	A base character; decode it
24.	STORE(P)	
25.	SWR(Code(P))	
26.	OR(Flg)	Combine current flag
27.	OR(Inshift)	current shifts
28.	OR(Diac)	current diacritics
29.	STORE(S(K))	and store
30. Blank:	SWR(Zero)	A base or a blank
31.	STORE(Diac)	Clear current diacritics
32.	INDEX(K, One, M, Get)	Move to next position
33.	GOTO(Overflow)	

Fig. 26—Program to recode a character string into an array of features

The result, when the current character is a shift, is to fill the working register with 0's except in the position assigned to this shift. By an OR operation, the new shift is combined with those already in force.

A shift terminator (line 14) cancels all current shifts.

A diacritic is decoded like a shift, and its bit is combined with any others presently waiting for a base character (lines 17–22).

A base character is decoded also; its cell in the *Code* sequence contains some convenient configuration in the rightmost character position. Thus, when that indication of the base character is combined with the current flag (line 26), shifts (line 27), and diacritics (line 28), the 1's from different sources necessarily go in different places.

The blank causes execution of the last few instructions of the routine for base characters. The current cell $S(K)$ is left empty. The diacritics are cleared, K is advanced, and control goes to a routine that obtains the next source character. If diacritics can occur without base characters, a slightly different program is needed.

The AND operation introduced above can be used in searching a feature array. For example, if the first capitalized character is wanted, the working register can be loaded with a bit in the proper position. Then $AND(S(K))$ yields zero if the character in $S(K)$ is not capitalized.

EXERCISES

1. Plan a keyboard for an exotic text. Assume that (i) the physical layout of Fig. 23 is mandatory, and function keys cannot be modified; (ii) new type can be purchased, so that printing keys can put any desired marks on paper.

2. Plan the necessary conventions to go with the keyboard of Ex. 1. Why are they needed?

3. Plan a line array for input from the keyboard.

4. Write conversion tables from paper-tape frames to the line array.

5. Write an Algol program to use the conversion tables.

6. Revise the program in Fig. 24 and combine it with that in Fig. 25.

7. Revise the program in Fig. 24 so that only base characters and blanks are copied.

8. Write a program to convert from lexical-segmental mode into continuous mode, with no flags. The source text ends with a filler.

9. How could the solution of Ex. 8 be modified to produce lines of text, each no longer than 72 characters? (No word breaking.)

10. Write an Algol program functionally equivalent to the one in Fig. 26.

REFERENCES

Computer Routines to Read Natural Text with Complex Formats (Patricia A. Graves, David G. Hays, Martin Kay, and Theodore W. Ziehe; RM-4920-PR, The RAND Corporation, August 1966) treats the acquisition of text from miscellaneous keyboard-actuated devices.

"Computer Editing, Typesetting, and Image Generation" (M. V. Mathews and Joan E. Miller; *AFIPS Conference Proceedings*, Vol. 27, Part 1, 1965, pp. 389–398) discusses copy preparation and introduces the method of character generation by composition of patches.

Computer Prepared Text: A Real-time/Time-sharing Multi-terminal Publication System (P. F. Santarelli; TR 00.1263, Systems Development Division, International Business Machines Corporation, April 1965) discusses elaborate and sophisticated methods.

"The RAND Tablet: A Man-machine Graphical Communication Device" (M. R. Davis and T. O. Ellis; *AFIPS Conference Proceedings*, Vol. 26, 1964, pp. 325–331) describes a way of communicating stylus motion to a computer.

Chapter 5

DICTIONARY LOOKUP

A dictionary is a file of information about small, repetitive elements of a language. The information is arranged in such a manner as to make it easy to find the properties of an element, given its shape. We would gain nothing in particular, and waste a great deal of space, by reminding ourselves at every point in this chapter that a phonetic or phonemic transcription can be looked up in a dictionary just as a written text can. Dictionaries keyed to phonological transcriptions have different headings from dictionaries for use with written text, but the working principles are the same. From now on, we refer to written material.

The need for dictionaries in automatic language processing is connected with what linguists call the arbitrariness of natural language. There is nothing about the spelling—nor, for that matter, about the phonological shape—of text to show, other than by a table lookup, what the grammatical or semantic properties of the text and its parts might be. From one point of view, dictionary lookup is a stratal conversion; but from any contemporary viewpoint, it is a necessary step, preliminary to grammatical and other analyses of text.

Before dictionary lookup, the input text is transcribed and fed into the computer. We will take it to be either standing in internal storage or ready in archival format. The dictionary likewise has been prepared, and is waiting in its standard format. When the lookup job is finished, the information obtained is left standing in storage or on magnetic tape in a format suitable for the next step.

The headings in the dictionary may be whole words, word parts, or what you will—provided you have a plan for matching headings with text. Each heading is a type; wherever it can be matched against text, there is an occurrence or token of that type. An occurrence (of a word or word part) has two main characteristics: its type and its place. Matching may be done with or without overlap. Matching without overlap means that every short segment of text is identified as an occurrence of one and only one type, and no part of the text belongs to occurrences of two types. Matching with overlap means that ambiguity is recognized; the type of an ambiguous occurrence remains to be decided by further work. Thus, if the dictionary asserts that the verb *lead* and the noun *lead* are different types, an occurrence of *lead* in text is ambiguously an occurrence of one or the other type, and will be matched with them both in dictionary lookup. Further processing may determine for each occurrence that it is of one and only one type. Hockett's famous remark that there is no *cat* in "catalog" reminds us that dictionary lookup may or may not identify boundaries in a text with absolute certainty.

There is this difference between looking up words and looking up word segments in a dictionary: if the headings are words, which must be bounded by spaces in text, the word occurrences in a text can be discriminated before dictionary lookup, shaken loose from one another, and handled independently. But if word parts are taken as headings in a dictionary, only dictionary lookup, and further processing if necessary, can decide how to make the cuts.

I. SEARCH METHODS: SIMPLE

The three most straightforward ways of doing dictionary lookup, one feasible with a small dictionary, the others with a dictionary of any size, are simple list search, text alphabetization, and address computation.

I.I. Searching a simple list

Let us pretend that each word in the dictionary is short enough to be stored in a single cell, and that the information about each word can be stored in a single cell also. We store the headings alphabetically in cells $DICT(0)$, $DICT(2)$, $DICT(4)$, and so on. In the cells with odd indexes, we store the information about them. Now to do dictionary lookup, we isolate the first word occurrence in text, up to the first space, and compare it with the first heading in the dictionary. If there is no match, we go on to the second heading, the third, and so on until we either match the first word of text or pass the place where it would stand in alphabetical order. If we make a match, we take the information from the following cell in the dictionary list and proceed to the second word in text. If we go past the place where the heading should be in the list, the word is unknown to our dictionary.

If the heading words are too long to be stored each in a single cell, we can use either a list structure or boundary markers, with the same search scheme. If the information about each word is larger than one cell, we can either allow a larger, but still fixed, amount of space for each entry, or a variable amount of space in the main dictionary list, or we can point from each heading to the beginning of the information about it in another list. If we take the latter course, the list of headings is separated completely from the list of information blocks, and the dictionary no longer resembles the sort of thing a person could use. This technique is eminently practical, and we shall develop it in Sec. 4.2.

Straight list searching is slow work, and we can do better. But even if we were willing to take the time, we would find in many cases that the mere list of headings is too long to be stored in the internal memory of a standard computer. A special-purpose computer built by IBM for the U.S. Air Force as a translating machine was equipped with a very large store, and serial search was used, with one important modification. Instead of beginning at the beginning of the dictionary, the machine began serial search at a place close to the storage location of the word to be looked up. One way to obtain this effect, although not the one actually used in the Air Force Translator, is by means of a directory. The directory could contain, for example, every thousandth word from the main list. The only information it gives about this word is its storage location, its index, in the main list. Searching is now done in two stages. The first step, carried out with the directory, is relatively fast, since the directory is a short list. The result is a starting location for the second search, namely the location of a word preceding the one to be found, but separated from it in the dictionary by no more than one one-thousandth of the dictionary entries.

If the whole list is in high-speed storage, a separate directory is unnecessary; the first scan of the list can test only every hundredth or thousandth entry. The scanning interval is reduced when the approximate location of the item sought is discovered. If the main list is in secondary storage, a directory in high-speed storage is needed.

1.2. Double sorting

A word occurrence in text is identified by its type and its position. In what we regard as normal format, the position is given implicitly. But a program can be designed to go through text, isolating word occurrences at spaces, and pairing them with consecutive occurrence numbers. Now the list of type-location pairs can be sorted into alphabetical order by type. There will be many repetitions of some types in ordinary text, but they must be retained. After the text has been alphabetized, it can be taken a little at a time from external storage, and the dictionary read a little at a time in step with the reading of the sorted text. While the first part of the text and the first part of the dictionary, both in alphabetical order, are in internal storage, matching goes as far as it can. On a new tape, the program writes triples consisting each of a location number, a type, and dictionary information. When the first block of text or dictionary is used up, another comes in from external storage to replace it. Thus no matter how large either the text or the dictionary may be, internal storage is never overtaxed.

After this stage has been completed, the program brings in the triples and sorts them by occurrence number. When sorting is done, the occurrence numbers can be made implicit once more, and the text consists of a sequence of word types in their original occurrence order, but now accompanied by the desired information from the dictionary.

This scheme has been used widely in computational linguistics, and certainly has the advantage of simplicity. The dictionary is easy to construct, and the program need not vary at all from one language to another. However, sorting is a very slow operation, and two complete sorts of any text are required when this plan is used.

I.3. Computed addresses

If storage were free, the most convenient way to look up a word in a dictionary would be by using its spelling as an index to its location. Every cell in a computer memory is indexed by a number, and words are spelled with letters; but the binary representations stored in computers are to be interpreted indifferently as numbers or letters, and therefore, by a monstrous pun, the spelling of a word can be taken as an index.

But for that to be practical, the memory would have to be large enough so that every string of letters shorter than the longest word in the language could serve as a cell index, and almost all the cells in the memory would be empty—since almost every letter string is a nonword. It would be pleasant to have free memories, in which we could waste almost all the available space, but even with expensive hardware there is a way to take advantage of the pun. The method that we are about to examine is sometimes called hash addressing, or random addressing, but what is characteristic about it is simply that the word to be looked up is regarded as a number, and an arithmetic computation performed on it.

The whole object of the computation is to reduce any word that may have to be looked up to a number that ranges over the possible addresses in the computer. If there is a place to store information for each number from 1 to 10,000, every word must be reduced to a number between 1 and 10,000 also. The information is put in storage, and then whenever we are given a word to look up we perform the numerical computation on it, get the address of a possible cell, and look there to see what we have.

The first thing that must be stored is clearly the spelling of the word itself. We cannot hope to find a computation that will reduce every word to a possible address and never reduce two different words to the same address. At least, no suggestion has yet been made that would have such a satisfactory effect. But if we can arrive at a cell after starting with either of two different words, we must make provision for both of them at that place; we do so by storing the spelling of one, with information about it, and a link address to another place where we will store the spelling of the second word and information about it. But we might arrive with three different words, and so it may be necessary to store a link address in the second place, and so on.

This scheme is efficient only if the address calculation can be designed so as to keep the number of different words pointing to the same place in memory at a low figure. For example, we might hope that ninety percent of the word occurrences in text would be matched against their entries in just one step, that almost all remaining words would be matched after an address computation and just one link, and so on. The address computation must be designed with care to achieve this result, and the memory must be relatively large.

If the computing system available includes both substantial disc or drum storage as well as an adequate amount of high-speed storage, address computation can be used to bring a portion of the dictionary from its permanent location in the disc file when it is needed. In high-speed storage, a directory is kept, and a space is reserved for a small block of dictionary. The address computation is performed on each word of text in turn. The resulting address is taken as an index in the directory. There, only an address to the disc file is given. The block with that address is brought into the space reserved in core storage, where it can be searched, perhaps in serial fashion, until the text item is matched. Depending on circumstances, a single block of dictionary might contain information about ten, a hundred, or even more word types. These blocks should not be excessively large, for two reasons: transferring a block from disc to core takes time, and space for a complete block must be reserved in core storage. It is desirable that the address computations bring out the correct block every time. However, thanks to use of the directory, every block can be almost completely filled; if the computation has a unique result for some word, that word can be combined with others and the address of the composite block stored in the directory for all the different indexes computable from words in it.

With a new language or a new computer, an address computation scheme is not the easiest to set up, but it is not the most difficult either. Some of the techniques described below will probably be more acceptable for large-scale work except under rather special circumstances.

2. SEARCH METHODS: ELEGANT

The way to obtain elegance in consultation of the dictionary is to organize storage so that the answers are obtained quickly. More complex storage structures generally require more space per unit of information, but not always. First we examine two forms of branching search processes, then a method using letter tables with which input is scanned from left to right.

2.1. Tree search

The sort trees discussed in an earlier chapter can be used for storage of a dictionary. In searching through one of these trees, the word given in text is compared with the word stored at a node. In case of identity, the object of the search has been found; otherwise, there are two possibilities, usually taken as going toward the beginning of the alphabet or toward the end. This method differs from searching a simply ordered list in that the list-scanning process goes inexorably downward; having two alternatives at every step shortens the number of steps to be taken by a very important factor.

Let us assume once more that the words to be stored fit into single cells. There are four units of information to be stored at every cell in the tree: a word, information about that word, and the addresses to be used in case the text word is earlier, or later, in the alphabet than the word stored at the node.

The word stored at the origin node of the tree is one that falls about midway in the alphabet. It may be best to go a little before or after the midpoint to get a word of high frequency, since matching the high-frequency word on the first test reduces the average number of tests to be made. The word reached by branching toward the beginning of the alphabet should fall about half-way between the beginning of the alphabet and the origin word in the tree; likewise, the word stored at the other location reachable on a branch from the origin should be about halfway between the origin word and the end of the alphabet. Again, high-frequency words in the appropriate neighborhoods may be chosen. In general, when a test is made, the word being sought is known to lie within a certain span; initially, that span is the whole alphabet, but thereafter it is from the earliest word tested to the latest. The next test should divide that span roughly in half, judging not by the length of the alphabet but by the length of the dictionary.

2.2. Binary search

The plan just described reduces by an important factor the average number of tests to be made when a word is looked up in the dictionary, but it does increase storage requirements. The two branching addresses of each node occupy valuable space. Approximately the same plan can be used, at the cost of a little more computing time, without occupying space for addresses. This plan is called binary search.

The words of the dictionary are stored in a sequence of cells, with information about them in the corresponding cells of a separate array. The beginning location of the list, the length of the list, and the midpoint are available to the search program. The search program goes initially to the midpoint. If the word being sought is found there, the search is over.

When a match fails, the program computes the midpoint of the allowable range. Initially, the allowable range is the whole list, hence the midpoint is the starting place. After one step, the allowable range runs from the beginning of the list to the middle, if the word being sought is earlier in the alphabet than the midpoint word, and from the midpoint to the end otherwise. The program computes the midpoint of the new range and makes another test. Should the test fail, the midpoint of a narrower range is computed, and so on. Ultimately, the allowable range consists of just one cell, and if the word is still not matched, it is not in the dictionary.

Binary search schemes have this effect on search time. The typical word requires *sequential* search through about half the entries of the dictionary. With binary search, if the number of words in the dictionary is between 2^{N-1} and 2^N, only N tests are needed. The difference in search time is therefore of great interest, especially where the number of entries is large enough to make the dictionary of practical use.

2.3. A binary-search program

A simple program for binary search is displayed in Fig. 27. The dictionary to be consulted is stored in a sequence of cells beginning at D(1). The length of the dictionary is stored in a cell called N. An index to the mid-point of the dictionary is stored in cell *Dict*. Another cell, *Dict*(1), contains zeros in all bit positions except one. Read as a number, the contents of *Dict*(1) is at least half the length of the dictionary, but not as great as the total length; this rule gives a unique value for its contents. With this prior setup, control goes to line 1. The contents of *Dict* is copied into cell P, where it can be modified; the contents of *Dict* is left unchanged for the next consultation of the dictionary, while P serves as a moving pointer. Likewise, the contents of the cell following *Dict* is transferred to M, where it can serve as a variable modifier, causing the pointer to move by successively smaller quantities. The word to be sought in the dictionary is available in cell

Location	Instruction	Comment
1.	SWR(Dict)	Initialize P
2.	STORE(P)	
3.	SWR(Dict(One))	Initialize M
4.	STORE(M)	
5. Test:	SWR(T)	Examine an entry
6.	TRANS(D(P), Down, Up)	Is it above or below text item?
7.	SWR(P)	Found an entry
8.	STORE(T(One))	Note where
9.	GOTO(Out)	Done; success
10. Down:	SWR(M)	Divide M by 2
11.	SRB(One)	
12.	TRANS(One, D-1, Out)	Is M still nonzero?
13. D-1	STORE(M)	
14.	ADD(P)	Advance P
15.	STORE(P)	
16.	TRANS(N, Up, Test)	Is P still valid?
17.	GOTO(Test)	
18. Up:	SWR(M)	
19.	SRB(One)	Divide M by 2
20.	TRANS(One, U-1, Out)	Is M still nonzero?
21. U-1:	STORE(M)	
22.	SWR(P)	Advance P
23.	SUB(M)	
24.	STORE(P)	
25.	TRANS(One, Test, Down)	Is P still valid?
26.	GOTO(Test)	

Fig. 27—Binary search

T, and at line 5 it is brought into the working register for comparison with the cell specified as D(P). If the current word in the dictionary is earlier than the text word, the pointer must be moved down; if it is greater, the pointer must be moved up. In case of equality, an entry has been found. What is needed by the program that called on the dictionary consultation routine is the index of the cell at which a match was made. The current pointer is stored in cell T(1), where it can be found, and control goes out.

To move the pointer down, beginning at line 10, the routine divides the contents of M by two, using a trick. The instruction SRB(*One*) shifts the content of the working register one bit position to the right. In a binary system, shifting to the right divides by two, just as scratching off one digit at the decimal point divides a decimal number by ten. The division would not be exact if the right-most digit were other than zero, but we have specified that it must be.

Now if M, after shifting to the right, is greater than or equal to 1, the process must continue. If the content of M is now 0, we have reached the position in alphabetical order of the text word being sought, without success; the desired entry is missing from the dictionary. Transferring control out of this subroutine without altering the contents of cell T(1) signals the main program that failure occurred. If the search must continue, the content of M is changed to the new value, and with M still in the working register the content of P is added. This moves the pointer down, as required, but it may move the pointer out of the dictionary. On the first try, the pointer moves from the mid-point of the dictionary down approximately one quarter the length of the dictionary; but if N = 17, then *Dict* must contain 9 and *Dict*(1) must contain 16. Thus P starts at 9 and the first move is half of 16, or 8. Adding 9 + 8 gives 17, which is still within the dictionary, then adding 4 more yields 21, which is beyond the last entry. After storing the new, tentative value of P, the program makes a conditional transfer on N. If the pointer is outside the dictionary area, control goes to *Up*. The result of this transfer will be to bring the pointer back as far as necessary before the next test is made. When the pointer is in a valid location, control returns to line 5 for another comparison of the text word with the dictionary entry.

The sequence of instructions carried out when the pointer is moved up is roughly the same, allowing for the necessity of subtracting M rather than adding it, and recognizing the fact that the first dictionary entry is reached with an index of one.

The operation of this program ends at line 9 if the search is successful, or at line 12 or 20 if the pointer can no longer be moved to a new place and an exact match is not found.

2.4. Letter tables

The various schemes considered up to this point have matched the entire word being sought against the complete heading of some entry in the dictionary; only the scheme for selecting the next heading to be matched has varied. Now we consider a plan which tests one letter of the text word at a time. There are no longer isolated, independent, headings in the dictionary, but rather a tree with *letters* at the nodes and dictionary information at the end points.

If a word can begin with any one of the 26 letters of the English alphabet, the first test has 26 possible outcomes, depending on which letter is in fact the initial letter of the word. The 26 different outcomes lead to as many nodes, where the second letter of the input word will be examined. Of course, there are many two-letter sequences that cannot stand at the beginning of a heading in an English dictionary. Among these are "tv," "qz," "bt," et cetera. There are 26 direct descendants of the first node, and there might in principle be 26 × 26 second-level descendants, but in fact there are many less. At the third level, there will be only a small fraction of the possible nodes, since most three-letter sequences are impossible at the beginning of an English word.

Once more we can take advantage of the fact that the same binary configurations are used for letters and for numbers, and use characters as indexes in cell sequences, as we did in the program of Fig. 26. An instruction like SWR(*First*(A)) brings into the working register the contents of the A-th cell in a list called *First*. Similarly, all the letters of the alphabet can be used to index from the origin of this list, and the content brought into the working register can control the selection of a table to be used in operating on the second letter of the word. The same can be done at every step, until the end of the word is reached.

Each entry in a letter table must tell the program several things. To begin with, it may have to state that there is no word in the dictionary beginning with the input sequence up to this point. For example, in an English dictionary, there must be a table to go to after reading "q" followed by "u". In that table, the entry for the letter "z" must inform the using program that there are no words in English beginning with "quz". Next, the entry may have to specify that there is a complete entry ending with the letter just supplied, and that information about it can be obtained at a certain place. For example, after reading "ta", the next letter table will contain in its entry for the letter "r" the fact that *tar* is a word and that information about it can be obtained somewhere. Finally, the entry must show whether any longer words begin with the proposed sequence, and if so give the address of the next letter table.

A much oversimplified version of the central search routine is shown in Fig. 28. The letter tables are supposed to be stored in a sequence of

Location	Instruction	Comment
1. Enter:	SWR(Origin)	Table origin
2.	ADD(T(I))	Plus character
3.	STORE(P)	Equals pointer
4.	SWR(Dict(P)/Six)	Get control
5.	TRANS(Test, X, Y)	
6.	SWR(Dict(P))	Get table entry
7.	SRC(One)	Drop control
8.	STORE(Origin)	
9.	INDEX(I, One, N, Enter)	
10.	GOTO(Out)	

Fig. 28—Simplified letter-table search

cells beginning at *Dict*. Initially, *Origin* contains 0. The text is stored one character per cell, beginning at T. Thus the first consultation (line 4) gets the entry for the first letter in text from the initial table. The rightmost character of an entry is a control; comparing it with the content of *Test* yields equality if search can continue. At location X, the case of a completed match is handled, and at Y the case of no possible continuation.

The remainder of each entry stores the origin of the letter table to be used for continued search; that number is put in *Origin*, and the procedure is iterated for the next character.

When this scheme is elaborated with sufficient programming elegance, it is not just faster than other types of dictionary look up, but actually requires less space in memory. The ordinary storage plans use one character position in storage for the first letter of each word in the dictionary; the letter-table plan uses one cell for each letter of the alphabet, no matter how long the dictionary. If there are on the average more than 6 words per initial letter, there is a saving. More space is required in the second position; a second-letter table must be stored for each possible initial letter. But thereafter the nonexistence of some letter sequences begins to have a favorable effect, and in the end the savings can be considerable.

3.   MATCHING TECHNIQUES

Linguists approaching the computer for the first time may be willing to deal with the problems raised by a system that forces them to cut a text at blanks, and only at blanks, and either recognize or not the letter strings that occur between them. A little experience suffices to show that the problems raised are far from trivial. Sound lexicography calls for entering as headings letter strings that extend across blanks and also segments that are not always bounded in text by preceding and following blanks. Treating certain punctuation marks as if they were blanks is no solution to these problems, although it can help if segmentation is to precede dictionary lookup. More powerful techniques are available, and most linguists will want to make use of them.

3.1. Longest match

We now take the input text to be a string of letters, other characters, and blanks; it may be a whole book, or just one sentence. In any event, we anticipate that parts of it can be found in the dictionary, but not necessarily the complete string. We wish to match it part by part, starting from the first character. We consider first a method that seeks to obtain a single best answer for each string; its output is a single string of dictionary entries, i.e., there is no ambiguity about the segmentation of the text.

Whether we start at the beginning of the string or at any point following matching of one or more dictionary headings against consecutive parts of the text, we wish to find the heading that covers the longest possible next span. Thus, we want to match all of "catalog" and not just "cat", or all of "in view of", and not just "in". The principle of longest match permits us to combine—in one alphabetic list—words, word parts, and word combinations. We will recognize no discontinuous stretches of text in this way, but otherwise we have considerable freedom to put in headings of whatever kind we like.

This matching technique is compatible with straight searching, with the use of a directory, and with letter tables. It cannot be used with binary search, unless the binary search is taken as a kind of directory procedure and used only to find a starting place for straight scanning. It cannot be used with double sorting, since the segmentation made depends on what entries are in the dictionary, and not on where specific characters occur in the text. It could be used with tree search of a complicated kind that we will not examine in detail.

Let us assume that each heading is stored as a string of letters followed by a boundary mark, which is later in alphabetic order than any letter of the alphabet. These headings are arranged in lexicographic order. Text is presented as a string of letters and spaces. Starting at any character position in text, we consult a directory and go to the indicated heading in the main list; starting there, our procedure is to scan downward comparing each entry in turn with the left-most part of the text string. If the heading is less than the text string, we move to the next heading; when the heading is greater than the text string, we make a further test.

Since the boundary mark used in dictionary headings never occurs in the text, the match of a complete heading against a text string can never lead to equality. The first heading in the dictionary that is larger than the text string is either a valid match for the left part of the substring or evidence that no match can be made to this string in this dictionary. For example, the dictionary might contain the following headings:

index#

internal#

in#

irony#

If the text string begins with "internally", the first heading is smaller, but the second is larger because the boundary mark is alphabetically later than the letter *l*. The procedure to be carried out with this heading consists of determining whether the match is exact up to the boundary mark. If it is, the correct heading has been found. If not, the search must go on. Thus, consider the text string "insignificant". Once again, the second heading in the list is the first that is greater than the text string, but now because the letter *t* follows the letter *s*. When a test for exact match up to the boundary mark is made, it fails. The search continues, and under certain circumstances it might go on for a long time. In this example, the immediately following heading yields the match, and the search is complete.

If the dictionary entry can be longer than the span on which a comparison can be made in one step, the first part of the heading must be compared with the first part of the text string and, in case of equality, the next part of the same heading tested against the next part of the text string. Taking the comparison as a whole, however, the procedure is the same as before.

Another way to perform longest-match search would be by maintaining separate lists for headings of different lengths. Scanning would be performed first in the list of longest entries. As soon as an entry of length k is reached that is later in lexicographic order than the initial part of the text string, scanning could shift to the k − 1 list. In fact, the complexity of the search logic could be increased considerably, but the principle of longest match is interesting largely because it is simple.

3.2. Arbitrary segments

The most attractive characteristic of the longest-match technique is that it yields an unambiguous result. The least attractive characteristic is that it does not allow for ambiguity except by devious and difficult means. If a stretch of text is ambiguous, it can be matched against one long heading which points to a collection of alternative interpretations. Examples of this kind of problem are found in languages like German, where the middle part of a word can belong to either the first part or the last. Thus, the word is XAY, where X and XA are valid headings, but Y is not. A dictionary designed for longest match consultation would have to include headings for X, XA, and AY, but also for Y; the Y entry would show that it must follow XA, and that the only valid segmentation was X-AY.

An alternative approach is to design the dictionary lookup system so that every heading in the dictionary is matched against every possible portion of text, leaving the elimination of mistaken matches to a subsequent stage.

Taking the letter-table approach, and assuming a text that can be matched accurately against the dictionary—that is, there is no heading missing from the dictionary that we would want to match against any part of the given text—the matching procedure goes as follows.

The first character of input is used as an index in the first letter table, and if a following letter table is indicated the second character is used as an index in it. This process goes on as long as further letter tables are named, but whenever a complete heading is marked two pieces of output are produced: Identification of the span of input text covered by the entry, and the information about it given by the dictionary. Whenever a heading matches a span of text ending with the k-th character, the (k + 1)-th character is used as an index in the initial letter table. The diagram in Fig. 29 shows how the output of dictionary lookup is constructed when this plan is followed.

h·i·s   c·a·t·a·l·o·g   i·s   u·n·t·e·s·t·e·d
0 1 2 3 4 5 6 7 8 9 10 11 12 13 14 15 16 17 18 19 20 21 22 23

Fig. 29—Ambiguous dictionary output

According to the figure, the only heading in the dictionary that matches the beginning of the text is *his*, and after it the blank is recognized. Starting at the next position, the dictionary recognizes *ca*, which is an abbreviation for *circa*; *cat*; and *catalog*. Following *cat*, the letter *a* is a heading, and then *lo* (an interjection) and *log* are recognized. From there to the end, the text is unambiguous. A diagram like this can be represented by a list of lists, the main list having an entry for each position where any match is completed. On each minor list, there are entries for the different segments matched, as in Fig. 30. Instead of the letter strings shown in Fig. 30, the output wanted for further processing would of course be the information given by the dictionary for each matched heading.

Wording backward from end point 11, for example, we can go directly to point 4 with *catalog* or to point 8 with *log*. From point 8, we can go to point 7 with *a* and from there to point 4 with *cat*. Now, this segmentation of "catalog" is unsatisfactory, whereas the segmentation of "untested" is desirable. To distinguish between these two cases requires some rules of morphology, that is, some grammar allowing segmentation only if the segments are of kinds, and in an order, that

Endpoint	List: Segment, initial point
3	his, 0
4	*blank*, 3
6	ca, 4
7	cat, 4
8	a, 7
10	lo, 8
11	catalog, 4; log, 8
12	*blank*, 11
14	is, 12
15	*blank*, 14
17	un, 15
21	test, 17
23	ed, 21

Fig. 30—Dictionary output as a list of lists

the language allows. Some linguists will write programs for morphological testing of dictionary output as independent units, and others will go directly to syntactic parsing (Chap. 6), making the "morphological" rules a part of their syntax.

The advantage of this kind of matching procedure is that it guarantees that all possible segmentations will be considered, without requiring peculiar dictionary entries; the disadvantage is that the output, prior to elimination of false analyses by morphological tests, is likely to be voluminous. For many purposes, many linguists are likely to feel that the advantage is overwhelming.

3.3. Flags, shifts, and diacritics

When continuous text is presented for dictionary lookup, it may consist of a string of alphabet flags, shifts, letters, punctuation marks, and diacritics. These different kinds of characters require varying kinds of treatment.

If all the characters in text were alphabet flags, letters, and perhaps blanks, it would be possible to construct either a single dictionary in which strings mixing these characters could be stored alphabetically, or a dictionary for each alphabet flag. In the latter case, there would be no alphabet flags in the dictionary; it seems natural for each flag to determine a separate dictionary. In fact, as Lamb has pointed out, it is natural to limit the alphabet of a given dictionary as much as possible; with a dictionary-lookup scheme of the kind he proposed, using five-bit characters would be valuable, since the number of entries in each letter table is reduced to 32. Taking into account diacritics, capitalization, and so on would increase the character set, but such elements of text need a different kind of treatment in any case.

Diacritics cause difficulties because in standard dictionaries they have a peculiar effect on alphabetical order. Naturally, it is not necessary for the dictionary as stored for automatic consultation to reflect the customary alphabetization practices of lexicographers. One plan is to convert the input text to an array of features, using the smallest feasible number of bits for identification of base characters. If the dictionary is organized for binary search, only the base characters are used to make the initial search. Once a heading is matched, an auxiliary heading can be consulted with the string of diacritic features. If the dictionary is organized as a system of letter tables, the advance from a given letter table can be made either to the next letter table or to a diacritic table in which only the diacritic part of the current character position is used.

Capitalization can be handled either as a feature present at certain character positions and absent at others, or else as a separate character, preceding other characters to which it applies. The special problem it brings with it is that it is sometimes a lexical element and sometimes not. A dictionary heading can specify that it matches only strings of text beginning with an initial capital, or in solid capitals, or regardless of capitalization. What a dictionary heading cannot say except in very unusual cases is that it matches only lowercase strings in text. For this reason, capitalization is best not used in primary search of the dictionary but rather isolated in an auxiliary position where it can be used to condition acceptance of a heading after a match has been made. Something of this sort is done in *Webster's New International Dictionary*, Third Edition, where the headings are lower case but sometimes accompanied by the mark "usu. cap."

4. SYSTEM ORGANIZATION

Searching and matching are the central operations in dictionary lookup, but they are only two operations required in the midst of what must be a large and complicated program. We now turn to the broader problems.

4.1. Batching

Dictionary lookup is not usually an end in itself, but rather part of a more complicated language-processing chore. A complete automatic language-processing system may involve many programs, tables of different kinds such as dictionaries and grammars, input text, and the output produced by processing. If all of the programs and tables can stand in computer storage simultaneously, the input can be read a little at a time, processed completely, and the final output transferred to external storage as it is produced. Ordinarily, high-speed computer memory is not large enough to permit adoption of such a plan; instead, major segments of the processing sequence must be isolated, the programs and tables for one segment put into storage, and text passed through. When the first step has been completed on a batch of text, the output from that step is taken as input to the next stage, where more programs and different tables are put into storage. Two, three, or many more stages may be necessary. The "batch" is the amount of text put through the computer while one segment of the complete system is in operation.

H. S. Kelly and T. W. Ziehe proposed a batching technique for dictionary lookup, which takes advantage of the fact that even a large batch of text contains tokens of only a few of the types that must be listed in a large dictionary. Obviously, the types that occur in one batch are not exactly the same as those in another; except for a few high-frequency items, each text makes a different selection from the vocabulary of its language.

In the first stage of processing for each batch, the headings occupy most of high-speed storage. They can take the form of letter tables, but need not. The text is read from magnetic tape, a little at a time, and matching is performed. Each heading ends in a certain cell, identifiable by its address or by its index relative to the origin of the dictionary. The identification number is written on magnetic tape to show the heading matched for each span of text. At the same time, a list of identification numbers is built up in highspeed storage; the list is kept in numerical order, possibly by means of a sort tree, so that duplication of entries can be avoided.

The next step is to read the dictionary from magnetic tape. Each entry in the dictionary includes the identification number of its heading; indeed, if a single entry is appropriate to several headings, it can include all their identification numbers. As each entry comes in, its identification number is checked against the list previously built up. Entries needed for the current batch are kept in storage, and unneeded entries disappear.

Since an entry can be of any length, the starting location of each entry is attached to the corresponding identification number. The entries can occupy the region of storage previously given over to headings, which are no longer needed.

Now the tape written during the first stage is read. It contains identification numbers in text order. Looking up an identification number in the list built during the first stage leads to an address; going to that address gets the dictionary entry applicable to the segment of text.

What happens next depends on the system. If there is space in high-speed storage, further processing can go on simultaneously. Otherwise, the dictionary entries must be written in text order on a new tape, to be read back in when space is free for the next task.

This scheme can be improved in various ways. For example, the identification numbers themselves should not be written on the first output tape. When a heading is matched in the first stage, the identification number is looked up in a sort tree; suppose it is found in $Tree(i)$. Then i should be written out. At the end of the first stage, the tree is linearized, for two reasons: to clear the left links, and to speed checking of entries as the dictionary is read. The left links can be used to store entry addresses; when the first output tape is read back, the numbers written on it index the left links, so that even binary search is obviated: $Leftlink(i)$ contains the address of the required dictionary entry.

4.2. Parallel files

For batch processing, where one job is done on a batch of material and then another job done on the results of that, and so on, it is not necessary to have all dictionary information in one place. All that is necessary is that if the information associated with one heading is scattered into several files, it can be recovered.

For example, let us suppose that a dictionary contains headings, morphological information, syntactic descriptions, and some kind of semantic information—perhaps translations into another language, or perhaps something quite different. The headings are needed for searching and matching; the morphological data are required for testing acceptability of the strings of headings matched. The syntactic information is needed for parsing complete utterances. And the semantic information is needed for some later stage. Since each of these stages may well occupy all available memory, each kind of information can be in a separate file.

Separation is more convenient for use of a dictionary than for maintenance. The additions and corrections needed from time to time—and very frequently during the early life of a new dictionary—are not easy to make if the dictionary is stored on several tape reels that must be kept parallel. A reasonable plan is to keep the dictionary in one file, say in catalog format, and maintain that. Then, as necessary, separate files can be extracted from the catalog, formatted as suitable for processing, and used until they become obsolete.

The notion of separating files can be carried even further, of course. It is not necessary that the parallel files be used one after another; they may be used some for one purpose and some for another. For example, syntactic information appropriate for parsing in accordance with two different theories of linguistics might be keyed to a single file of headings, so that linguists could use the same basic dictionary even though they wanted to encode their knowledge of syntax in different ways.

4.3. Online processing

Batching is a happy way to organize a large computing job if there is no reason to intervene from time to time. But there are systems, some of which are discussed in later chapters, that require processing of text one sentence at a time, on every level of linguistic and substantive analysis, with human intervention after the processing of each sentence. These systems are the kind that must be operated online; the user is seated at a console and types in one fact, instruction, or question. After it has been processed, the computer system causes an answer or some kind of response to be typed out on the console, and the user continues.

With such a system, the key parts of the complete program always remain in storage; they call in as necessary the smallest possible segments of program or data required for processing a given segment of text.

With regard to the dictionary in particular, its central portion might be stored. If the letter table method is being used, the first few letter tables would be available in core storage, and then a few more at a time would be brought in selectively depending on initial results. If a binary search tree is used, the origin and a few steps out on some branches might be stored, and the next segments brought in as needed. Or an address computation might be performed to bring in a small block of dictionary information.

In all these cases, the secondary storage would certainly have to be discs, drums, or some other kind of random access memory. Both user and computer are waiting while the secondary storage device operates to locate and transfer the desired information.

5. MAINTENANCE

A dictionary of a natural language stored in a format to be processed by a computer is more than one segment of an automatic language-processing system. It will be used, if it is good, not in one system but in many, for different purposes. It will be consulted by linguists doing research on the language even if they have no computers; it will serve as a storehouse for the linguists who use it, allowing them to put away facts that they ultimately hope to use in research reports, in processing schemes they have not developed yet, in teaching students, or elsewhere. To serve all these purposes the dictionary must be more than a set of parallel files in which headings can be looked up and the corresponding information brought out. It must be possible to present the dictionary in a form linguists can use conveniently, and it must be possible to add, remove, or alter information in it.

5.1. Internal and external versions

Of all the internal versions of dictionaries considered heretofore in this chapter, the one least likely to succeed as a presentation format for direct examination by linguists and others is that of letter tables. Lamb, as a matter of fact, recognized from the start that linguists should not be required even to set up the letter tables, much less ever to use them. Letter tables are an internal organization of information that should be presented in an entirely different way, and an adapter, a program for converting between the form a linguist can use and the letter tables, is necessary.

This is an extreme case but in fact the internal versions we have considered are all different from what a linguist would want. In fact, it would be unusual for a situation to arise where a dictionary prepared at one research center could best be shipped to another in the form used by the first for dictionary lookup. Perhaps the best version of a dictionary to take as basic is one in catalog format. Its map reflects, at higher levels, whatever hierarchical organization the designing linguist chooses to recognize. For example, the data class on level 1 might be that of root morphemes. On the next class there might be bases, words, or some other composite forms obtained from roots by derivational processes. This hierarchical structure could continue for as long as the linguist chooses, but below it, and partially parallel to it, there would be additional data classes containing the different kinds of information pertinent to units of different orders. Some linguists would perhaps want to attach directly to the root morphemes on the highest level the sources he ascribed them to. English roots could thus be identified as to the language from which they came. English bases would be identified as formed from their roots by certain affixes or other attachments or changes, as belonging to a certain century, as belonging to a certain fundamental syntactic category, and so on. Deeper in the map, there would be minor morphological, syntactic, and perhaps semantic data.

If a dictionary is stored in catalog format, an adaptation program must be run whenever it is transferred to core storage for consultation. This program selects the kind of information needed, omitting such things as source or data of first appearance if they are not needed for the job at hand. What it takes it reformats and perhaps recodes to prepare for consultation with the search methods and matching techniques preferred.

A different program would be used to arrange and present the information for human inspection. Several different versions might be wanted on paper, including one for publication and wide distribution and another for reference when changes are to be made. If a linguist or his technicians must write long lists of alterations, they deserve to be given a method of shorthand reference to entries in the dictionary.

5.2. Updating

To produce a dictionary for use in automatic processing, a linguist may begin with some published dictionary, or he may begin by collecting items from a corpus of text. Whichever he does, when he begins processing new text he will find unmatchable segments. Sometimes he may choose to disregard what he cannot recognize, but often enough he will want to add new headings to his dictionary. Even if he were to attain complete coverage for his language, if it is in widespread use it is changing, and after a decade more or less he would be forced to revise his dictionary or to admit that it is obsolete—or historical. In fact, alterations of the dictionary will be made for many different reasons.

A dictionary created by one group of linguists for one purpose will be adopted by another group as the basis for a different kind of study. Looking at its map, they will undoubtedly find that they must add new classes of data to contain the new information they propose to collect.

As research on a new problem begins, pertinent information may be at hand for a few of the relevant items in a dictionary, but not for all. In that case, the new data class is introduced and data are added to the catalog where possible, but subsequently information will be developed for new items of the same kind and new data of an old class will have to be added.

Sometimes information will be put into a dictionary, of a certain kind and with respect to a certain item, without absolute certainty of accuracy. Then, when further study produces a more precise answer or simply falsifies the one that had been supposed correct, it will be necessary to remove or alter an existing datum.

When new elements—words, morphemes, or roots, etc.—are discovered, they must be inserted, and information about them added as it can be obtained.

These are the processes of updating a dictionary. The RAND catalog system is supposed to provide basic operations with which updating programs can be constructed easily. The complexity updating systems are sometimes forced to is a reminder that the computer may process text automatically, but does so as the obedient servant of the linguist and designer; dictionary updating is one form of teaching that linguists must accept if they want their computers to be true disciples.

EXERCISES

Write the following programs in Algol. Assume arrays *Text*, *Dict* (the headings), and *Gram* (the grammatical information wanted). Thus, if $Text[i] = Dict[j]$, then $Gram[j]$ applies to $Text[i]$.

1. Perform simple list search.

2. Search with a directory.

3. Assume that the text has been alphabetized. *Loc* is an array of text locations. For each i, the value of $TL[i]$ is the smallest such that $Loc[TL[i]]$ is a location of word $Text[i]$, and $TL[i + 1] - 1$ is the largest. Match text with dictionary and prepare for sorting by location.

4. Perform tree search.

5. How many second-letter tables would be needed for a dictionary of English (or some other language)? How many third?

6. Write a program to eliminate false segments from an output like that in Fig. 30, using only the requirement that no part of the text can be unaccounted for.

7. Write a control program to initiate searches and create arrays of results like those in Fig. 30. The search program sets three parameters: the character position at which a matched string ends, the length of the matched string, and the identity of the dictionary entry. Maintain a list of positions at which searches must be initiated; after each search, start a new one at the earliest remaining place. An endpoint list (one line in Fig. 30) can be closed and written on an output tape as soon as it is impossible to add to it; when is that stage reached? When can a stretch of input text be released to make room for more?

REFERENCES

"Influences of Context on Translation" (A. D. Booth; *Information Theory*, Colin Cherry, ed., Academic Press, New York, 1956, pp. 181–183) explains direct addressing, sequential scanning, and binary search.

Final Report on Computer Set AN/GSQ-16(XW-2) (Thomas J. Watson Research Center, International Business Machines Corporation; RADC-TDR-63-100, September 1963) describes a special computer for translation built around a digital store using photographic recording.

"Glossary Lookup Made Easy" (Hugh S. Kelly and Theodore W. Ziehe, *Proceedings of the National Symposium on Machine Translation*, H. P. Edmundson, ed., Prentice-Hall, Inc., Englewood Cliffs, N.J., 1961, pp. 325–334) uses the method of separating files of information of different kinds.

"A High-speed Large-capacity Dictionary System" (Sydney M. Lamb and William H. Jacobsen, Jr.; *Mechanical Translation*, Vol. 6 (November 1961), pp. 76–107; *also* RALP pp. 51–72) explains the letter-table method.

Consultation d'un Dictionnare et Analyse Morphologique en Traduction Automatique (Gerard Veillon; doctoral dissertation, University of Grenoble, 1965) contains a revised version of Lamb's method.

Chapter 6

PARSING STRATEGIES

Several linguistic theories link certain sets of strings with simple grammars in a particular way. For example, the grammar can consist of a set of expansion formulae. Each formula (rule) has, say, one symbol on the left and a string of symbols on the right. A string can be expanded if it contains the lefthand symbol of any expansion rule; the expansion is performed by replacing that one symbol with the corresponding string. Symbols are of three kinds: starting symbols, internal or nonterminal symbols, and terminal symbols. A terminal string is associated with a particular grammar of this context-free phrase-structure type if it can be obtained from a starting symbol by successive expansions. To put it another way, we can think of the expansion rules, used backward, as reduction rules. A terminal string is associated with the grammar if it can be reduced to a starting symbol by a sequence of reductions.

The structure of a string is a representation of the reductions that must be performed on it to reduce it to a starting symbol. Obtaining a structure for a given string, relative to a given grammar, is called parsing. For some strings, and some grammars, multiple structures are possible; the string is said to be ambiguous relative to the grammar, and it has turned out with the grammars proposed heretofore that most strings corresponding to sentences of natural languages are ambiguous, often remarkably so. Many programs have been proposed for parsing; in this chapter, we consider some specific programs and also some general features of parsing programs.

I. SOME BASIC TECHNIQUES

To begin with, let us examine a few parsers that may not be practical for any purpose, but that have fairly simple organization.

I.I. Simple reduction

Assume that a string is stored in a list, with each entry containing the representation of one terminal symbol. There must be available a grammar, that is to say, a list of reduction rules. Each reduction rule is a pair, composed of a string of symbols and a single symbol. Our strategy is to find any string of symbols in the grammar that matches any part of the given string. Replace that part of the given string with the single corresponding symbol, and go on.

Initially, the pointer to the head of the list points to the first terminal symbol in the given string. The link from that entry points to the second symbol, and so on to the end of the list and the string. Now suppose that the grammar includes a formula by which the first three symbols in the original string can be reduced to a single symbol. We construct a new entry for the list; the content of this entry is the single symbol obtained from the grammar. The pointer to the head of the list now points to the new cell, and the new cell points to the fourth terminal. The first two diagrams in Fig. 31 show how this change is made. The

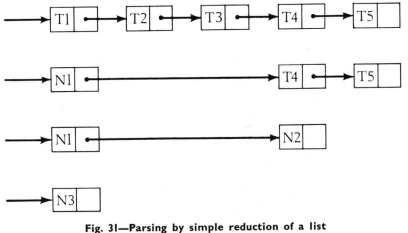

Fig. 31—Parsing by simple reduction of a list
T = Terminal, N = Nonterminal

next diagram in the figure shows what will happen if a reduction formula applicable to the fourth and fifth terminal symbols of the original string is applied next. Finally, the string of two nonterminals is reduced by another formula to just one, and if it is a starting symbol the parsing is successful.

A string is reduced when a formula can be found that applies somewhere in it. Where should the first reduction be made? Where next? A systematic answer to questions like this, determining the exact sequence in which reductions will be made to any particular string, is the basis for a parsing strategy.

For example, our strategy might be to start always at the head of the string. If the grammar contains any formula applicable beginning with the first element of the present string, apply it. Thus, Fig. 31 shows an initial reduction applied beginning with the first terminal. Following this strategy, the next thing to try for would be a reduction involving N1. Now, there may be no formula in the grammar reducing a substring beginning with N1 and continuing with T4. In that case, a subsidiary rule must be provided. Namely, if no formula applies at the first position, go to the second position and try there. In general, given any string, apply a reduction formula as early in it as possible. The second reduction in the figure would be made, under this strategy, only if no formula in the grammar were applicable to N1-T4-T5.

This strategy is realized by the algorithm presented in Fig. 32. The input string is stored as the first L components of an array called *Str*,

```
           Head := 1; J: = L + 1;
Entry:   i := Head;
CTest:   if CT(Str, Next, i) ≠ 0
            then begin   Str[j] := CT(Str, Next, i);
                         if i = Head then Head := j else Next[Prev] := j;
                         Next[j] := Next[Last];
                         j := j + 1;
                         goto Entry
                  end

            else begin   Prev := i;
                         i := Next[i];
                         goto if i ≠ 0 then CTest
                                  else if Next[Head] = 0 then Done
                                               else Fail
                  end
```

Fig. 32—A string-reduction parser

beginning with *Str*[1] and ending with *Str*[L]; more components are specified during parsing. Another array, called *Next*, furnishes the links. At any time, *Str*[*Head*] is the first element in the string, whether reduced or not, and when *Next*[*Head*] = 0 the string is reduced to a single element. At any step, the object is to find a reducible substring beginning at *Str*[i], and a variable called *Prev* is used to keep track of the element pointing to *Str*[i].

A procedure, CT(X, Y, Z), is used to consult a grammar; how such connectability tests work is considered in Chap. 7. This one is given the names of two arrays, *Str* and *Next*, and the current index, i. It returns CT = 0 if no rule is found, and otherwise gives the symbol for the whole string and the index of the last item covered (as the value of *Last*). This is our first use of an Algol procedure, but the way it fits into the program is simple and obvious.

The algorithm initializes *Head*, and sets up j to point to the first undefined component of *Str*. Whenever the algorithm goes to the label *Entry*, it sets i to the value of *Head*, attempting to reduce a phrase at the beginning of the string. Now the question is whether a phrase can be reduced, and CT(*Str*, *Next*, i) gives the answer. If it is affirmative, the new symbol is made the value of *Str*[j], and the previous element now must point to this place; if there is no previous element (i = *Head*), the new symbol stands at the head of the string. The new symbol points to the successor of the phrase it replaces, and j advances. Since a phrase was reduced, control goes to *Entry*, and parsing resumes at the head of the string.

If no phrase beginning with *Str*[i] can be reduced, parsing moves on to *Next*[i], after *Prev* is assigned a new value. Control goes to one of three places. If i = 0, parsing has reached the end of the string, and it would be pointless to go to *CTest*. But there are only two ways to reach the end of the string; one is by reducing it to a single element, in which case parsing is done successfully, and the other is to scan the whole string without making any reduction, in which case parsing has failed.

Another strategy would be to start on the right, at the end of the string, and make reductions as close to that end as possible. With that strategy, all the pointers ought to be reversed; the origin of the list should be the end of the string, and each entry should point to the preceding symbol in the string.

These two strategies could only be compared, and one of them preferred to the other, on substantive grounds. A linguist might like one better than the other if his knowledge of language in general, or some language in particular, caused him to do so; using a computer for parsing would not make one better than the other. But suppose that in some language phrases were generally formed of a main word followed by a subordinate word or phrase. If any such language exists, parsing it from the right would be preferable to parsing from the left.

There are other strategies, which we will examine later.

1.2. Use of a pushdown store

A Dyck language is written with paired terminal symbols; let X1 be paired with Y1, X2 with Y2, and so on. For each pair of terminals, there are four reduction formulae: X1-Y1, Y1-X1, X1-0-Y1, and Y1-0-X1 all reduce to 0. The unique nonterminal is 0, and a Dyck language is the set of strings reducible to 0.

Deciding whether or not a given string belongs to a Dyck language is easy. Take each terminal symbol in turn, from left to right or right to left. Put the first in a store; thereafter, compare each new symbol in the string, say t, with the last one put in the store, say s. If s and t are paired, discard s; otherwise, put s back and add t to the store. If the store is empty after the last character has been read, the string belongs to the Dyck language, and otherwise not.

A store used in this way is called a pushdown store. Fig. 33 shows the parsing of a string in a Dyck language, but with suitable elaboration a pushdown-store parser can be constructed for any context-free language.

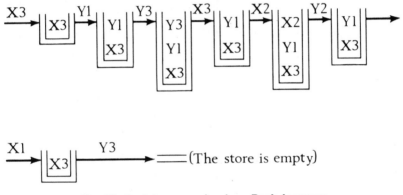

Fig. 33—Pushdown parsing in a Dyck language

Another simple example is furnished by mirror languages with center markers. Any string in a mirror language is unchanged when read backward; the choice of terminal alphabet is completely free, except that one character appears at the midpoint of every string, and nowhere else. A pushdown parser works by copying the first half of a string, then, after receiving the midpoint marker, erasing characters from the store if they match those in the string.

The parser in Fig. 34 uses the value of t as midpoint marker, and sets $T = 1$ when the marker is read. While $T = 0$, each character is stored by a procedure called *PDput*. Every procedure must, of course, be defined; this one is defined by

procedure PDput(X); **begin** p := p + 1; PD[p] := X **end**

Thus, the pushdown store is an array, and p points to its open end. After the midpoint has been passed, the program in Fig. 34 continues taking characters of input, but compares them with the ones stored

$$T := 0; j := 1;$$
$$\textbf{for } i := 1, j \textbf{ while } T = 0 \textbf{ do}$$
$$\textbf{if } Str[i] = t \textbf{ then } T := 1$$
$$\textbf{else begin } PDput(Str[i]);$$
$$j := j + 1$$
$$\textbf{end};$$
$$\textbf{for } i := j + 1 \textbf{ step } 1 \textbf{ until } L \textbf{ do}$$
$$\textbf{if } PDtop \neq Str[i] \textbf{ then goto } Fail;$$
$$\textbf{goto if } p = 0 \textbf{ then } Done \textbf{ else } Fail$$

Fig. 34—Mirror-language parser

previously. *PDtop* is another procedure, defined by

$$\textbf{procedure } PDtop; \textbf{ begin if } p = 0 \textbf{ then } PDtop := 0$$
$$\textbf{else begin } PDtop := PD[p];$$
$$p := p - 1$$
$$\textbf{end}$$

If the pushdown store is empty when a character is read, or if its top symbol does not match the current terminal, parsing fails, as it does also if the store is not empty after the last character has been read.

The example given so far shows how a pushdown store operates, but not how it can be used with more complex context-free grammars. The illustration of Fig. 31 can serve as an introduction.

This time, we begin with the starting symbol, N3, in the pushdown store. On reading the first terminal, T1, consult the grammar. If there is no formula expanding N3 into a string beginning with T1, but a formula expanding N1 into T1-T2-T3, go on to see if there is a formula expanding N3 into a string starting with N1. There is, and the remainder of the expansion is just N2. Under these circumstances, do the following: Delete N3 and write N2 in the pushdown store, and on top of it T3 and T2. Accept T1. The pushdown store now has the second of the configurations shown in Fig. 35.

When the next terminal symbol is read, it matches the top symbol in the pushdown store, and in this case the action taken is different. The terminal read is accepted, and the top character is erased from the

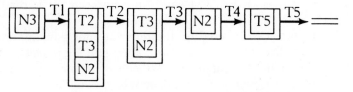

Fig. 35—Parsing with a pushdown store

pushdown store. The same thing happens for the next terminal in the string, as shown in the figure. When the fourth terminal is read, the top symbol in the pushdown store is not a terminal, but there is an expansion formula that has the symbol in the pushdown store on one side and a string starting with T4 on the other side. That formula is completed by T5; the latter symbol is written in the pushdown store, after the one standing there has been erased. When the last terminal symbol of the string has been read, matched with the top symbol in the pushdown store, and the usual action taken, the pushdown store is empty and the string is accepted.

In general, parsing begins with a starting symbol in the pushdown store. At each step, a character of the input string, say t, and the character most recently put in the store, say s, are compared. There are two cases:

(i) When s is a terminal. If $s = t$, s is erased and parsing continues. Otherwise, the string is not accepted.

(ii) When s is a nonterminal, the grammar is consulted.
A sequence of rules must be found such that the first expands s, t is the first symbol in the expansion of the last, and all intervening steps are expansions of first elements of expansions. Fig. 36 shows a typical situation; T1 is reached in the input string with N1 in the store. The grammar includes a formula expanding N1 into N2-X1-X2 (whether each X is terminal or nonterminal is irrelevant). It also includes an expansion of N2 into N3-X3 and of N3 into T1-X4-X5. These rules account for the appearance of T1, given N1, provided X1 through X5 appear later. Rhodes speaks of predictions, and we adopt her term. If the items predicted are terminals, they must appear in the input string; if they are nonterminals, they must be connected with subsequent terminals by expansion rules. Note that the predictions must be satisfied in the order X4-X5-X3-X1-X2; they are stored in reverse order.

In Fig. 36, three rules are used. The number can be larger, but for any context-free grammar a limit can be set. This limit establishes the amount of storage needed outside the pushdown store. Conceptually, a pushdown parser consists of a finite machine supplemented with an indefinitely expansible store whose use obeys the rules already explained. To recapitulate: Only the most recently stored symbol can be read, and when it is read it is erased. One and only one symbol is read from storage each time an input character is read.

Pushdown stores can be used in different ways for parsing, and it is known that they are, in a certain sense, adequate for parsing all context-free phrase structure languages. We can see from the example in Fig. 35 one of the problems that must be solved, whether with a pushdown parser or any other kind.

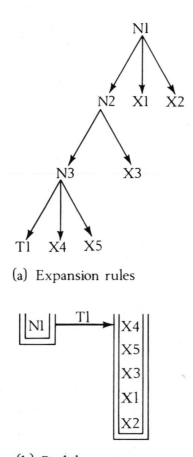

(a) Expansion rules

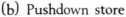

(b) Pushdown store

Fig. 36—Management of a pushdown store

Suppose that there were two different expansion rules in the grammar both associating N1 with strings beginning with T1, but continuing in different ways. If that were true, we would not know what to do when reading the first terminal symbol. The pushdown configuration shown in the figure will give a correct result if the second terminal in the string is T2, but a different configuration would be needed if the second character were something else. Even looking at the next symbol in the terminal string might not help, since the rules could match at that point also. Suppose that one of the rules includes T3, and the other differs only by leaving it out. The symbol T3 is present in the terminal string, but might be there not to accompany T1 and T2 as the expansion of N1, but rather as part of the expansion of some other symbol. Thus, the truth is that only complete parsing of a string reveals that any part of a tentative parsing is correct. In some special cases it may be possible to say that only a certain special parsing of a certain special substring is possible, whatever the rest of the sentence, but if a parser is to be widely applicable it must make provisions for doubtful cases. We return later to other parsing strategies, to see what difficulties they get into.

1.3. A dependency parser

Some linguistic theories operate with government formulae instead of expansion formulae. A nonterminal symbol can depend on or conversely can govern other nonterminal symbols. The structure associated with a string by a dependency grammar is a set of relationships like that.

A government formula names one symbol as governor and lists a set of possible dependent symbols. The order of governor and dependents relative to one another is fixed by the formula also. A dependency grammar states further what symbols can occur without dependents, and which ones can be allowed as governing but ungoverned elements of a sentence. In general, a sentence has only one ungoverned symbol.

Besides these government formulae, a dependency grammar includes a list of correspondences between terminal and nonterminal symbols. Each terminal is paired with at least one nonterminal, and possibly with several; in a given occurrence, a terminal must be identified with just one nonterminal, but choosing which one is an aspect of parsing. In the following simple example, we assume one-to-one correspondence between terminals and nonterminals.

A dependency parser can be almost identical with a phrase-structure parser, but let us instead consider one as different as possible from the example given above. Once more let the elements of a string be stored in a list. When a dependency structure is found, it must contain just one ungoverned element, and that element must be acceptable to the grammar. Start by searching the list for a symbol that can occur ungoverned, and take it as the ungoverned element of the given string. With it, start a new list, with two links per entry; this one will grow into a dependency tree.

Next, find in the grammar a formula in which the governor is the selected ungoverned symbol and all the dependents named in the formula appear in the string to be parsed, in the correct relative order. In Fig. 37, the string to be parsed consists of five terminal elements, the ungoverned element is T2, and it governs T1 and T5. The ungoverned element in a sentence is the origin of the sentence's dependency structure; at one step removed from that origin are the dependents of the

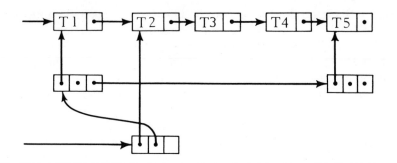

(a) T2 governs T1 and T5

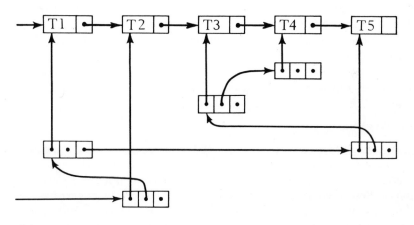

(b) T5 governs T3; T3 governs T4

Fig. 37—A dependency parser

ungoverned element, here T1 and T5. Let us take as our strategy working outward from the origin step by step; we are now ready to work at step 1, and when we finish there we will go to step 2. The dependents of a given element X must lie between certain limits. On the left, there is the beginning of the sentence, the governor of X (perhaps), and any descendants of X's governor that lie between the governor and X; on the right there are the end of the sentence, the governor of the given element if that is there, and any dependents that lie between. Thus, any dependents of T1 must lie between the beginning of the sentence and T2, which governs T1. There are of course no available terminal symbols in that region, and therefore T1 can govern nothing. The parsing started is not valid unless T1 is of the kind allowed by the grammar to have no dependents at all. The dependents of T5 must lie between T2, which governs T5, and the end of the sentence. In that region there are T3 and T4. Suppose that the grammar allows T3 to depend on T5. In that case, we can proceed to the next step, where only T3 is to be examined; if it governs T4, and if at the next step T4 is found to be the kind of element that need have no dependents, the parsing is complete, as shown in Fig. 37b.

In Fig. 37b, the top row is the original list of terminal symbols in the string to be parsed. The lower part of the figure shows a link structure reflecting the dependency connections in the sentence. Entering the structure from the left, we go to an entry for the ungoverned origin of the sentence; the first part points to a terminal in the original list, the second to a dependent, and the third to another dependent of the same governor. Following these linkages in the figure reveals the dependency structure described above for this string.

Whereas the other parsers considered till now have generally operated more or less from left to right on the string, or from right to left, this one operates by choosing, so to speak, the top of the dependency structure, and working downward from there. This is not the only way a dependency parser could work, as we shall see.

1.4. Organizing phrase structures

Almost anyone using a computer for language processing will want to know the structure of any string he submits to a parser, and not merely whether the string is acceptable to it or not. The dependency parser described in Sec. 1.3 produces a structure of government relationships, but we have not yet considered how to store phrase structures.

Fig. 38 shows how a linked array can be used to store the structure of a string relative to a context-free phrase structure grammar. There

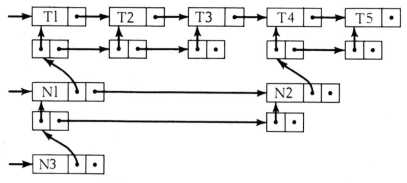

Fig. 38—Phrase structure stored in a linked array

are several entries to this array, one for each level, where level is measured by distance from terminal symbols. On the first level, there are the terminals themselves. On the second level, there are constitutes made up exclusively of terminal elements. On the third level, there are constitutes each having at least one constituent on level two; and so on. The constitutes on each level are linked, so that there is a separate list for each level. Each constitute is also linked to a list of its constituents; a list of constituents is composed of entries each pointing to a constituent. This complicated form of storage is justified by considerations we have not touched on yet.

We saw in Sec. 1.2 that a pushdown store can go astray. Ambiguity can lead any kind of parser into trouble, but parsing strategies can be designed to overcome any difficulty that ambiguity can cause. It is necessary, however, to be able to recognize overlapping constitutes. In Fig. 38, constitute N1 covers terminals T1, T2, and T3. The constitutes on level two do not overlap, since there is no terminal symbol covered by both of them. Naturally, if they overlapped, they could not be part of the same parsing of the terminal string, but they might be formed at a time when it was not possible to determine—on account of ambiguity—which of them would be used in a full parsing. By maintaining a list of constituents for each constitute, it is possible to avoid confusion between a constitute as a phrase in itself and the same constitute as constituent of another on a higher level. Hence the same constitute can be constituent of two different higher level phrases, and a strategy can be invented with enough power to find every possible structure for a given string relative to a given grammar. We turn to problems of that order next.

2. PARSING VARIABLES

Throughout Sec. 1 of this chapter, we examined different ways of working backward from a given string of terminal symbols to a nonterminal starting symbol, relying on a grammar. From time to time, we have talked about consulting a grammar, but without seeing how that consultation would be performed; all such questions are left for Chap. 7. A parsing program can in fact be divided into two components, one embodying a certain parsing logic, the other a method for doing connectability tests. The parsing logic, which we are discussing in the present chapter, can be further analyzed into a strategy and a storage plan. A strategy is concocted by deciding how to nest or interlace iterations on several variables.

Let us see what some possible variables are.

2.1. Position and length

A terminal string is composed of a certain number, say n, of terminal symbols. Let us say that they occupy positions 1 through n respectively.

If a nonterminal symbol is expanded by a formula into terminal symbols, it can be said to cover those instances of the terminal symbols obtained by applying it. In Fig. 38 above, the nonterminal N1 covers T1, T2, and T3; likewise, N2 covers T4 and T5. In general, a nonterminal symbol in the structure of a string covers the terminals covered by the nonterminals in its expansion, plus any terminals that appear directly in its expansion. For example, in Fig. 38 nonterminal N3 covers the entire string.

Let us define the position of a nonterminal, relative to a given string, as the position of the first terminal symbol it covers. The length of a nonterminal is the number of terminal symbols it covers. If a nonterminal symbol occurs at position P, with length L, then the next terminal symbol available to be covered by a different nonterminal is at position P + L.

These two variables can be used as the control variables for a parsing strategy. Thus, for example, the major iteration variable might be length, with iteration on position nested. That is, all constituents of length 2 will be formed first, then those of length 3, those of length 4, and so on up to the length of the whole string. At each length, strings starting at position one are considered first, then position two, and so on. If the string to be parsed is of length n and constituents of length L are being formed, the last starting position to be considered is n − L + 1.

Position and length can be nested the other way, but with a somewhat different plan. Starting with position 1 and length 1, form all constitutes of length L ending at position P. When all values of L less than or equal to P have been considered, go on to position P + 1, and consider all lengths from 1 to P + 1.

Since no two constituents can have the same length and either begin at the same position or else end at the same position, it is obvious that a plan based on these two variables must consider every possibility and will never consider any possibility twice. What may not be instantly apparent, but will be obvious once mentioned, is that every constitute that might be a constituent of another constitute is formed before the latter is considered. In a word, these plans arrange for things to be made before they are needed.

2.2. Level

In terms of phrase structure, let the level of a constituent be one greater than the level of any of its immediate constituents. Thus, as stated above, the level of terminal symbols is 1, the level of constitutes composed entirely of terminal symbols is 2, the level of a constitute that has at least one level-2 constituent is 3, and so on. In terms of dependency theory, let the level of a structure be one greater than the number of links from its origin to the terminal symbol furthest removed. Thus, a dependency structure with just one node has level one, a governor has level 2, a governor with a dependent that has in its turn another dependent is of level 3, and so on.

Level can be used as a control variable. Naturally, structures with smaller level numbers must be formed first. In both phrase-structure and dependency grammars, the greatest possible level number for any structure associated with a string of length n is n. It is not necessary to use length as a control variable in a strategy based on level. Level and position might be used together; given that there are constitutes of a given level at certain positions, they must all be considered, and taken in combination with appropriate possible partners on either side.

Position and level can be interchanged. Working at position P, form constitutes of all levels up to P ending there, then go on to position P + 1.

2.3. Combinations

A constitute with given length, L, and given position, P, can be formed in various ways. Let us consider first the situation that obtains if every formula in the grammar has just two symbols in its expansion.

In this case, a constitute has two constituents, whose lengths add up to its own length. The first of them can be of length 1, 2, . . . , L − 1; the second, correspondingly, must be of length L − 1, L − 2, . . . , 1. With the constitute at P, the first constituent must also be at P, and the second at P + k, where k is the length of the first constituent.

Now, releasing the restriction to binary expansions, we must consider the possibility that a constitute has two or any larger number of constituents. If the constitute is to be of length L, the first constituent can be of length 1, 2, . . . , L − C + 1, where C is the number of constituents under consideration. If k is the length of the first constituent, the second can be of length 1, 2, . . . , L − k − C + 2.

Where length and position are taken as the main variables in a parsing strategy, all possible combinations must be considered for each setting of length and position.

2.4. Grammatical interpretations

In any practical application, the terminal symbols in the string to be parsed come not from raw input directly, but from some previous step such as dictionary lookup. But as we have seen, the result of a dictionary lookup may be a set of alternative interpretations. That is to say, we may begin parsing with a string of sets of terminal symbols.

One way to handle such ambiguities is to choose just one terminal string by taking one interpretation at each position. To be sure of obtaining all possible parsings of the original string, every possible combination of choices must be made. If there are two interpretations at one position, two interpretations of the whole string must be parsed; if there are two interpretations at each of three positions, eight strings must be parsed; and so on.

Instead of proceeding in this manner, it is more economical to make grammatical interpretations a low-order control variable. When a constituent is to be selected with given length and position, or given level and position, a list of constitutes with the required properties, but with different grammatical interpretations, is run through. Taking length, position, combinations, and grammatical interpretations, gives the Cocke parsing logic, which is apparently the first to be invented that guarantees to find all allowable interpretations of any string relative to a context-free phrase structure grammar.

3. STORAGE STRUCTURES

In Sec. 1 we saw several ways of storing information during parsing. Here we consider two more, slightly more elaborate and better adapted to practical requirements.

3.1. Parsing lists

Storage structures and parsing strategies are slightly more bound together than parsing logics are bound to grammar consultation procedures. To explain and to illustrate the use of parsing lists, we take the Cocke strategy. The main iteration variable is length of the constitute to be formed; next comes position, then combinations, then grammatical interpretations. Whenever a constitute is formed, an entry is added to the parsing list. To form a constitute, the identities of certain constituents are specified, and the parsing list is consulted to see if they are there. If they are not found, the proposed constitute cannot be formed; if they are, the grammar is consulted.

The entries on a parsing list are indexed, but that index need not be stored explicitly, naturally. In each entry are stored length, position, grammatical description (or an address leading to a grammatical description), and finally either a link to a list of constituent addresses

Index	Length	Position	Grammatical Description	Constituents Left	Constituents Right	(Word)
1	1	1	Pronoun			They
2	1	2	Copula			are
3	1	2	Aux			are
4	1	3	Adj			flying
5	1	3	V-prog			flying
6	1	4	Noun			planes
7	2	2	Verb	3	5	
8	2	3	NP	4	6	
9	3	1	Sent	1	7	
10	3	2	VP	2	8	
11	3	2	VP	7	6	
12	4	1	Sent	1	10	
13	4	1	Sent	1	11	

Fig. 39—Parsing list: "They are flying planes"

or else, if the grammar is binary, pointers to left and right constituents—the pointers are indexes in the parsing list. Figure 39 shows an example.

The first several entries on a parsing list are terminal symbols. The individual grammatical interpretations of terminals are given one by one, distinguished by position number. That is, the list begins with entries of length one, starting at position one, and has one entry for each grammatical interpretation of that item. After the last grammatical interpretation of the last length 1 item, descriptions of constitutes begin. The parser forms them one by one.

After the list is well developed, say when constitutes of length 7 are being formed, searches of the list are made in this way. L = 7, p = 3 for example, and therefore the following pairs of constituents must be tested (identify each by length and position, in that order): 1, 3 with 6, 4; 2, 3 with 5, 5; 3, 3 with 4, 6; 4, 3 with 3, 7; 5, 3 with 2, 8; and 6, 3 with 1, 9. The parsing list is ordered by length and within length by position. However, there is not an entry on the list for every pair of length with position so it is not possible to index on these variables. Instead, some other technique must be used for search: Running down the list from the top; entering by a directory, which can be indexed on length and perhaps on position, and which then provides indexes to initial list entries for length or length-position blocks; or linking from every entry on the list to the next entry with the same value of P.

A program requiring a directory with both length and position as entry variables is presented in Fig. 40. As might be expected, it works by means of five nested iterations. They control, in order beginning with the outermost, length (L) and position (P) of the constitute being formed; the length of the lefthand constituent (LLC); and the grammatical interpretations of lefthand and righthand constituents.

```
for L := 2 step 1 until N do
   begin Index[L − 1, N − L + 3] := k;
      for P := 1 step 1 until N − L + 1 do
         begin Index[L, P] := k;
            for LLC := 1 step 1 until L − 1 do
               for i := Index[LLC, P] step 1 until Index[LLC, P + 1] −1 do
                  for j := Index[L − LLC, P + LLC] step 1
                     until Index[L − LLC, P + LLC + 1] −1 do
                  begin Gconst := CT(G[i], G[j]);
                     if Gconst ≠ 0
                  then begin Lg[k] := L;
                             Pos[k] := P;
                             G[k] := Gconst;
                             LC[k] := i;
                             RC[k] := j;
                             k := k + 1
                     end
               end
         end
   end
```

Fig. 40—A parsing program: Length, position, parsing list

The directory is an array called *Index*; the sentence is not longer than N positions, and the *Index* array is N × (N + 1). Each component *Index*[L, P] has as value the first index for an entry in the parsing list with location L and position P. Each component *Index*[L, N − L + 2] is equal to *Index*[L + 1, 1]; this device simplifies consultation of the directory, as we shall see.

The iterations on L, P, and LLC are obvious. The grammatical interpretations of the lefthand constituent are found in the parsing list, as the program says, beginning at *Index*[LLC, P] and ending on the line before the next group begins: *Index*[LLC, P + 1] − 1. If the extra directory entries mentioned above were not provided, special conditions would arise here for the last position within each length. The iteration over interpretations of the righthand constituents has the same form.

When a pair of entries is chosen, a connectability-test routine is called on to assign a value to *Gconst*. If that value is 0, the grammar disallows the combination, and nothing happens. If the proposed constitute is grammatically viable, an entry is added to the parsing list; k serves as pointer to the next position. The parsing list consists of arrays *Lg, Pos, G, LC,* and *RC*; as in Fig. 39, these contain length, position, grammatical description, and the indices of left and right constituents.

The directory must be developed by the parser. Each time a new value of P is considered, the current value of k is assigned to *Index*[L, P], whether or not any entries were written in the parsing list for the previous value of P. Hence two adjacent entries, e.g. *Index*[2, 4] and *Index*[2, 5] can be equal, and in that case the entry that would be selected for, e.g., L = 2, P = 4 would not be valid. However, the iterations on i and j prevent examination of invalid entries. If *Index*[LLC, P] = *Index*[LLC, P + 1] = X, the iteration is from i = X to i = X − 1, and that is impossible with a positive increment; not even one step is performed. The final, dummy component of *Index* for each value of L is filled in as the iteration begins with the next value of L.

3.2. Path tables

The structure of a sentence, as defined by phrase-structure theory, is a collection of phrases or constitutes. Phrases are bound together into a tree by relationships of constituency. They are also related by virtue of the fact that each covers a specified portion of the sentence: Any phrase is followed by any other that covers the contiguous, following portion. If all or part of a sentence is ambiguous, all of the constitutes that can be formed on it are related in these ways—if not by constituency, at least by succession.

A parsing path is a sequence of phrases, each following the one before. Figure 41 shows a parsing structure in which paths can be

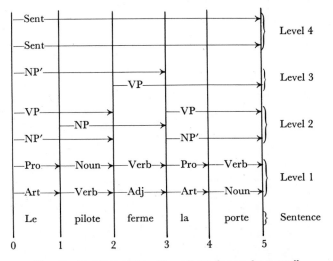

Fig. 41—Parsing paths: "Le pilote ferme la porte"

	1				2				3				4				5			
	G	Orig	CL	CR	G	Orig	CL	CR	G	Orig	CL	CR	G	Orig	CL	CR	G	Orig	CL	CR
1	Art	0			Verb	1			Verb	2			Art	3			Verb	4		
2	Pro	0			Noun	1			Adj	2			Pro	3			Noun	4		
3	0				VP	0	2	1	NP	1	2	2	0				VP	3	2	1
4	0				NP'	0	1	2	NP'	0	1	3	0				NP'	3	1	2
5	0				0				0				0				Sent	0	4	3
6	0				0				0				0				VP	2	1	4
7	0				0				0				0				Sent	0	4	6
8	0				0				0				0				0			
	Le				pilote				ferme				la				porte			

Fig. 42—Path tables for a position-length parser

traced; the vertical lines between word occurrences mark boundaries of coverage, and each arrow shows the portion of the sentence covered by one phrase. (To keep this figure simple, constituencies are not shown.) Thus a phrase of type VP covers "ferme la porte"; its arrow runs from line 2 to line 5. Also, a phrase of type NP' covers "Le pilote"; its arrow runs from line 0 to line 2. Since the NP' ends at the line where the VP begins, the phrases are contiguous.

A set of tables equivalent to a path chart can be used as a basis for parsing. One such parser is due to Martin Kay, another to Frederick B. Thompson. Kay's takes position as major control variable, and we follow his algorithm rather closely; Thompson's uses level, as we do in our final context-free parser, but the one we examine differs considerably from his.

To parse by sentence position, we set up a table for each position and list in it all phrases ending there. Initially, each table contains only the results of dictionary lookup; as it happens, the first two lines of each table in Fig. 42 come from that source, but any number could. Four items are given on each line. G stands for grammatical type; *Orig* stands for origin, corresponding to the line in Fig. 41 where the phrase begins; CL is the count, or index, of the lefthand constituent of the phrase; and CR is that of the righthand constituent. By means of the CL and CR entries, the constituencies omitted from Fig. 41 are displayed here. For example, the NP on line 3 of table 3 has CR = 2; since the righthand constituent is always in the same table with the phrase, in this case it is the Adj. But for that Adj, *Orig* = 2; since the two constituents must be contiguous, the lefthand constituent is to be found in table 3, and, since for the NP phrase itself CL = 2, the item sought is of type Noun. Hence the NP is composed of Noun followed by Adj, and the constituencies of all other phrases can be traced in similar fashion.

If the tables were to be used with a grammar permitting more than two constituents per phrase, constituency relationships would have to be stored differently. Instead of CL and CR, each table would contain a column of addresses for lists of constituents. In those lists, each constituent could be identified by a count as in the present CL and CR positions.

In Algol, we define four arrays, G[i, j], *Orig*[i, j], CL[i, j], and CR[i, j] where i is table (or position) number, and j indexes entries within the table. The position-dominated strategy is to form all possible constitutes ending at position i, then go on to position i + 1. The first position to require attention is i = 2, unless the grammar includes rules that replace one symbol with another single symbol. The outermost

```
for i := 2 step 1 until N do
    begin P := Desc[i] + 1;
        for j := 1, j + 1 while G[i, j] ≠ 0 do
            if Orig[i, j] ≠ 0 then
                for k := 1, k + 1 while G[Orig[i, j], k] ≠ 0 do
                    begin Const := CT(G[Orig[i, j], k], G[i, j]);
                        if Const ≠ 0 then
                            begin G[i, P] := Const;
                                Orig[i, P] := Orig[Orig[i, j], k];
                                CL[i, P] := k;
                                CR[i, P] := j;
                                P := P + 1
                            end
                    end
    end
```

Fig. 43—Parser: Position, length, path table

iteration in Fig. 43 begins at the second position and ends at N, the last in the sentence.

A pointer, P, identifies the first available place in the current table. The vector *Desc*[i] is provided by the program that puts dictionary results into the tables; each entry tells how many descriptions the dictionary gave for the current item.

The iteration at each position keeps trying to build phrases ending there as long as new righthand constituents can be tried: they can be tested as soon as they are constructed. In table 3 of Fig. 42, the first two lines come from the dictionary. The program deals with them one by one, adding a third line; going on to the third line, it adds a fourth; but testing the fourth line adds nothing, so G[3, 5] remains zero and the program goes on to i = 4.

For each item, the program tries all ways of forming constitutes with the item as righthand constituent. If the item has *Orig* = 0, there is nothing on its left. Otherwise, the item is contiguous to all items in table *Orig*[i, j]. For example, take i = 4, j = 2 (in Fig. 42), and note *Orig*[4, 2] = 3. Each G[3, k] must be paired with G[4, 2] = *Pro* and tested against the grammar, but all give null results. The CT procedure gives 0 for unrelated pairs, or a phrase type otherwise.

When a new phrase can be formed, a line is added to the table. For example, take i = 5, j = 6, k = 4 in Fig. 42; then *Orig*[5, 6] = 2, G[2, 4] = NP′, G[5, 6] = VP, and CT(NP′, VP) = *Sent*. Since P is the pointer to an available line, and i designates the current table,

G[i, P] takes as value the grammatical type of the new phrase. The origin of the new phrase, assigned to $Orig[i, P]$ is the origin of its lefthand constituent. The indices k and j identify the constituents, and P is advanced to the next place in the table for the current position.

Because the number of lines used varies from table to table, the algorithm in Fig. 43 wastes storage space. An Algol compiler must be given maximum values for i and j; it reserves enough space to store the maximum number of lines in each table. Thus, if sentences of up to 100 occurrences are to be handled, and if some tables are expected to need 20 lines (a modest estimate), 2000 entries must be allowed to each of G[i, j], $Orig[i, j]$, CL[i, j], and CR[i, j]. One cell is taken for every entry in every array by most Algol compilers. (If grammatical descriptions are too large for such treatment, additional arrays must be defined; see Chap. 7.) Since the grammar must be stored during parsing, this requirement for path tables is large enough to merit attention. A different, somewhat more complex algorithm would use singly indexed arrays. In each, the entries for position 1 would be followed immediately by those for position 2, and so on to the end of the sentence. The iteration controls would be different, and the algorithm would have to copy dictionary information into its array on moving to its new position.

In practical use, a parser may have to determine sentence boundaries as it goes. Punctuation sometimes marks boundaries unambiguously, but not always. A parser that moves from position to position can check punctuation as it goes and decide when to cut off a sentence (and clear its storage) on the basis of grammatical types and punctuation jointly.

3.3. Parsing by level

The storage scheme presented in this section is a table of paths and constituencies, but it lists phrases in order by level. An elementary unit, say a word, is of level 1; the level of any phrase is higher by 1 than the highest level of any constituent.

With level as a major control variable, a parser forms all phrases composed of elementary units; these phrases are on level 2. Then it forms those on level 3; each must have at least one constituent on level 2, but can also have lower level constituents.

In Algol, several arrays are used. G[i] stores the grammatical descriptions of phrases. Assuming two constituents per phrase, IL[i] and IR[i] store the indices of left and right constituents. The coverage of a phrase is indicated by FP[i], the first position covered by it in the sentence, and LP[i], the last. But level, not length or position, is the major variable, and so phrases beginning or ending at a certain position are not necessarily adjacent in the array. To simplify the task of finding such a collection of phrases, the algorithm presented below uses two arrays of links: LF[i], links on first position covered, and LL[i], links on last position covered. An example is given in Fig. 44a; its content is identical with that of Fig. 42.

Index	G	IL	IR	FP	LP	LF	LL
1	Art			1	1	2	2
2	Pro			1	1	11	0
3	Verb			2	2	4	4
4	Noun			2	2	13	11
5	Verb			3	3	6	6
6	Adj			3	3	17	13
7	Art			4	4	8	8
8	Pro			4	4	14	0
9	Verb			5	5	10	10
10	Noun			5	5	0	14
11	VP	2	3	1	2	12	12
12	NP'	1	4	1	2	16	0
13	NP	4	6	2	3	0	16
14	VP	8	9	4	5	15	15
15	NP'	7	10	4	5	0	17
16	NP'	1	13	1	3	18	0
17	VP	5	15	3	5	0	18
18	Sent	16	14	1	5	19	19
19	Sent	12	17	1	5	0	0

(a) Path table

Index	Entry
1	1
2	11
3	16
4	18
5	20
6	20

(b) Level Entries

Index	HLF	HLL
1	1	1
2	3	3
3	5	5
4	7	7
5	9	9

(c) Heads of position lists

Index	PLF	PLL
1	19	2
2	13	12
3	17	16
4	15	8
5	10	19

(d) Pointers to position lists

Fig. 44—Modified path table and directories for a level-position parser

Five directories are used. One gives the starting point in the main arrays for phrases of each level (Fig. 44b). Two are starting-point lists for coverage lists; HLF, the head of linkage by first position covered, indicates the earliest entry in the main array that has coverage beginning at the selected position, and HLL does the same with respect to last position (Fig. 44c). Starting with HLF[j], moving to LF[HLF[j]], and so on, carries us through a list of phrases all covering portions of the sentence beginning at position j. The last entry in such a list has LF = 0; the index to that entry is kept, as a pointer, in PLF[j]. Similar pointers are kept for last-position lists in PLL (Fig. 44d).

The parser (Fig. 45) takes *Level* = 1, to form phrases of level 2, and goes on from level to level as long as possible. The program that fills in dictionary information sets *Entry*[1] = 1 and assigns the proper value to *Entry*[2]. On finishing level 1, the parser assigns a value to *Entry*[3]; all phrases on level 2 have been recorded. The pointer P moves up when a phrase is added to the list; if no phrases of level L

for Level := 1, Level + 1 **while** Entry[Level] ≠ Entry[Level + 1] **do**
 begin for i := Entry[Level] **step** 1 **until** Entry[Level + 1] −1 **do**
  begin if FP[i] ≠ 1 **then**
    for j := HLL[FP[i] − 1], LL[j] **while** j ≠ 0 ∧ j < Entry[Level +1] **do**
     begin Const := CT(G[j], G[i]);
      if Const ≠ 0 **then**
       begin G[P] := Const; IL[P] := j; IR[P] := i;
           FP[P] := FP[j]; LP[P] := LP[i];
           LF[PLF[FP[j]]] := LL[PLL[LP[i]]] := P;
           PLF[FP[j]] := PLL[LP[i]] := P; P := P + 1 **end**
    end;
    if LP[i] ≠ N **then**
    for j := HLF[LP[i] + 1], LF[j] **while** j ≠ 0 ∧ j < Entry[Level] **do**
     begin Const := CT(G[i], G[j]);
      if Const ≠ 0 **then**
       begin Ġ[P] := Const; IL[P] := i; IR[P] := j;
           FP[P] := FP[i]; LP[P] := LP[j];
           LF[PLF[FP[i]]] := LL[PLL[LP[j]]] := P;
           PLF[FP[i]] := PLL[LP[j]] := P; P := P + 1 **end**
    end
  end;
  Entry[Level + 2] := P
 end

Fig. 45—Parser: Level, position, modified path table

are added, *Entry*[L] = *Entry*[L + 1]. The major iteration stops, since no phrases of any higher level can be formed.

The second iteration goes through entries of the current level. For each of them, it must try to add partners on both left and right. Imagine a 4-word sentence in which only one phrase is found on level 2; if it covers positions 1 and 2, it must be coupled with the word in position 3, whereas if it covers positions 3 and 4, its partner is at position 2. But suppose two phrases are found, covering positions 1 and 2 (phrase A) and 3 and 4 (phrase B), respectively. Then several pairs must be considered: Phrase A with word 3, word 2 with phrase B, and phrase A with phrase B. Hence each phrase on a given level must be paired with contiguous phrases on the same level or lower; but to avoid testing pairs on the same level twice, a trick is required. In Fig. 45, the trick is based on left-to-right order, but order in the main array could be used.

Given a phrase on the current level (its index is i), the parser looks for partners to its left unless (FP[i] = 1) it begins in the first position of the sentence. The possible partners are those phrases with last position FP[i] − 1; the index of the first comes from a directory, HLL[FP[i] − 1], and the rest are obtained by using LL links. For example, take i = 17 in Fig. 44; then FP[17] = 3, HLL[2] = 3, LL[3] = 4, LL[4] = 11, LL[11] = 12, and LL[12] = 0, so that the possible partners of phrase 17 are 3, 4, 11, and 12. The iteration can end, as in this illustration, with a zero link, but it also ends if it reaches an entry on a level higher than the current one—thus two phrases on the same level can be tested here. (The symbol ∧ means that the conditions before and after it must both be true.)

For each pair considered, a CT procedure is carried out. If the grammar allows the combination, a new phrase is added. P is the pointer to an available line; the grammatical type put in is that attributed to the phrase by the grammar, the indices of the left and right constituents are j and i, respectively. The first and last positions covered by the new phrase are the first and last covered by its left and right constituents. Now the linkages must be extended. PLF and PLL point to the current last entries; those links are made to point to the new phrase, which becomes the last entry for its first and last position lists. Finally, the pointer in the main array is advanced.

As the two outermost iterations focus on each phrase, it is paired not only with phrases preceding it, but also—if its last position is not the last in the sentence—with those following. The section of the algorithm that does this is parallel to that already discussed, except for changes caused by left-right reversal of phrases i and j, and also the restriction that the possible partner be on a lower level. Thus partners on the same level are paired once, not twice.

Choice of level as major control variable gives the programmer the option of clearing part of storage before parsing of one sentence is finished. The Cocke algorithm allows only a few constitutes, near the center of the sentence, to be dropped; for example, after length 4 has been dealt with, words 3 and 4 and any phrase covering only them cannot be used again in the parsing of a sentence of length 6. Again, if position is the major variable, whole sentences can be recognized and cleared from storage as they are found. The situation is somewhat better if level is used.

Every constitute on levels higher than L must contain at least one constituent on level L. Hence, after phrases on level L have been formed, other phrases can be used only if they can be combined in larger structures with those on level L. Since two phrases cannot be parts of a single structure if they overlap, a phrase of level lower than L is useful only if it is nonoverlapping with at least one phrase on level L. Now, consider all the phrases on level L, and determine the largest value of FP (say A) and the smallest value of LP (say B); a phrase of lower level must be retained if either its last position is less than A or its first position is greater than B. The time required to examine each phrase and eliminate it if possible would probably lead the programmer to initiate the procedure only when the space available for the parsing list is full.

EXERCISES

1. Write a Dyck-language pushdown parser.

2. Polish prefix notation allows strings such as +ab, meaning the sum of a and b. Grammatically, each symbol is a predicate (P), or a variable (x). Assume each predicate takes two arguments, either variables or predications: Pxx, PxPxx, and PPxxPxx are well formed. Write a pushdown parser.

3. In general, a context-free phrase-structure grammar can be converted into a set of predictions of this form: If terminal T occurs with nonterminal N predicted, the prediction of N is satisfied and symbols x . . . x are predicted. The list of predicted symbols can be vacuous. A string is parsed successfully if the total list of predictions, beginning with a stated symbol, is empty for the first time after the last character has been read. Write a pushdown predictive parser.

4. Set up a linked array as in Fig. 38 for Algol processing. Write a program to find a complete structure for the terminal string, assuming that the array has been developed with multiple analyses and possibly overlapping constitutes.

5. Reorganize the program in Fig. 40 to make position the major control variable; revise the treatment of position and length appropriately.

6. Write an Algol program to list all paths covering a full sentence, using a storage array like that in Fig. 42. (This operation is part of transformational parsing; see Chap. 8.)

7. The parser in Fig. 43 has position as its major control variable, but length is not its secondary control; what is, and what difference does it make?

8. Revise the parser in Fig. 43 to use one-dimensional arrays like those used in Fig. 44.

9. Sketch the controls necessary to make a parser that moves over positions in a text decide sentence boundaries.

10. How would the parser in Fig. 43 have to be modified for use with a grammar having more than two symbols in some expansions?

11. Write an Algol program to find constitutes that can be dropped from an array like that in Fig. 44; list the indices of items dropped (this is an available-space list); maintain first and last-position linkages.

12. Write an Algol program to trace all complete sentence structures in one of the parsing arrays. Start with phrases of type *sentence*, covering the whole sentence, and list constituents in an order suitable for presentation to a linguist.

REFERENCES

"Parsing" (David G. Hays; RALP pp. 73–82) introduces the topic, and explains backtracking, a method not discussed in the present chapter.

"Dependency Theory: A Formalism and some Observations" (David G. Hays; *Language*, Vol. 40, No. 4, October-December 1964, pp. 511–525) gives an introduction to this approach.

"The Use of Machines in the Construction of a Grammar and Computer Program for Structural Analysis" (K. E. Harper and D. G. Hays; *Information Processing*, UNESCO, Paris, 1960, pp. 188–194) describes an early dependency parser.

Studies in Machine Translation—10: Russian Sentence-structure Determination (D. G. Hays and T. W. Ziehe; RM-2538, The RAND Corporation, April 1960) describes the first RAND parser in detail.

"A New Approach to the Mechanical Syntactic Analysis of Russian" (Ida Rhodes; *Mechanical Translation*, Vol. 6, November 1961, pp. 33–50) was probably the first publication on predictive parsing.

"The Predictive Analyzer and a Path Elimination Technique" (Susumu Kuno; *Communications of the Association for Computing Machinery*, Vol. 8, No. 7, July 1965, pp. 453–462, *also* RALP pp. 83–106) treats predictive parsing much more fully than the present chapter does, and shows methods for making it an efficient approach.

The Harvard English Syntactic Analyzer Manual (Carlton DeTar, Inez B. Hazel, and C. Cynthia Tukis; *Mathematical Linguistics and Automatic Translation*, Report No. NSF-14, The Computation Laboratory, Harvard University, July 1965) is a detailed and technical presentation of a predictive parser.

"Formal Properties of Grammars" (Noam Chomsky; in *Handbook of Mathematical Psychology*, R. D. Luce, R. R. Bush, and E. Galanter, eds., Wiley, New York, 1963, Vol. 2, pp. 323–418) covers theoretical questions of phrase-structure grammar, as well as other topics.

PARSE: A System for Automatic Syntactic Analysis of English Text (J. J. Robinson and S. L. Marks; RM-4654-PR, The RAND Corporation, September 1965) uses the Cocke parsing logic, cover symbols, and pattern-of-ambiguity coding.

Chapter 7

TECHNIQUES FOR STORING AND USING GRAMMARS

Each of the parsers described in Chapter 6 turns at the moment of decision to a program not described there. Parsing logic determines what strings of items are to be referred to a grammar, but it does not determine how the grammar is to be stored or consulted.

According to the simplest view of phrase structure grammar, each rule has two parts. In a context-free grammar, one part is a single, unanalyzable symbol; the other part is a string of symbols. When the parser presents a string of symbols, the question is whether that string appears anywhere in the grammar; either the answer is negative or else a symbol is paired with the string in some rule.

For both practical and theoretical reasons, many linguists choose a different formulation. The grammatical description of a single item is for them not a single symbol but a set of components. Now a rule of grammar can pair a statement about item descriptions with a string of such statements. Each statement can specify components that must be present, or components that must be absent, or alternatives of which one must be present, for example. The theoretical argument in favor of such a position is generally an assertion that complex symbols allow the linguist to make more valid statements about natural languages than he could otherwise express. The practical argument is that for many languages, if not for all, grammars are easier to construct, to remember, and to process if they use complex symbols. The linguist's resources, including both his own time and the computing capacity he can obtain, are always so limited in comparison with the task of describing a natural language that he must conserve them in every way he can. This chapter is about the conservation of resources in handling grammars.

I. ELEMENTARY METHODS

Before beginning to consider sophisticated methods, we had best look at some elementary problems.

I.I. The grammar as an array

Any grammar has to be used by both the linguist and the computer. However, it need not take the same form for both. For the linguist, all of the terms in the grammar should be easy to remember. For the computer, the important considerations are compactness of storage and speed of consultation.

To exemplify this point, let us imagine a linguist with a small number of grammatical categories and a computer with adequate storage space. In the first instance, let us suppose that each of his formulae pairs exactly one symbol with a string of exactly two symbols.

For external use, this linguist can use whatever representation he considers attractive for each of his category symbols. In his dictionary, he can store such an external representation in the entry for each syntactic unit, but then he must translate them into internal representations after dictionary lookup. If he chooses, he can instead store the internal representation in the dictionary, and perform the necessary conversion when he adds an entry to the dictionary and, in the opposite direction, whenever he prints the dictionary for inspection. Likewise, his grammar will be presented as a list of rules expressed as strings of external representations of categories, but it will be converted to a different form for use during parsing.

As internal representation, he can use the first n integers, where n is the number of categories to be represented.

When the parser consults the grammar, it supplies two integers. The grammar consultation program, if it were written in Algol, would just take the given integers as indices in an array, obtaining from the array either 0 if no rule links the given categories, or the integer designating another category if the rule exists. Whatever the programming language, consultation of the grammar in this situation is trivial.

Next, let us consider grammars with only this much more complexity: that some rules still contain strings of two category symbols, some strings of three, but none longer. The grammar consultation program can still take a given string of three category symbols as subscripts for entry to an array. However, when parsing logic supplies a string of three symbols and the first two match a two-place rule but there is no rule involving all three, something further is required. One plan is to store the two-place rules using a two-dimensional array, and consult it twice—once with the first two and once with the last two of any string of three symbols. The three symbols are also taken as indices to the three-dimensional array. Another plan is to store in each cell of the three-dimensional array all the necessary information. For example, each cell could contain the symbol, if any, paired by a rule with the full string of three symbols; in addition, it could contain another symbol—or perhaps the same symbol—paired by a formula with the first two of the three symbols; and in a third segment the same entry could contain the symbol paired by some rule with the last two symbols.

But suppose the grammar contains just 100 categories; with two-place rules, the grammar array has 10,000 entries, and with three-place entries the number is 1,000,000. A grammar with one hundred categories and something on the order of a million rules is unbelievable. Hence, we must suppose that almost all of the array is empty. If some rules contain more than three symbols, the situation is worse, and even a million cells cannot be provided in any real computer.

This is the same kind of situation that led to consideration of more complicated methods for dictionary lookup. Some of the same plans can be used in the storage of grammars.

1.2. Compression of formula lists

Consider the case of a grammar limited to binary expansion formulae. Let us assume that when the grammar is to be consulted the parsing logic puts forward a pair of symbols. If the number of different symbols is not too great, the first can be taken as index in a list; each entry in this list is 0 if there is no formula having an expansion that begins with the given symbol, and otherwise the entry gives the origin of a table. Direct indexing in the new table would require too much storage. Instead, if the list of expansions beginning with a given symbol is typically short, straight searching may be simplest; if many of these lists are long, binary search can be used.

If the grammar includes expansion rules leading to strings of three or more symbols, the first step is the same, and the second step differs only in that the contents of an entry in a second-symbol list would be more complex. If an expansion can stop with the second symbol, the associated symbol must be given. If the string can continue to a third place, the origin of a new table must be given. If the parsing logic, on supplying a string, wants to know whether any substring is obtainable by an expansion formula, consultation of the grammar must be performed beginning with every symbol in the string except the last.

Perhaps the most burdensome aspect of working with a grammar of multiplace expansion rules is the necessity of forming and testing long strings of phrases that might comprise new constitutes. In terms of position parsing, each phrase ending at position p, with origin p', must be combined with every phrase ending at p'; if one of those has origin p'', the string of phrases must be extended in every possible way by addition of phrases ending at p''; and so on. This burden can be reduced, by closer interlocking of parsing logic with connectability testing. Let the parser run through phrases ending at position p, and submit the grammatical type of each to the connectability-test program, which selects a list of possible continuations, if there are any. The parser runs through its list of contiguous phrases; for each one on the list of possible continuations, the CT program replies either that a new constitute (of a certain type) is formed, or that another step must be taken—or both. This procedure is like the letter-table method for dictionary lookup (Chap. 5, Sec. 2.4); the number of strings tested is reduced to the extent that the grammar blocks continuations.

2. GRAMMARS WITH COMPLEX SYMBOLS

A simple grammar uses a discrete symbol for every class of strings it defines, whether these strings be elementary or composite. In various ways, elegant grammars use complex symbols. Since grammars published for human consumption are invariably elegant, complex symbols are familiar. When someone writes that an item is "a noun in the genitive case, singular, masculine, governs noun clauses" he is giving values for five attributes: part of speech, case, number, gender, and special government. In a context-free phrase-structure grammar, each formula couples one complex symbol with a string of them. Storage and consultation of a grammar in this form is more difficult than if each symbol is unanalyzable, yet it would be more awkward still to deal with an alphabet of unanalyzable symbols as large as any natural language would require.

2.1. Internal and external coding

Some grammatical attributes are best considered as having only two values, present and absent. Thus, the attribute of governing a noun clause could be treated that way. On the other hand, some linguists think it more natural to take gender as an attribute with three distinct values, in a language that differentiates masculine, feminine, and neuter. Other linguists would surely prefer to identify two attributes, and say that a neuter word possesses neither of them, that one is present for both masculine and feminine words, and that the other is present only in (say) feminine words. Similarly with case, some linguists will prefer to work with a single attribute having many values, as many as there are cases in his language; others will choose to define as many attributes as necessary, each attribute being present or absent.

In making up a dictionary, the linguist must write down a grammatical description for each entry. It goes without saying that he wants to encode the information he must supply in a way that is easy to remember but also compact. True, he could write "part of speech:

noun" beside each noun entry, and that would be easy to remember. But the amount of handwriting necessary to the preparation of a large dictionary would be excessively tedious. He might also write "PS:N" and do much better, since he is unlikely to forget that the PS means part of speech and the N means noun. On the other hand, if every grammatical description is to include a symbol for part of speech, he might do better still to begin always with "N" for a noun, "V" for a verb, and the like; the first character in every description is part of speech—position alone is enough to identify what attribute is being mentioned.

Perhaps no attribute other than part of speech belongs in every complex symbol; there are probably some that must be mentioned in the description of any noun, however, and the linguist preparing a dictionary of Russian might choose to write "NM", "NF", or "NN" for masculine, feminine, and neuter nouns, always taking the second position for gender. Some different attribute, common to all verbs, might occupy the second position following V. Now the linguist must remember, as he codes the dictionary, not just what symbols he is using for the components of complex symbols, but also where to put them. Perhaps he has gone too far now in the direction of abbreviating.

If this much abbreviation in external encoding is excessive, it is probably not too much for internal use. Three natural units of computer storage are the bit, the character, and the cell. If every attribute has just two values, a bit position can be identified with each attribute and a 1 stored in it if the attribute is present, 0 otherwise. If some attributes are multivalued, it may be most convenient to identify a character position with each attribute, and to store a character corresponding to each value in that place. The definitions of character positions can be conditioned to part of speech, and if just six attributes are enough for any part of speech, each complex symbol need occupy no more than one cell. In practice, more attributes will often be required, and therefore some complex symbols will occupy two or more cells.

2.2. Cover symbols

Natural languages all contain instances of random ambiguity, as when *cleaner* turns out to be both agentive noun and comparative adjective; there seems to be no connection. The linguist designing an encoding system is best advised to neglect such random combinations, assigning two distinct grammar-code symbols to an item if need be. But there is also systematic, or patterned, ambiguity, and for this the linguist may want to have a systematic treatment.

In Russian, noun inflection presents a score or so of patterns of ambiguity. One affix is used at several places in the paradigm, for example in the nominative singular, accusative singular, and genitive plural positions. The linguist can identify these patterns of ambiguity and assign a symbol to each pattern. A pattern-of-ambiguity symbol must fit into the space allocated to an ordinary symbol for the value of one attribute. Thus, if N stands for nominative, A for accusative, and G for genitive, a single number or letter must suffice as the symbol for "nominative or accusative." Note that if case is one attribute and number another, a pattern of ambiguity that links them, putting together one case in singular and another in plural, cannot be treated in this way.

Now there is a formula in Russian that couples a nominative singular adjective with a nominative singular noun, if both are of the same gender. The patterns of ambiguity for adjectives and nouns are similar, but not identical. The linguist has a list of symbols for noun case and number, and another list for adjective case and number, each including pure types and patterns of ambiguity. If the grammar lists every acceptable combination of noun symbol with adjective symbol, the list is extensive. Cover symbols are a help in shortening grammars.

A cover symbol is one designed for use in a rule; it signifies that any of several distinct symbols in the description of an item satisfies the rule. Thus, a cover symbol to be used for nouns, and intended to signify nominative case, would be interpreted as indicating that any purely nominative noun, but likewise any ambiguous noun including the nominative as one possibility, is acceptable. By means of cover symbols, the number of grammatical descriptions assigned to individual items in the dictionary can be kept small, while the number of rules to be listed is not made regrettably large.

Cover symbols can be processed in several ways. The grammar can be maintained by the linguist with cover symbols, but expanded by replacement of cover symbols when the grammar is read into machine storage. The linguist's time is conserved, but space in machine storage is not. Of course, he must memorize the cover symbols as well as the symbols for single values of attributes.

Another possibility, but an unattractive one, is to expand the symbols in the dictionary after they have been attached to items in text but before parsing; now only pure types are symbolized, but the multiple descriptions attached to individual items lead to a number of intermediate results in parsing that may be intolerable.

A third possibility is to match pattern-of-ambiguity symbols with cover symbols at the time the grammar is consulted. The parsing logic presents a string of complex symbols; in any complex symbol, any component can stand for a single value of an attribute, or several. The formulae of the grammar contain cover symbols. It is therefore impossible to do binary search, since an exact match between a complex symbol in text and a complex symbol in the grammar cannot be demanded. In a system programmed at RAND in 1959 by Theodore W. Ziehe, the formulae to be stored were expanded so that no cover symbols were used for part of speech. Now, a directory of part of speech strings can be constructed. Extracting the part of speech from each complex symbol in the string offered by the parser, the program can either index to an entry in the directory or perform binary search. The directory refers to a block of storage where all rules having the required parts of speech can be found. Within that block, every formula must be compared with the string of complex symbols presented for testing.

The matching proceeds component by component. One way to perform the match is to convert the symbol stored for a component of a complex symbol in the grammar into a list of the symbols for values or combinations of values it covers. Then, if the symbol given by the parser is on the list, the match is accepted and the test proceeds to the next position.

This third plan keeps space requirements for both the table of grammatical rules and the lists of partial parsing results small, but uses computing time when table lookup is called for.

2.3. Organized tables

If it were true in practice that most grammatical rules referred to only one or two components of grammatical descriptions, it would be easy to write and use grammars, even without cover symbols. We could store each rule as a specification of what attributes to examine, and what values to accept. In fact, almost any rule worth writing mentions several. Since many components can be ambiguous for many items, the length of the rule table is enlarged multiplicatively if cover symbols are not used. However, multiplication of table length can also be avoided by separate inspection of individual components.

Martin Kay has designed a system of this kind. The first stage is to determine what sort of grammatical relationship is being proposed. In terms of phrase structure, Hockett has named them construction types; in dependency grammar, the term syntactic function is used. In general, examination of the parts of speech of items taken from text provides an indication of what construction types or syntactic functions might connect them. Thus, a table of part-of-speech pairs is given, and part-of-speech components are extracted from grammatical descriptions and looked up in this table. The table directs the system to proceed by extracting certain components from the grammatical descriptions and naming the table in which they can be looked up. This guidance is possible only because construction types or grammatical functions demand agreement, in a broad sense, with respect to fixed components. In the end, there may be alternative patterns of agreement even for a given function and a given part of speech, but when there are the table can indicate that a successful lookup, either in table A with given components, or in table B with other components, is acceptable.

Depending on the language being parsed, it may be most satisfactory to use the table of part-of-speech pairs to guide the entire test on a pair of items, or to allow subsequent tables to do so as well. It would be possible, for example, to state in the adjective-noun entry of a part-of-speech table that one of two functions, either government of the noun by the adjective or modification of the noun by the adjective, is possible. Furthermore, the entry could show that in the case of modification there must be agreement with respect to gender, number, and case, these being three separate components findable in a certain way within the grammatical descriptions of adjectives and nouns respectively, and tested by reference to three tables: one for each component. The same main-table entry would show further that if the adjective governs the noun, the noun must be in the case governed by the adjective; this pair of components would be extracted according to instructions given in the part-of-speech table or elsewhere and tested with the case-government table.

No full-fledged illustration of this method appears in the literature, but preliminary studies clearly show that the number of tables needed for a natural language, and the number of entries needed in each make for a much smaller storage requirement than that imposed by a system putting a complete grammar in one table.

2.4. Transfer of components

If complex symbols are used for phrases as well as for terminals, the grammar must provide them. However, some of them can be copied from the descriptions of constituents into the description of the constitute. In that case, the grammar can be compressed if instructions for copying are given instead of duplicate symbols.

For example, a linguist might choose to say that English adjective and noun are constituents of a noun phrase, and that article + noun (or noun phrase) constitute a determined noun phrase to which no other determiner can be added. Perhaps the description of a noun has many components, of which few are relevant to combination with adjective or determiner. But perhaps many of them are relevant to combinations that must be made later, as with a preposition or verb. The internal coding for a grammatical rule can provide one symbol which, used in the phrasal side of the formula, means that the given component is to be copied from the textual description of one of the constituents of the formula. This symbol, used in the rule for combining adjective with noun, could transfer all the unaffected properties of the noun constituent to the constitute.

The rule for attaching article to noun or noun phrase must do something different, however. The description of a noun phrase must show whether or not a determiner is present, and therefore the value of this attribute must be stored as part of the formula and transferred from the grammar to the text when the rule is used.

A different way of producing a component for the grammatical description of a constitute is needed when agreement is invoked between two possibly ambiguous attributes. If a Russian adjective can be genitive or some other case, but not nominative, and if a noun can be nominative or genitive but not any other case, they must be said to agree in case—but then the case of the phrase is surely genitive. In a situation like this, the appropriate value of the attribute for the constitute is some function of the sets of values of the constituent.

3. CATEGORIAL GRAMMAR AND CODE MATCHING

A categorial grammar is a system of categories. Each category bears a symbol which, by design, reflects its ability to combine with others. When two items can be put together into a constitute with definite properties, a categorial grammar assigns to one of them a simple symbol, say x, and to the other a compound symbol combining x with a symbolization of the properties of the combination. Formation of a compound symbol is done by means of an operator that tells whether the simpler element must precede or follow the one with compound symbol. We examine two cases, one with relatively simple categories and extremely simple parsing procedure, the other with more elaborate category descriptions and a necessarily more elaborate parsing routine.

3.1. A categorial parser

Lambek wrote about categorial grammars using two elementary symbols, n and s. An intransitive verb has the symbol "Pns", meaning: When preceded by an n, this item forms a composite of type s. Thus, "John runs" has the grammatical description n–Pns, but upon applying the rule of cancellation, a composite is formed of type s. A transitive verb has the symbol FnPns, so that "John ate breakfast" would have the description n–FnPns–n. One cancellation yields n–Pns, and since the second and third symbols were cancelled "ate breakfast" is a phrase. Another cancellation yields s as before.

Kay's categorial parser uses a parsing logic such as that invented by John Cocke. In the course of parsing a sentence, therefore, a list of intermediate parsing results will be produced, and each entry on this list will be the description of a constitute, including the identities of its constituents. The list of grammatical descriptions of single items obtained during dictionary lookup stands at the head of the constitute list. Categorial grammars are noteworthy because they make the customary table of construction formulae unnecessary. However, in a practical application, it must be expected that many dictionary items will be highly ambiguous, and that many of the categorial symbols will be extremely complicated. If symbols for patterns of ambiguity were introduced, the whole point of the categorial idea would be lost.

Kay escapes from the unwelcome demands for large storage by making a list of categorial symbols in a form that saves storage space and simplifies the matching process. This category list is prepared anew for each sentence, before parsing begins, and belongs to the CT routine, not the parsing logic. Note that every compound symbol has the form Rxy, where R is an operator, either P or F, and x, y are category symbols—elementary or compound. The category list is composed of three arrays, R, x, and y; the values of x[i] and y[i] are indices to other entries in the category list.

The CT procedure is defined by

procedure CT(i, j); **begin** CT : = **if** R[i] = F ∧ x[i] = j **then** y[i]

else if R[j] = P ∧ x[j] = i **then** y[j]

else 0 **end**

Here i and j are the grammatical descriptions of two words or phrases; they are, in fact, indices in the category list. The phrase with symbol i precedes the one with symbol j. Hence if symbol i is compound, with operator F, it has the form Fx[i]y[i]; followed by x[i], it forms a phrase of category y[i]. But it is followed by a phrase with symbol j; if x[i] = j, a phrase can be formed. Likewise, if the second phrase is compound, with operator P, it has the form Px[j]y[j], and a phrase can be formed if i = x[j]. Both conditions cannot be true of the same pair of phrases, since simpler category symbols must always cancel parts of more complicated symbols.

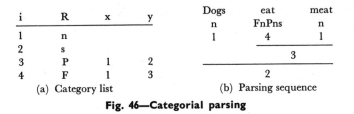

Fig. 46—Categorial parsing

An example is shown in Fig. 46. The first two entries in the category list are the elementary n and s. The third is Pns, and the fourth is FnPns. Now consider a sentence like "Dogs eat meat," with symbols n–FnPns–n. The CT procedure accepts the second and third symbols, 4–1, to yield 3; it then accepts 1–3 to yield 2, and the sentence is parsed.

But before a sentence can be parsed, a category list must be created for it. Simultaneously, the category symbols obtained by consultation of a dictionary—strings composed of operators and elementary category symbols—must be converted into a form suitable for use in parsing. We can neglect the housekeeping details and attend only to conversion of single symbols. Given arrays R[i], x[i], and y[i], incompletely developed, and a category symbol stored in an array S[j], the problem is to augment the category list as necessary and furnish the index of S[j] in the augmented list. The algorithm in Fig. 47 does these things, relying on I as a pointer to an available line in the category list, and using three procedures. Two of them, *PDput* and *PDtop*, operate a pushdown store (Chap. 6, Sec. 1.2); the third, *find*(A, B, C), searches the existing part of the category list for a line with R[i] = A, x[i] = B, and y[i] = C.

The algorithm examines a category symbol from right to left; if the symbol to be converted is FnPns, K = 5 and S[5] = s. It puts each

```
for k := K step −1 until 1 do
    if S[k] = n then PDput (1)
    else if S[k] = s then PDput (2)
    else begin op := S[k]; arga := PDtop; argb := PDtop;
              cat := find (op, arga, argb);
              if cat = 0 then begin cat := I; R[I] := op;
                  x[i] := arga; y[i] := argb; I := I + 1 end;
              PDput (cat)
    end;
if p ≠ 1 then goto Error;
T: = PDtop
```

Fig. 47—Program to build a list of categories

elementary symbol into the pushdown store. Upon reaching an operator, it reads out the top two entries in the store and searches the category list. Thus, in converting FnPns, it first tries *find*(P, 1, 2). Suppose, as in Fig. 46a, that only the two top lines of the category list are filled. Then the search routine is unsuccessful, and *cat* is set to zero. But that causes the third line of the list to be filled in, and *cat* is set to 3 and put in the pushdown store. In the illustration, the next search is *find*(F, 1, 3); this category is added to the list, and the pushdown store finally contains, as it must for any well-formed category symbol, just one entry. The algorithm assigns the value of that entry to T, and stops.

Because the CT procedure is fast and simple, the categorial formalism is attractive. Use of category lists reduces the storage required for grammatical descriptions of phrases during parsing.

3.2. Code matching

Were it not for agreement variables, the simple categorial idea would be extremely satisfying. In fact, however, agreement variables are a widespread phenomenon in language, and the categorial notion alone is ill-adapted to situations where certain agreement variables are used, in different combinations, at many places in the structure of the language, and where there are numerous patterns of ambiguity to be deciphered.

There are as we have seen many ways to store information, including putting zero or one in a certain position to represent presence or absence of a given feature. This is the idea behind code matching. For example, let us designate six positions to correspond to the six cases of Russian nouns, and describe a given noun, which may be ambiguous with respect to case, by putting a one in each position corresponding to a case that the noun may be in. Thus, if a noun is ambiguously nominative or accusative, we put ones in the nominative and accusative positions for it, and zeros elsewhere. But what if the noun is ambiguously genitive singular or nominative or accusative plural? In that case, an accurate representation can be made only if twelve positions are defined, corresponding to the twelve possible combinations of six genders with two numbers. So there is one position for genitive singular, another for nominative plural, and a third for accusative plural; the noun form has a description with ones in those three positions and zeros in the nine others.

To determine whether an adjective agrees with a noun, we match the encoded descriptions of adjective and noun. If there is at least one position in which both adjective and noun carry ones, they agree, and the construction is interpreted as being in the case and number where the common one is found. If two or more positions match, the constitute is ambiguous. But if either the noun or the adjective has a one in a place where the other member of the combination has a zero, that much ambiguity is eliminated by formation of the constitute.

The logic of this kind of combination is that of the Boolean "and." Two ones make a one, but any other pair of integers makes a zero.

This scheme is very natural for the processing of agreement variables where there are numerous patterns of ambiguity, partially resolved in various combinations. It can also be used for government situations, as where a verb governs a noun in a certain case, since the patterns of ones and zeros associated with the verbs can be regarded as specifying its case requirements, rather than its own nature.

The principal difficulty about code-matching schemes is that they require voluminous storage. The description of a word or phrase includes a central part, fixing its major syntactic properties: the functions it serves and governs, or the construction types it enters. The remainder of the description consists of as many strings of ones and zeros as necessary for agreement tests; for some kinds of words and phrases, many long strings are needed. Thus, a Russian noun needs one string in which its case, number, and gender are encoded—some 36 bits. But a noun can govern another noun, and a similar string is needed to encode the properties of the noun governed. One tentative scheme called for about 500 bits per word. If this much storage is used for each phrase, and thousands of phrases are formed as a sentence is parsed, the storage capacity of a large computer can be exceeded.

One partial solution is to omit from the description of a phrase any segment that would be identical to the corresponding segment of the description of a constituent. If the omitted information is needed later, the CT procedure can use the parsing lists or tables to find the constituent where it is stored. In fact, Lecerf has suggested that the governing member of a phrase is just the one where most information that could be needed is located.

EXERCISES

1. Assign category symbols to the words of the following sentences in such a way that they would be parsed in the manner shown by the parentheses. Write the category list as it would be formed for each sentence, and show the parsing sequences (cf. Fig. 46). (a) ((Sweet Sue)(has(eyes(of blue)))). (b) (Probably(Brutus(killed Caesar))). (c) (I(believe (Brutus (killed Caesar)))).

2. Imagine a language with nouns (N), verbs (V), and adjectives (A). All parts of speech have singular (S) and plural (P) forms. Nouns and adjectives are masculine (M) or feminine (F); nominative (N), genitive (G), dative (D), or accusative (A).

Verbs are intransitive (I), transitive (T; govern accusative objects), or doubly transitive (D; govern accusative and dative). Adjectives precede the nouns they modify and agree in number, gender, and case. Genitive nouns modify preceding nouns. Subjects agree with predicates in number, and precede. Objects follow verbs.

(a) Lay out a form for grammatical descriptions, using a 36-bit cell for each full description and a 6-bit character for each meaningful part.

(b) If a rule is composed of three complete grammatical descriptions, two for constituents and one for the phrase formed, how many rules are needed for adjective-noun phrases?

(c) How many extra rules would be added to deal with the following patterns of ambiguity? For nouns: nominative or accusative (X; occurs with all numbers and genders); genitive or dative (Y; occurs in singular feminine only). For adjectives: X and Y as for nouns; accusative or dative (occurs in feminine only).

3. Write a set of tables (cf. Sec. 2.3) for the grammar of Ex. 2. What are the construction types of this grammar?

4. How would a CT routine be written in Algol to use the tables of Ex. 3? In machine instructions?

5. Assume that the nouns in the language of Ex. 2 are classifiable into animate (A) and inanimate (I), and that some verbs take only animate subjects, some only animate objects. How does this classification change the answers to Exs. 2a, 2b, and 3?

6. If a linguist studying the language of Ex. 2 were to claim that the predicate should be handled with a single rule, how could that part of the grammar be organized? The predicate consists of (i) an intransitive verb alone, (ii) a transitive verb followed by an accusative noun, or (iii) a doubly transitive verb followed by accusative and dative nouns in either order.

REFERENCES

"An Algebraic Thesaurus" (A. F. Parker-Rhodes; presented at an International Conference on Mechanical Translation, Cambridge, Mass., 1956) suggests code-matching techniques.

"Connectability Calculations, Syntactic Functions, and Russian Syntax" (David G. Hays; *Mechanical Translation*, Vol. 8, No. 1, August 1964, pp. 32–51; *also* RALP pp. 107–125) gives many details of a code-matching procedure for Russian.

The Tabular Parser: A Parsing Program for Phrase Structure and Dependency (Martin Kay; RM-4933-PR, The RAND Corporation, July 1966) presents the method described in Sec. 2.3.

"The Mathematics of Sentence Structure" (J. Lambek; *American Mathematical Monthly*, Vol. 65, No. 3, 1958, pp. 154–170) is an early statement on categorial grammar.

A Parsing Program for Categorial Grammars (M. Kay, RM-4283-PR, The RAND Corporation, September 1964) gives the algorithms sketched in Sec. 3.

Chapter 8

CONTEXT-SENSITIVE AND
TRANSFORMATIONAL PARSING

Whether to produce a more accurate characterization of the syntactic structures he sees in language, or to extract from natural-language texts the content they carry, leaving behind the accidental features of individual grammars, the contemporary linguist often demands more than context-free phrase-structure or dependency parsing. At least three different approaches have been suggested.

Transformational grammar, as Chomsky has elaborated it, uses operations on complete phrase-structure diagrams. A comparatively simple phrase-structure grammar produces deep structures with associated terminal strings. The transformations operate on these, yielding surface structures with associated strings that can be converted into written sentences or spoken utterances. The task of a transformational parser is to determine the deep structure of any sentence presented to it.

Eugene D. Pendergraft has proposed a different way of elaborating phrase-structure grammar. Just as a constituency diagram characterizes the grammatical relationships obtaining among units of a sentence, so can a second-level constituency diagram characterize relationships among the parts of a syntactic constituency diagram. Pendergraft intends these second-order relationships to reflect semantical structures. For each level there is a grammar. A given sentence can have a well-formed syntactic structure relative to the first grammar, but if that structure is itself ill-formed relative to the second grammar, the sentence must be taken to be grammatical but meaningless. This degree of independence between the two levels makes it seem likely that Pendergraft's theory offers about as much power as Chomsky's.

Like Chomsky's approach, Lamb's stratal theory establishes multiple, parallel representations of any text. Lamb says that each representation belongs to an independent stratum. The theories differ mainly in two respects: the means used to pass from one stratum to another, and the structural schemes used on strata more distant from the surface (what Lamb calls higher, and Chomsky calls deeper). Stratificational grammar is considered further in Chap. 9.

The present chapter is devoted to techniques for transformational parsing, after a preliminary look at context-sensitive grammar.

I. CONTEXT-SENSITIVE PARSING

The phrase-structure grammars considered heretofore are called context-free because each formula is usable in any context whatsoever. A single symbol is expanded into a string; whatever may be happening in the rest of the structure is irrelevant. Every complete parsing logic described in Chap. 6 is based on a plan for making sure that the constituents are ready when a constitute is to be formed. Length and level provide two different ways of doing this.

Context-sensitive formulae pair strings. Again, these are expansion formulae, but the longer string consists of a duplicate of the shorter, except that one symbol in the shorter string is expanded into a substring of the longer. The remainder is a statement of the context in which the expansion can be performed. Since the context is not itself being expanded, the statement of context can involve terminals, or constitutes of any length or level. It is not possible to make certain that every constituent wanted will be available before a constitute is formed; the context may not be recognizable, during parsing, when it is needed.

I.I. Analysis and resynthesis

We can regard a context-sensitive grammar as a context-free grammar with restrictions applied to some rules. By adopting this point of view, we can obtain a scheme, although not an economical one, for context-sensitive parsing. It was invented by John Cocke.

First, we transcribe the grammar, omitting all context restrictions. Obviously, the new grammar parses every string acceptable to the old one and if the restrictions are not vacuous it either assigns extra structures to some acceptable strings or accepts some additional strings, and may do both. If we parse a string using the new grammar, we can be sure of obtaining every true structure, but we may obtain some false ones.

To eliminate erroneous parsings, we attempt to synthesize the sentence, using the original context-sensitive grammar. When this stage begins, one or more highest level constitutes are stored. Each is described as having a certain type, and being composed of certain parts. If any of those parts are expanded, at least one in any parsing must be expanded in the context of the others as they stand. If none of the context-sensitive rules is capable of doing that, the parsing is fallacious and can be discarded. If at least one expansion can be made, the process can be continued. In every case, parsing has already determined what constituents a constitute is to have; the synthesis stage can only be allowed to try various contexts.

1.2. Path tables

Instead of treating a context-sensitive grammar as if it were a context-free grammar with restrictions superimposed, we can treat it as if it were a set of rules for rewriting strings. True, all but one of the symbols on the short side of the rule are copied as themselves on the long side. But we can regard that as a matter of secondary importance.

In a path chart of the kind introduced in Chap. 6, Sec. 3.2, there are as many endpoints as elements in the terminal string. Every phrase has an endpoint and an origin; it covers the part of the terminal string between those points. In that chapter, the rules considered are context-free, each pairing a symbol (corresponding to a long phrase) and a string (corresponding to a sequence of phrases covering the same part of the terminal string). To represent the pairing of strings by formulae of a context-sensitive grammar, we permit the introduction of new endpoints. Starting at one side of the chart and choosing any phrase that starts where a chosen one ends, we always arrive at the other side of the chart by means of a path in which every phrase could serve as part of the context for the rewriting of any other on the same path. For example, consider the paths in Fig. 48a. Constituent E appears to be followed by either C or F; thus, if a context-sensitive grammar is in use, and it rewrites E as AB when E is followed by C—or by F—all is well. But suppose the required context is F, and that EC is reduced to G, and GD to H. Then F does not appear in the final parsing of the sentence; the parsing is not a true reflection of what the grammar has to say about the terminal string.

The introduction of line 5 in Fig. 48b avoids any such unwitting mistake. Thinking of the critical rule as coupling EF with ABF, we draw the path from 0 through 5 to 4. Line 5 is introduced just for this purpose, and we must take due note that whereas E (on the arrow 0–5) has constituents A and B, the F on arrow 5–4 has the same constituents as the F on arrow 2–4. Recalling that a constituent is followed by any other that begins where it ends, we see from Fig. 48b that E is followed by F, but not by C. Hence no constitute can be formed out of E and C.

A parser using this storage scheme can be controlled by position, much the same as the one in Fig. 43; its outermost iteration is over endpoints, and halts when it has gone through the last of the ordinary endpoints (e.g., 4 in Fig. 48).

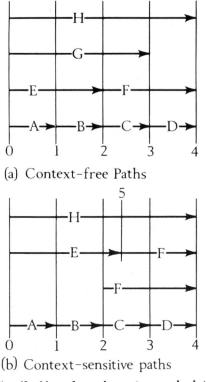

(a) Context–free Paths

(b) Context–sensitive paths

Fig. 48—Use of supplementary endpoints

The secondary iteration is on phrases (ending) at the current end-point. As new phrases are constructed, they are added to the list, just as in the parser of Fig. 43.

Given one of these phrases as rightmost possible constituent, the parser seeks partners, using the rule that endpoint of partner must equal origin of chosen phrase. Sequences of all lengths are tried, using a CT routine of suitable form. When a sequence of phrases satisfying the grammar is established, the CT routine gives a signal, indicating whether the expansion formula is context-free (CF) or context-sensitive (CS). If CF, the CT routine gives a single symbol, the grammatical description of the phrase, and the parser adds it to the path table, along with a list of its constituents.

When a CS rule is used, the CT routine gives a string of symbols, and the parser must create new endpoints. For example, when ABF is reduced to EF in Fig. 48b, the current endpoint is 4 and the next available endpoint number is 5. There is an old F in the table, with endpoint 4, origin 2, and a reference to the list of its constituents (they are C and D). The parser now adds a new phrase with grammatical description F, endpoint 4, and a reference to the same list of constituents, but the origin of this phrase is 5. If the rule were that ABCD reduces to ECD, two endpoints would have to be created; more might be needed, but at last the new path reaches a pre-existing endpoint—the origin of E is 0 in the figure.

The outermost iteration of this parser is over endpoints, but its progress is erratic. Perhaps the clearest way to express the rule is to say that the original list of endpoints goes into a pushdown store, in reverse order; the first out is endpoint 1 (or rather 2). Now when a new endpoint is created, the current endpoint is put back in the pushdown, and on top of it the new one, or, if several new endpoints are created by application of one formula, all of them go in. When work stops at the current endpoint, the next is taken from the pushdown store.

For example, suppose the current endpoint is an original, number 7, with number 8 at the top of the store. Now create a new node, say 13; 7 goes above 8, and 13 above 7. When nothing more can be done at 7, the next one taken is 13; let a sequence of endpoints be created, numbers 14 and 15, such that a phrase has its endpoint at 14 and its origin at 15. Now 13 goes into the store, with 14 above and 15 on top. If no new endpoints are created, the endpoints taken are 15, 14, 13, 7 and 8.

The secondary iteration needs a control to eliminate some useless work. In the foregoing example, endpoint 13 was created during the search for phrases ending at 7; hence a phrase with origin 13 is placed in the endpoint 7 table. To seek partners for that phrase during the same major step would be premature; first all phrases ending at 13 must be formed. Therefore, whenever iteration over phrases ending at a certain point begins, the parser notes the first available endpoint number and stores it as a characteristic of the endpoint; phrases with that origin or a higher one are skipped over. The next time the iteration reaches the same endpoint, the parser finds a previous limit and fixes a new one; it seeks partners only for phrases with origins greater than the previous limit but less than the new one.

2. TRANSFORMATIONS

Linguists who use transformations often wish to write down grammars, that is to create them in one way or another, in a form suitable for the production of sentences, then to rearrange their grammars so as to be able to parse sentences. This reversal, as we have seen, is trivial for phrase-structure grammar. Not so with transformational grammars; the form commonly used, which was invented by Noam Chomsky, cannot be inverted from production to recognition or vice versa by any algorithmic procedure now known.

Faced with this problem, a linguist can choose among various alternatives. For one thing, he can choose between production and recognition, write his grammar in accordance with his choice, and make no attempt to carry out the other process in an exactly corresponding fashion. Some linguists have in fact made this choice for themselves, generally opting for production and disregarding the problem of recognition. When he particularly desires to do both things, the linguist can seek a new form for transformation rules, aiming at one that can be converted into production and recognition versions more readily than the change can be made with Chomsky's rule forms. But this is a choice to be taken by theoreticians. Another approach is to seek a parsing procedure that demands no more of the user than he is capable of doing. Two attempts to follow this approach are described below.

2.1. The form of transformational grammars

For our purposes, the standard formalization of transformational grammars distinguishes just two components. The first is a phrase-structure grammar, which may be context-free or context-sensitive, with or without recursive rules. It constructs constituency diagrams, with complete node labeling, and delivers them to the second component.

In the second component, the transformation rules are applied. Each rule is applicable to a subset of the constituency diagrams that can be produced either by the basic phrase-structure grammar or by application of transformations to such basic diagrams. A transformation rule then consists of a statement characterizing a subset to which it is applicable and a statement of operations to be performed on any diagram in that class. A certain transformation rule may apply to a given diagram not at all, or in just one way, or in more ways than one. For each distinct way of applying a transformation to a diagram, there is a unique resulting diagram. In this sense, each transformation rule maps a class of structural diagrams onto another class. However, it is more germane to computational issues to see how applicability is to be determined and what kinds of processes are to be carried out on accepted diagrams.

As for applicability, the basic notion is that of a path, as described in Sec. 1.2. Given a finished parsing of a terminal string relative to a given grammar, but with just one parsing standing in the diagram—all

useless incomplete parsings, and all ambiguities, must be removed—
the applicability of a given transformation is determined by looking
for a certain kind of path. It is not necessary, however, that the statement of applicability for a given transformation rule specify this path
completely. Chomsky's conception of transformational grammar permits the use of variables in statements of applicability. Thus, a transformation might be applicable to a given structural diagram if any path
in it could be found beginning with a certain symbol, continuing with
any symbol on a specified list, continuing thereafter with any sequence
of symbols whatsoever, and ending with a specified, single symbol.

Note that in a statement of applicability, according to this description,
no constituency relations can be required. Thus, one cannot say that a
transformation is applicable to a structural diagram containing a given
constitute only if that constitute is expanded into stated constituents.
But this is a puristic conception, and writers on transformational grammar often add what they call restrictions to statements of applicability.
These restrictions often amount to constituency requirements.

The puristic conception of the kind of change a transformation can
work is that it operates exclusively on the path it matches. Having
found a path, and marked certain segments of it as satisfying the segmental requirements of the transformation rule, we may be required
to permute those elements, to introduce new ones, to replace one of
them with a new element, or to delete one. Changes in structure above
or below the path followed are supposed to be made in accordance
with universal principles, and therefore should not have to be mentioned
in individual transformational rules.

Note that no provision is made for expansion of a symbol introduced
by a transformation rule. Hence, the only symbols that can be introduced are terminal. In some versions of transformation theory, there
are double-base transformations, operating on two sentences at a time.
Such a transformation can break down the structure of one sentence
and insert all or part of it at a specified place in the structure of the
other. This is a way of introducing more than a terminal node, but
some versions of transformational grammar do not permit it.

The universal principles adumbrated in arguments against explicit
statement of structural changes have not been set forth in sufficient
detail to guide programmers. For the present therefore, it is more
convenient to work with transformation rules that state explicitly what
structural alterations the linguist intends to be effected by his rules.
It can certainly be assumed that substitutions work no structural
changes. One element simply replaces another at a given position in
the structural diagram. Deletions can be taken to make only the

obvious changes. When an element is deleted, its constituents and
everything it covers down to the terminal string go with it, and so do
any single-branching nodes from which it descends. Permutations can
best be broken down into smaller components. In addition to these
elementary operations, two more seem to be needed. Having marked
a given element in a structural diagram, a transformation rule may need
either to add a co-constituent, forming part of the same constitute the
marked element belongs to, or to add a constituent of the marked
element as constitute. It is probably convenient to have positional
variants for these operations. A co-constituent might be added immediately to the right or immediately to the left of the marked element,
and a constituent of the element as constitute might be added either
leftmost or rightmost among its immediate descendants.

This discussion of transformation rules, which is incomplete, should
give some hint as to why transformational grammars are hard to invert:
The applicability statements must be recast so that they characterize
the structures producible by the associated transformations, and the
structural changes must be made to work backward. Two procedures
for transformational parsing are discussed below; the problem of getting
suitable grammars is left out. The reader who is interested more than
casually will want to consult the literature on this subject.

2.2. Intermixed parsing

Transformation rules operate on structural diagrams, not on terminal
strings. Hence to say whether any transformation should be applied
in reverse to a given string, it is necessary to associate a structural
diagram with the sentence first. For that purpose, parsing with a
phrase-structure grammar would be suitable except for the fact that
no grammar assigning just the right structural diagrams may be possible. One way out of this dilemma is to find a way of parsing enough
of a given string to determine the applicability of a transformation.
When even one transformation has been applied in reverse, a little
more phrase-structure parsing may be possible. This plan was followed
by Petrick.

For this strategy, a path chart is convenient as the storage structure,
and the standard preliminaries of dictionary lookup furnish the initial
entries. Then control is given to a parser. It uses a context-free or a
context-sensitive grammar, developing constructions as far as it can.
When it is no longer able to establish any new constitutes, control
passes to a transformational parser, which seeks all possible matches
between paths in the stored charts and applicability statements of
transformation rules (which are, of course, stored in reversed form).

How it makes its search is described in Sec. 3.1. Whenever it applies a transformation, it establishes a new partial path in the chart. The path begins with the first constituent about which the applicability statement makes any specific requirements, and the new path continues, including copies of everything necessary, through the last such constituent. The arcs on the new path are labeled, and marked as being identical to, or having as constituents, symbols previously on the chart. If a reverse transformation puts in any symbol that is neither identical with nor composed of symbols previously on the chart, then of course the nullity of these relationships must be noted.

When the transformational parser has examined every possible path in the chart, the phrase-structure parser is applied once more. It would be wasteful to start from the beginning, since the parser has previously done everything that could be done without including some of the results of reverse transformation made on the most recent call of the transformational parser. Like the parser controlled by level (Chap. 6, Sec. 3.3), this one can work on new phrases only, seeking partners for them and yielding to the transformational parser when it can do no more.

2.3. Use of a covering surface grammar

In general, it is not possible to construct a context-free grammar that recognizes all and only the strings produced by a stated transformational grammar, assigning to each just those structural diagrams that the transformational grammar would assign. However, it is certainly possible to devise a grammar that recognizes at least the strings produced by a given transformation grammar, and assigns at least the structural diagrams that it would assign. The guarantee is carried by the possibility of recognizing all strings over a finite alphabet, and assigning to each string all structures using a finite set of labels. With this argument, the guarantee is worthless, since the computing time and storage space required would be inordinate. It is by no means obvious, however, that the difficulty of handling the cases of interest— the natural languages of our world—would be intolerably great. In fact, it is entirely possible that rather tidy surface grammars, not recognizing many unacceptable strings and not assigning many inaccurate structures, can be developed.

A research group at the MITRE Corporation, led by Donald E. Walker, undertook to do transformational parsing in this way. Their system begins with a surface parser. After dictionary lookup, they apply a context-free or context-sensitive phrase-structure grammar. Any string not recognized by this grammar is rejected, and for any string the parser recognizes it provides one or more complete phrase-structure diagrams.

These diagrams, which can conveniently be stored in path charts, are submitted to the· reverse transformational system. It operates in the manner described in the previous section, but when it stops, parsing is finished. There is no recourse to a phrase-structure grammar once transformational parsing begins. The final step is checking, as described in Sec. 1.1, including both the base grammar and the transformations.

The same difficulties that arose to plague us with the parser of Petrick's type are with us here again. How to obtain a surface grammar that does the best possible job, leaving what the transformational parser requires but not too much more, is perhaps more difficult with a system of the MITRE kind. Obtaining a set of reversed transformations is no easier.

However, the approach of the MITRE group does suggest a different plan of work for the practical linguist. For the theoretician, there may be advantages in thinking about production systems. For the linguist who is required to recognize sentences in order to verify that his grammar covers what native speakers actually say, or in order to extract the content for further processing, it may be more sensible to write his grammar in the first place as a recognition system. Given a flow of text, writing a surface grammar with which to recognize all its sentences and obtain structural diagrams is perhaps a tedious task, but not a hopeless one. There is no algorithm for doing it, at least none that can be used in practice, but what is called for is the kind of job linguists have long been accustomed to attempting. Developing a good transformational system in recognition form is perhaps not much more difficult than developing it in production form to begin with. In principle, elimination of the checking step may be doubtful; in practice, the linguist may choose to do without the checking step from the beginning, and to get exactly the structures he wants by refinement of his surface grammar and recognition-form transformations.

3. CONSULTATION OF TRANSFORMATION RULES

A transformational grammar is a list of transformation rules. Each rule consists of a statement of applicability and instructions for change of structure. Such lists must be stored and consulted; let us see some of the available techniques.

3.1. Applicability

A statement of applicability is a string of segments. Matching proceeds segment by segment; the first segment of the applicability statement must be matched against the first part of a path through a parsing chart, the next segment must be matched with a contiguous portion of the path, and so on.

The segments of applicability statements fall into two main types, matching (i) single words or phrases and (ii) strings, respectively. A segment of type (i) can be written as a single grammatical symbol, a list of symbols, or a list of one or more features that must be present in a complex symbol. A segment of type (ii) can be written with an arbitrary but unique symbol, indicating that any string whatever is acceptable; or a specification can be made, for example that a string containing a noun phrase is not acceptable.

One method of transformational parsing is to consider the rules of the grammar in turn, applying each, wherever it is applicable, to a stored collection of constituency diagrams. Customarily, applicability statements are required to match complete paths, covering the entire terminal string; since both first and last segments of a statement can be of type (ii), this requirement is essentially vacuous. Nevertheless, let us examine an algorithm that relies on it, temporarily neglecting the problem of type (ii) segments.

Consider the path tables in Fig. 42. Matching can best proceed from right to left; the rightmost segment of the applicability statement must match a symbol in the table for the rightmost sentence position. If it does not, the rule is inapplicable. If it matches any, take the first one found as current match for the Kth (rightmost) segment, and seek a match for the $(K - 1)$th segment. The next match must be at the origin of the constituent currently matched to the Kth segment; if that origin is the beginning of the sentence, the procedure is blocked.

This algorithm iterates on segment number, beginning with the Kth (say, with k = K); it achieves a success if it finds a match when k = 1 such that the matched constituent has origin 0. In case of success, the iteration is from k to $k - 1$; in case of failure, from k to $k + 1$. But failure thus leads to re-examination of constituents previously searched unless the path-table entry currently matched to the $(k + 1)$th segment is used as starting point.

For example, suppose the applicability statement is *Art-Noun-VP*. In Fig. 42, the first *VP* in table 5 has origin 3; setting $k = 3 - 1 = 2$ leads to a search for a *Noun* in table 3, where there is none. This failure causes k to be set to $2 + 1 = 3$; again a *VP* is sought in table 5, beginning after the one previously found. The other *VP* has origin 2; with k = 2, a *Noun* is found in table 2, with origin 1. Thanks to this success, the next search is with k = 1, and an *Art* is found. Since its origin is 0, the algorithm has achieved a success.

When a complete match is established, it is delivered to the part of the program that performs transformations (Sec. 3.2). However, the first complete match is not necessarily the only one possible. The procedure therefore continues just as if the constituent matched for $k = 1$ had failed to match; it has delivered all possible matches when the iteration sets $k = K$ and no additional matches to the Kth segment can be found.

The occurrence of a type (ii) segment complicates the algorithm, not merely because it can match any constituent, but because it can match any string of constituents, including the null string. What a type (ii) segment does is permit the next segment to match at the current position or any beyond it. Suppose a match has been made to the kth segment, and that the $(k - 1)$th segment is of type (ii), carrying no special restrictions. Suppose furthermore that the constituent matched to the kth segment has origin i. Then the $(k - 2)$th segment must be compared with all constituents in table i; then in the tables corresponding to their origins; and so on. The only limit that can be set is that the remaining segments have to be paired with something; for example, if the type (ii) segment is third in the applicability statement, it is pointless to compare the second segment with entries in table 1—unless the first segment is also of type (ii).

3.2. Structural changes

When an applicability statement is matched against a path, type (i) segments are matched against individual constituents, and type (ii) segments against sequences of them. This correspondence is available for use in carrying out structural changes.

The structural change performed by a complete transformation can be regarded as a program, in which the only operators used are *copy*, *add constituent, add co-constituent, and delete*. If the first segment of the applicability statement is of type (ii) and unrestricted, construction of a new path can begin after the part of the stored path matching that segment. Likewise, construction of a new path can end before a final part matched against a type (ii) segment. Between those places, endpoints have to be inserted, as in Fig. 48. To begin with, the old path can be copied, with its constituents lying between new endpoints. Then, the first instruction in the transformation program can be carried out. If it calls for deletion, the symbol to be deleted is found on the new path; if its endpoint is i and origin j, i is replaced by j wherever it occurs as origin. Likewise, an insertion can be handled by changing pointers and adding labels as called for by the transformation. Substitutions are done by changing labels. Permutations are made by copying constituents into their new places, then deleting them from their old ones. If a new constituent of one of the constituents on the new path is to be inserted, it is put on the proper endpoint and constituency lists. The change program is carried out step by step, and when it is complete the transformation has been applied.

EXERCISES

1. Write an algorithm to find all constitutes adjacent to a given one, using a parsing list (Fig. 39). What purpose does this algorithm serve in context-sensitive parsing by analysis and resynthesis?

2. Show, by means of a phrase-structure diagram, that a constitute is sometimes shorter than the one providing context for it. Use this grammar:

$$S \rightarrow AB, A \rightarrow AD, A \rightarrow CD, C \rightarrow CD, A \rightarrow EF, C \rightarrow GH, CDB \rightarrow CDIJ,$$
$$I \rightarrow KL, ADB \rightarrow ADKM, M \rightarrow LJ$$

3. Some theories of grammar require that rules be ordered. In the production of strings, each rule (if applicable) is applied as many times as possible, but not after a later rule has been applied. A rule can take the form $A \rightarrow \{BC, DE\}$, i.e., the simple formulae $A \rightarrow BC$ and $A \rightarrow DE$ have the same place in the ordering. How might a context-sensitive parser take into account the ordering of rules?

4. Using the parser of Sec. 1.2 and the grammar of Ex. 2, show the steps in the parsing of "EFDDKLJ."

5. Assuming the grammar of Ex. 2, in what ways does the structure of "GHDDKLJ" satisfy the applicability statement $C - X - B$, where X is any string? Does "GHDDKLJ" have a unique structure?

6. Given a storage structure like the one in Fig. 42, write algorithms (in Algol) to (a) copy a path, (b) delete an item from the new path, (c) insert a new element.

7. How must a program for determining applicability operate if some segments of applicability statements consist of (i) a symbol to match the label of a phrase, together with (ii) an applicability statement that must match the immediate constituents of the same phrase?

8. Sketch a program for production of sentences with a transformational grammar (cf. Sec. 2.1).

REFERENCES

"Three Models for the Description of Language" (Noam Chomsky; *IRE Transactions on Information Theory*, Vol. IT-2, No. 3, 1956, pp. 113–124) sets forth models of finite-state, phrase-structure and transformational theories.

A Recognition Procedure for Transformational Grammars (S. R. Petrick; doctoral dissertation, Massachusetts Institute of Technology, 1965) describes the method of intermixed phrase-structure and transformational parsing.

"The Mitre Syntactic Analysis Procedure for Transformational Grammars" (Arnold M. Zwicky, Joyce Friedman, Barbara C. Hall, and Donald E. Walker; *AFIPS Conference Proceedings*, Vol. 27, Part 1, 1965, pp. 317–326) introduces their method.

English Preprocessor Manual (SR-132, The MITRE Corporation, December 1964) contains a full statement of the system.

"Basic Methodology" (Eugene D. Pendergraft; in *Symposium on the Current Status of Research*, W. P. Lehmann and E. D. Pendergraft, eds., LRC-63-SR1, Linguistics Research Center, The University of Texas, October 1963, pp. 15–60) outlines the author's approach.

"The Grammar of Specifiers" (David A. Dinneen; excerpts from *A Left-to-right Generative Grammar of French*, doctoral dissertation, Massachusetts Institute of Technology, 1962; *also* RALP, pp. 127–136) applies another method of separating the grammar of a language into two or more components.

Chapter 9

STRATAL CONVERSION

The theory of linguistic stratification is supported by much the same kind of argument that brought certain linguists to the theory of grammatical transformations. In practical terms, the phenomena of natural languages are simpler to describe if they are sorted out; each kind of phenomenon is explained on one level, where the mechanisms used to account for other kinds of phenomena do not interfere. In theoretical terms, there is the belief—which must someday be tested— that processing of language in the human brain is organized in approximately this manner. The linguist who decides on a stratal description must decide how many strata there are in language, name them, allocate the patterns of language to the several strata, and show how the mechanisms of each stratum account for the patterns allocated to it—and how the strata are connected.

Typical problems for which the linguist must have computer programs if he employs a stratal theory are conversion from one stratum to another and characterization of well-formed structures on each stratum.

I. THE FORM OF A MULTISTRATAL SYSTEM

For our purposes, we need not decide specifically how many strata are needed for the description of any language in particular, or all languages in general. We can exemplify the computational problems that arise if we think of four strata, which we can call the phonemic, the morphemic, the lexemic, and the sememic. Each stratum must have an alphabet. The alphabetic elements of these four strata are, respectively, phonemes, morphemes, lexemes, and sememes.

When we say that the alphabetic elements are morphemes on the morphemic stratum, we of course imply that individual morphemes are unanalyzable, indivisible units. A morpheme may be represented, on the phonemic stratum, by a combination of phonemes. But representation and composition are different relationships; the strata are distinguished from one another precisely in order to provide for the coexistence in language of two kinds of units, or four, or still more. Phonemic units enter into phonemic combinations, according to the rules of phonemic grammar, or phonotactics. Morphemic units enter morphemic combinations, according to rules of morphotactics. Likewise, the description of a language must include lexotactic and semotactic rules if all four strata are identified.

In addition to variation in alphabet, a stratal theory provides for variation in geometry of occurrence. An utterance, or stretch of discourse, is represented by a string of phonemes. The same utterance is represented, on the morphemic stratum, by a string of morphemes, or perhaps by a tree of morphemes, or possibly by a string of trees of morphemes. On the lexemic stratum, the same utterance is represented by a tree, or string of trees, of lexemes. Finally, on the sememic stratum, the utterance is represented by a graph or network of sememes.

1.1. Conversions

A stratal conversion is a mapping or transduction of the representation of an utterance on one stratum into the representation of the same utterance on an adjacent stratum. The conversion is said to be upward if it converts a string of phonemes into a morphemic representation, or morphemic into lexemic, or lexemic into sememic. A conversion is said to be downward if it operates in the opposite direction.

Upward and downward conversions are different in a very important sense. Since ambiguity is widespread in natural languages, an upward conversion can always in principle have two or more results, not equivalent to one another. One string of phonemes may represent two different morphemic configurations, and therefore be ambiguous; or, representing only one morphemic configuration, the phonemic string is still ambiguous if the second upward conversion leads to two or more distinct lexemic representations. Finally, one lexemic configuration may represent two different sememic networks. In the opposite direction, there is no ambiguity, but there may be free variation. Starting with a fixed sememic graph, a downward conversion may yield two different lexemic configurations, but if it does they are in free variation and equivalent.

1.2. Sketch of a multistratal system

Let us suppose, for the sake of having a definite example, that a multistratal theory describes a language with exactly four strata. A multistratal linguistic system has two purposes: (a) To characterize the set of well-formed sememic networks, and convert each, by a sequence of stratal conversions, into any of its equivalent phonemic representations. (b) Given any arbitrary string of phonemes, to determine whether it represents any well-formed sememic network, and to find, by a sequence of upward conversions, ending with a test for well-formedness of the sememic graph or graphs obtained, those it does represent. Because the two directions are asymmetrical, each downward conversion beginning with a fixed sememic graph leads to one acceptable phonemic representation, but different choices during the sequence of conversions might lead from the same sememic graph to some other phonemic representation, whereas each upward conversion starting with a fixed phonemic string must lead to all attainable sememic graphs, that is, those that are well-formed and represented by the original phonemic string.

Figure 49 displays the major components of such a system. The transducers in the diagram have the function in conversion that parsing and connectability-test programs have in parsing. They provide the operational structure, but the substantive detail is in the tactic and conversion rules. Theoreticians who use a model of this kind regard the structures of the different transducers as linguistic universals, from which it follows that a single system of computer programs would do the job of recognition or production of sentences for any natural language, given adequate lists of rules.

The diagram in Fig. 49 assumes that each transducer, with suitable conversion rules, always converts well-formed input into well-formed output. Thus, it is unnecessary to test the grammaticality of a morphemic graph, if it was obtained by transduction from a lexemic graph which was itself well-formed. It must also be assumed that ill-formed input is rejected by each transducer, operating in either direction. The only uncontrolled producer of well-formed representations is the one at the top, which produces sememic graphs, and the only device testing well-formedness is the same element of the system, operating in the reverse direction. In fact, even this device is shown only for formal reasons; the diagram is intended to cover the scope of linguistics, leaving out a psycholinguistic transduction at the top which would couple the linguistic processes with those of cognition, etc. The graph also foreshortens the analysis at the bottom, where further linguistic theory might be applied to articulatory and auditory mechanisms.

The transduction between morphemic graphs and phonemic strings is, approximately, a dictionary process. We have already examined some of the ways in which it is possible to program dictionary lookup. Phonemic strings enter the transducer, in the upward conversion, and are segmented, perhaps with ambiguity, into strings representing

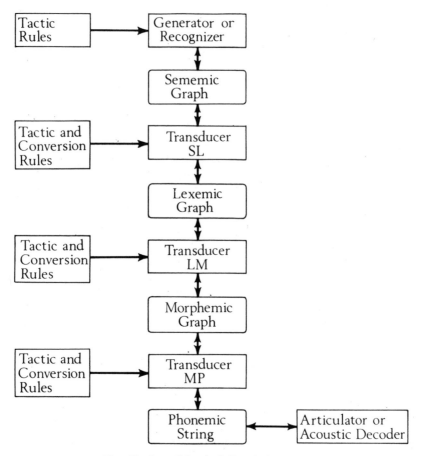

Fig. 49—A multistratal linguistic system

morphemes. On the phonemic stratum, the sound patterns of the language are accounted for. To fit those patterns, morphemes change their shapes; they take on one or another shape according to the environments in which they are placed. By means of the conversion upward to the morphemic stratum, such variability is eliminated; each morpheme has just one shape, since the morphemes are the alphabetic elements of this stratum. In the opposite direction, the dictionary conversion provides a set of alternative representations for each morpheme, and criteria for choosing the appropriate representation in a given environment.

The allocation of linguistic phenomena to the morphemic and lexemic strata is not statable in such familiar terms as those used in explaining the phonemic stratum. We had best be content with a somewhat oversimplified discussion that reveals approximately what kind of problems must be faced. The morphemic representation of a text is a string; the lexemic representation is a tree or string of trees. The only phenomena best allocated to the morphemic stratum are those that fit well into a tactics of strings. In many languages, there are regularities that involve pairs of neighbors: A grammatical formula involves two kinds of morphemes that, according to the formulae of the language, are unrelated if they are separated. In recognition, some of the ambiguities left by transductions from the phonemic stratum can be eliminated, through the tactics of the morphemic stratum, thanks to such formulae. If these tactic formulae are embodied in the dictionary, any ambiguities that they are capable of eliminating are suppressed during the phonemic-to-morphemic conversion.

The transduction from the morphemic stratum to the lexemic is like parsing. The lexemic representation of a simple utterance is a tree, namely a dependency tree, of the kind already familiar. A longer, more complicated utterance may be represented by a graph consisting of a string of trees. By and large, the patterns ordinarily called grammatical can be allocated to the lexemic stratum. More precisely, since the organizing principle on the lexemic stratum is not the simple ordering of elements in a string but the direct interconnection of grammatically related elements that would have to be separated in a string, much of grammar goes into the conversion between the morphemic and lexemic strata. Morphemes that serve to show the connection of separated elements, and word order itself—which helps to show the connections that are implicit in strings, but explicit in dependency graphs—have no place in a lexemic representation. Downward conversion, from lexemic trees to morphemic strings, introduces the function morphemes and imposes the occurrence order that the grammar of a natural language uses to show relationships. Upward conversion (parsing) makes use of those elements and properties to determine relationships, perhaps with ambiguity. On the lexemic stratum, the variations that can be attributed to the differing environments in which certain grammatical relationships must be expressed have been eliminated.

To put the matter very crudely, semantic phenomena are assigned to the sememic stratum. A precise discussion of this matter would be lengthy, and in truth there is a distinction to be made between the linguistic phenomena assigned to the sememic stratum and the semantic phenomena which are outside language. The problems of transduction between sememic and lexemic strata are new; we turn to them in the next section.

2. TRANSDUCTIONS BETWEEN GENERALIZED GRAPHS AND TREES

A lexemic graph is a tree or string of trees. A sememic graph is an arbitrary network. In the transduction between them, some combinations of lexemes are recognized as representations of single sememes, and relationships that went unrecognized on the lexemic stratum are made explicit.

2.1. Dictionary lookup in a tree

Let us recapitulate the letter-table method of segmenting strings of phonemes. The first token on the lower stratum is matched by type against the first-letter table. The type of the second token is matched against the particular second-letter table identified by the contents of the matched entry in the first-letter table. A corresponding technique is operable when the representations on the lower stratum are trees. Instead of segmenting the lower level string into unbroken sub-strings, we must segment the lower-stratum tree into connected subtrees.

Given a tree, therefore, we start with the label at the origin, that is, with the type of the origin token. We have, as it were, an origin-lexeme table in which to match it. Because the number of different lexemes is very large, it may be impractical to do a direct lookup using the lexeme as address.

However the match may be performed, when an entry in the table is found it either identifies the lexeme as the monolexemic representation of a sememe, or recognizes it as the head of a tree constituting the multilexemic representation of a sememe. Indeed, because of ambiguity, the two cases can obtain simultaneously, and a given lexeme can head more than one representation tree, taking part in the representation of more than one sememe.

If the original lexeme is head of at least one representation tree, the original-lexeme table must contain two pieces of information: where to find the second-lexeme table, and what function to follow in the input tree. In a lexemic tree, one governor can have several dependents. The dependents have different functions, and only the dependent with a given function can be matched in the second-lexeme table. Note that in a string each token is followed by exactly one other, and therefore this kind of information is unnecessary in the letter-table entries.

As long as the lexemic representation of a sememe consists of a governing lexeme, with a dependent of a given function, which in turn may have a dependent with a given function, and so on, the search continues from table to table. However, the representation of a sememe can consist of a certain governing lexeme with two or more direct dependents, each having a certain function and a certain identity. They in turn can have dependents, and so on. At any branch point, it is necessary to continue down one path, but without forgetting that a match will require testing another path as well. For example, consider a sememe represented by a certain verb with an adverbial modifier and a noun object, the object being modified in turn by a certain adjective. When a lexemic tree with the verb at its origin is looked up in the sememic dictionary, the type of the verb is matched in the origin-lexeme table. Two functions, modifier and complement, are listed. If the verb in the lexemic tree governs a modifier, the type of that modifier is matched in the appropriate table, but the fact that a complement is needed is remembered. In the appropriate second-lexeme table, matching the type of the modifier furnishes the information that nothing else is needed along that path. The program returns to the original node, and finds the information that a complement was also called for. If the verb in the lexemic tree governs a complement, its type is matched in the appropriate second-lexeme table, and upon obtaining a match the information is obtained that a dependent modifier (an adjective) is needed.

When the left part of a string has been matched in a dictionary, the remainder is taken for lookup, beginning at the next place. When a tree is being looked up in a dictionary, the first successful lookup can yield two or more unconnected subtrees. Lookup must continue in all of them, that is, there is more than one next place for the continuation. Furthermore, the connections among the lexemes must be remembered, so that the output of the transduction is a tree of sememes.

When a complete lexemic representation of a sememe is established, the dictionary furnishes the information about it that will be needed in further processing. The next step, which is closely related to parsing, is the subject of Sec. 2.2.

2.2. Recognition of graphs

A sememic graph consists of nodes, each labeled with a sememe, and of connections between nodes. Each connection joins two sememes, and is directed: it runs from one of them to the other. The connections themselves can be labeled; they would thus be typified as agencies of action, goals of action, qualifiers, and so on. According to Lamb, however, the connections are unlabeled, and therefore such notions as agency are represented by sememes or possibly by components of sememic node labels.

Conversion of a lexemic tree into a sememic graph can include both the establishment of new connections, which are only implicit in the lexemic tree, and identification of two nodes as sememically identical.

As an example of a situation where establishment of a direct connection is desirable, consider any language in which quantifiers are substantivized. For example, "I drank a little of the wine." Here *little* is used with an article and a dependent preposition. What was drunk was wine, and the word *little* is introduced to say how much was drunk. A linguist would probably expect a direct sememic connection between the drinking and the wine; he might also expect the connection between "little" and "drink" to be broken.

Many common situations call for recognition of sememic identities. Personal and relative pronouns, and many other sorts of words in different languages, are surrogates for their antecedents. Because utterances are strings of their elements, it would often be confusing to try to say everything one had to say about a given thing, event, or abstraction without representing it repeatedly. If a noun is subject of a verb in a main clause, and object of another verb in a subordinate clause, the restriction of lexemic graphs to trees is maintained if the noun is represented by a pronoun in one of those two relationships. In a sememic graph, two direct connections can be made with only one token of the noun.

One way of performing upward conversion is to have a collection of formulae, each specifying some part of a lexemic tree and some part of a sememic graph. Such a formula can be used in a particular conversion whenever and whereever its lexemic prescription can be matched. The formula must show how the part of a sememic structure that it introduces is connected with other parts already introduced by the rules. The logic of such a conversion system is to seek in every way possible to apply all the rules wherever they match portions of a given structure. If the rules are ordered, they must be applied in order. If multiple results are obtained, the lexemic structure submitted is ambiguous. As in other processing, the converter must provide for local ambiguity that can only be resolved in the final result of conversion. In the opposite direction, the same kind of system can be provided. It compares its formulae with a given sememic network, and when it finds a place where one is applicable it introduces part of a lexemic tree. As Martin Kay has pointed out, such formulae can be conditioned to existing situations in both the sememic graph that is to be converted and the lexemic tree that has been established (in part) by application of previous formulae.

EXERCISES

1. Write an algorithm (in Algol) to transduce strings of one stratum into those of another: Read one character of input; consult a current table; get (i) output (any string), (ii) name of table to be used for next character.

2. How could the algorithm of Ex. 1 be used to produce the correct form of the regular English plural (written variety)? Assume input such as "bookZ" or "storyZ".

3. The problem of Ex. 2 is simplified if two consecutive passes are made: the input string is fed to the transducer in left-to-right order, to obtain an intermediate product that is then fed, in right-to-left order, to a second (different) transducer. How would this plan work for English plurals (e.g., "busZ") and regular past-tense and participial forms (e.g., "shamD" becomes "shammed", not "shamed").

4. Write an algorithm for the central logic of dictionary lookup in a tree (cf. Sec. 2.1). Assume one of the tree-storage plans used in Chap. 6.

REFERENCES

"The Organization of Languages—A Stratificational View" (H. A. Gleason, Jr.; *Report of the 15th Annual Round Table Meeting on Linguistics and Language Studies,* C. I. J. M. Stuart, ed., Georgetown Monograph Series on Languages and Linguistics, No. 17, 1964, pp. 75–96).

"On Alternation, Transformation, Realization, and Stratification" (Sydney M. Lamb; *Report of the 15th Round Table . . .* , pp. 105–123).

"The Sememic Approach to Structural Semantics" (Sydney M. Lamb; *American Anthropologist,* Vol. 66, No. 3, Part 2, June 1964, pp. 57–78).

"Prolegomena to a Theory of Phonology" (Sydney M. Lamb; *Language,* Vol. 42, No. 2, April–June 1966, pp. 536–573) offers an approach to stratal conversion using networks of logical units instead of algorithms such as those considered in the present chapter.

"Automatic Phrase Matching" (Gerard Salton; preprints of the 1965 International Conference on Computational Linguistics; *also* RALP pp. 169–188) explains a technique for looking up syntactically related words in a dictionary, and is therefore closely related to stratal conversion.

Chapter 10

CONCORDANCES

The concordance is the indispensable research tool of the novice in linguistics, and every linguist is a novice when he begins work on a new language. The classic method of linguistic research is the study of distributions, and a concordance is nothing else but a tabulation of the distribution of whatever items the linguist chooses to study.

The simple concordance has its place in linguistic research, but so do variations on it. Its near relative, the index verborum, is a simplification; if there is only one way to simplify a concordance, there are countless ways to make it more complex—and, in general, more useful. What shall the unit be? What is the environment of an occurrence? What features of the environment of an item shall control the arrangement of occurrences in the concordance? A concordance is merely a list, arranged in convenient order, of the occurrences of items, each occurrence surrounded by an appropriate portion of its context. But let the definitions of item, context, and arrangement be sufficiently elaborate, and both the cost and the value of the concordance can be made almost as high as the researcher pleases.

I. ITEMS AND CONTEXTS

A concordance is made from a text. If the making of the concordance is to be delightfully simple, the text should be transcribed in printable characters with two levels of boundaries; let us call these unit and context boundaries respectively. We still have great flexibility, for the printable characters can be identified with the phonemes of a language, the graphemes of a writing system, or what have you; and the stretches set apart by context boundaries can be sentences, utterances, lines of poetry, verses of the Bible, or almost anything else. If the text is stored in a catalog structure, each unit between context boundaries will probably be the whole content of a single datum. Unit boundaries can set off words, morphemes, syllables, or any other units of interest.

I.I. The simplest concordances

A simple algorithm for the making of simple concordances has three parts. The first part prepares the text for sorting, the second part is the sort itself, and the third part is listing.

To prepare a text, take one contextual span—that is, a stretch between consecutive boundary marks. If this stretch consists of K unit occurrences, the first stage result will comprise K outputs, each composed of a sorting key and a copy of the complete stretch. Starting at the beginning of the stretch, look for the first unit boundary; take what lies within the stretch up to that boundary and copy it out as a separate record, the sort key; set aside the sort key and a copy of the complete stretch, perhaps adding an identification of the position of the full stretch in the text of the whole. Now, beginning at the unit boundary just reached, take the characters up to the next boundary, make a sort key of them, and proceed as before. The output of this stage is much larger than the input; a contextual span consisting of 7 units goes into the output 7 times.

The sort itself can be accomplished by any reasonable plan. The sort operates only on the sort keys, carrying the associated stretches with them. Some lexicographic order must be assumed, so that the notion of arranging the strings of characters contained in the sort keys alphabetically is meaningful. If the concordance is simple, most of the computing cost comes in this stage.

Listing is another entirely simple operation, given all that we are currently supposing. The sort has brought together all the contextual spans with a common sort key. Print the first sort key in some obvious place; perhaps flush left, perhaps centered, perhaps flush right. Leave blank space above and below it, then begin printing the contextual spans with that sort key, one after another. If all or almost all of them occupy one line or less, print them single spaced; otherwise, leave a blank space after each. Print the identification number of each contextual span at the margin on left or right. After the last contextual span for a certain sort key, print—if you like—the number of occurrences of the unit and then leave blank space before printing the next sort key. The concordance is now finished, and belongs to the ages.

1.2. Simple variations

If a concordance is being made for lexicographic purposes, it may contain an uninterestingly large number of occurrences of a few different units. Thus, for example, the prepositions, conjunctions, and auxiliary verbs are so frequent in most text as to render unnecessary complete listings of their distributions. If the linguist knows what items will be excessively frequent in his text, he can prepare an exclusion list, as it has been called, which adds no great complexity to the operation. As the text is being prepared, each stretch between unit boundaries is compared with the contents of the exclusion list. If it matches an entry on the list, it is not taken as a sort key. This simple device, when its use is appropriate, can reduce the length of the concordance by a third.

Another class of items that may not be interesting is that of hapax legomena. These are the units that occur just once each, and although their occurrences are not a large proportion of any large text, they may amount to half of the distinct units if we count by type, rather than by token. If the simple plan described above is being used, these items cannot be excluded until the stage of listing has been reached, but even listing is an expensive operation, and—if appropriate—perhaps ten percent of the listing can be eliminated by omitting items that are found to occur only once each.

A somewhat more interesting situation is the one that arises when the linguist knows what he wants. If he is studying a definite problem, perhaps a group of words with a common attribute, he can list them for inclusion in the concordance. To implement his wishes, the program that prepares the text compares each unit occurrence with the items on the inclusion list and makes up a sort key only if it is successful. Only a few minutes of computing time is needed to scan a reel of tape on which over a million words of text can be stored. If the inclusion list is short, an enormous amount of text can be screened at relatively little cost, since the major job—sorting—is performed only on the desired material.

If the linguist is studying affixation, it is no great trick to reverse the sort keys, so that the last character of the unit is most significant in the sort. After the sort is completed, the sort key can be turned around again before printing; even if the linguist is working on the terminal portion of his units, he will find it more natural to read them in the ordinary way.

2. CONCORDANCE OF ANNOTATIONS

Concordances are not always made from raw text. Simple strings of characters can be altered or annotated by one or more of several different procedures. One of the simplest is consultation of a dictionary. Since, as we have seen, consultation of a dictionary imposes a segmentation on the input, unit boundaries in the original text no longer have the same status if dictionary lookup is to precede the making of the concordance. The information that can be obtained from a dictionary can enrich the text in many ways; still more is possible with automatic parsing or with annotation by informants.

2.1. Using morphological and lexical information

If the language under study is one with an inflexional system that makes word-and-paradigm analysis appropriate, dictionary lookup can provide for each item both an indication of the word it represents and the place it occupies in its paradigm. Even if the concept of words being inflected through paradigms is not adopted, segmentation into morphemes may well produce an encoded distinction between base, root, or stem elements on the one hand and affixes on the other. This distinction can be used in the preparation of a concordance from the text. If the concordance is being made for lexicographic purposes, the distributions of affixes—or, correspondingly, the distribution of para- digmatic categories—may be of secondary interest. In such a case, the linguist calls for exclusion of affixes when concordance lines are being prepared. All his sort keys are words in one model or stem elements in the other. Since the grammatical information may or may not be of interest, the concordance can be prepared with affixes or grammatical indicia in secondary place in the sort key, or they can be excluded from it. Perhaps, for some purposes, the linguist will give the stem element first place in the sort key, and follow it secondarily with the next following stem element from the text. He might equally well choose the next preceding stem element, for that matter. On the other hand, if the concordance is being made principally for syntactic purposes, the affixes—which may be expected to serve grammatical functions—may be the only elements for which concordance entries are to be prepared. In that case, the linguist will provide an inclusion list of them.

Whatever his purpose, the linguist must deal with the fact that ambiguity is widespread. Most often, consultation of a dictionary leads, at least for some stretches of the text, to ambiguous results. Either a certain stretch can be segmented in more than one way, or, with a fixed segmentation, it is impossible to decide whether a certain seg- mented unit belongs to this word or that, is representing one morpheme or another. Depending on what will be done with the concordance, the linguist may choose to call on an informant here. After the con- cordance has been sorted out, the entries for ambiguous stretches can be listed on work sheets. Informants must then answer the implicit question, resolving each ambiguity in accordance with his (the informant's) understanding of the context. These choices are input to the computer, collated with the concordance, and used to eliminate false segmentations or interpretations; the complete concordance is printed without ambiguities. If the concordance is to be used for local research, and not published, the resolution of ambiguities may be carried out at the same time as other kinds of analysis. Note, however, that sort keys must be prepared in such a way that an ambiguous stretch is sorted into place with other identically ambiguous stretches.

Consultation of a dictionary can also furnish, for example, translations of individual items into another language. The translations can be taken as major or as minor segments of the sort key. The problem of ambiguity arises here also; between any pair of languages, there will be units that are translated with one item in one place and with another item in another place. Again, annotators can be asked to choose the correct translation from a partial concordance in advance of the main print run.

A dictionary can contain an encoded semantical analysis of individual items. For instance, this can take the form of a hierarchical classification of meaning, somewhat like the organized listing in Roget's thesaurus. If the place of the item in the hierarchy is used as sort key, all instances of a given item will be collected together. They will be preceded and followed by occurrences of items with most closely related meaning, and not far away there will be other items with related but slightly more distant meanings. The problem of ambiguity is of course the same as before.

For whatever reason he may use dictionary lookup, the linguist must decide whether the output of dictionary lookup replaces or supplements the input text. The principal argument against supplementation is that the information is redundant. If the dictionary is properly constructed no information is lost when the input text is completely replaced by a string of dictionary entries. On the other hand, the argument in favor of supplementation is that the concordance is to have intensive use by many persons, some of them not thoroughly familiar with the organization of information in the dictionary. If the dictionary output is attached to the input text, so that the concordance contains both, it is accessible to the widest possible audience.

If two or more kinds of information are included in a concordance listing, it is usually wise to keep each kind of information on a separate line. The sortable unit then must consist of the sort key itself, a stretch of input text, and the corresponding items of information taken from the dictionary. These items can readily be placed across the page in such a manner as to fall directly beneath the input unit to which they apply. If appropriate, the line on which the input text is printed can be spaced out, with blanks between words or with blanks between segments identified during dictionary lookup, so as to make the display of associated information more convenient. If a stretch is ambiguous, the alternative segmentations or interpretations can be one under the other.

2.2. Syntactic information

The limit on what can be done with a dictionary is just this: each unit must be interpreted individually. If the interpretation of an item, whether as an individual item or in relation to others, or the arrangement of item occurrences in the concordance, is to depend on context in a direct way, syntactical analysis must be carried out. Automatic parsing, or syntactic parsing by informants, may thus precede the making of a concordance.

The two major virtues of parsing as a preliminary to concordance-making are on the one hand that syntactic function can be used as a controlling variable in the arrangement of concordance entries, and that the context used in sorting can be fixed syntactically, rather than by spatial adjacency.

Dependency theory has one significant advantage over immediate-constituent theory in the making of concordances. It states overtly what elements are adjacent. Each unit in a text has a governor, or else is syntactically independent; each unit can have certain dependents. One very natural way of establishing a concordance is to take the lexical identities of items, the lexical identities of their governors and dependents, and the syntactic functions they serve for one another as controlling variables. These elements can be put into the sort key in different orders for different purposes. For one purpose, the major sort might be by syntactic function; for another, lexical identities might be the major sorting element. But let us take one case for concreteness of illustration. We have input text, performed dictionary lookup, and carried out automatic parsing. We are principally interested in the verbs of the language, which are either independent syntactically or else depend on subordinate conjunctions or the like. As major sort variable, we take the lexical identity of the verb. As secondary key, we take the lexical identity of the item serving subjective function. We may even introduce a tertiary element in the sort key, namely, lexical identity of the first complement. Each entry in the concordance is headed by printing out the verb. Then, flush left on the line, we cause to be printed a subject noun. Beneath that, slightly indented, we print a first complement. Then we show all the contexts in which this verb occurs with this subject and this first complement. Now we list another complement, more contexts, and so on until we have finished with one subject noun; we proceed with other subjects of the same verb, and so on.

We have now come a long way from the simplest concordances. The notion of one level of sorting, i.e. with a sort key containing just one unit occurrence, with a uniform plan plan for making a concordance from everything in a text, seems inadequate. The simplest concordances serve the simplest purposes, and when research on a language begins they are the appropriate tool. Sooner or later, the linguist goes beyond them. At an intermediate stage, a selective concordance, prepared on text that has been processed through a dictionary and perhaps parsing, sometimes with additional annotation by informants, arranged according to a plan specific to the purpose at hand, is the best that can be done. Since a great deal of linguistic research has to be carried out at this intermediate level, calling for study of vast amounts of text, very elegant programs for making tailored concordances are well-justified.

3. PROCESSING TECHNIQUES

The simplest way to make a concordance is one we have already seen. The text is read, unit and context boundaries are identified, sort keys are prepared, and the sort is carried out by a standard program. This plan is workable even for the most sophisticated concordances, but is not necessarily the best. A sort tree (Chap. 2, Sec. 5.1) can be used effectively. The general plan for this kind of sort is to process text until core is filled, write the results on an intermediate tape, and proceed until the whole text has been handled. Then the intermediate outputs are merged, bringing everything into its final arrangement in one sequence.

We must assume that the input, encoded perhaps as described in Chap. 4, contains shift characters and punctuation as well as alphabetic characters. Let us suppose furthermore that shifts and punctuation are not to influence the arrangement of the concordance; but all occurrences of *the* are to be grouped together, whether they appear in the text with initial caps, all caps, no caps, underscoring, preceding quotation marks, and so on. Let us consider what happens if dictionary lookup is not to precede the making of the concordance.

Two large working areas are reserved for the concordance. In the first, a sort tree is developed. In the second, text is stored, but in a special form. As the text is read in, character by character, shifts and punctuation are stripped away. The stretch of alphabetic characters between unit boundaries is processed through the sort tree until the proper cell is found; it is stored therein. The address of that cell is stored in the next available cell in the second, or text, region. If there is any punctuation or shifting attached to this occurrence of the item, the next cell is used to store information about it. Such a cell must be marked, since its content cannot be interpreted as an address. When memory is full, the sort tree is converted into an alphabetical list. Only the links are changed; the stored items remain where they were, hence the addresses in the text list are still valid. Now the first item in the alphabetical list is taken, and the entire text list is scanned for occurrences added. Whenever one is found, an item is constructed, just as we have explained before, complete with sort key; the sort key will be used to control subsequent merging. This scheme requires that the text list be scanned once for every different unit put into the sort tree. Of course, the scanning takes time, and can be avoided, but at the cost of occupying more storage space. For example, a list of occurrences can be attached, by a link, to every cell in the sort tree. After the sort tree has been constructed and rearranged in alphabetic order, these addresses provide immediate access to all its occurrences. Occupying more space at this stage means making more passes during the subsequent merge operations. A balance must be struck, and as computers change—particularly as larger and larger high-speed memories are made available—the appropriate balance changes.

Compromises are certainly possible. For example, only partial addresses can be stored in the list reached from the sort tree; these addresses are taken as starting points for searches, which are therefore shortened.

If two or more kinds of information are being carried, e.g. a source language text and its translation, or input text and the results of dictionary lookup or parsing, an additional block of storage must be provided for the parallel material. If the sort key is to be made up of two or more different kinds of information, perhaps from different categories of input (e.g., from the lexical identity of an item as obtained by dictionary lookup and from grammatical properties of its dependent as computed during parsing) the sort tree may have two distinct levels. It will be remembered that in the ordinary sort tree there are two links: one left and one right. Now it is necessary to provide three links: left and right links to other items of the same kind, and an additional link to the head of a sort tree containing material of a different type. If the tree has only two levels, the lower-level tree has only two kinds of branches. Upon reading in the information about an occurrence, we take the primary information, such as lexical identity, and go through the sort tree to its proper location; there we take the third link and go through the subordinate sort tree with secondary information, for example the grammatical description of a dependent.

4. SOME GENTLE WARNINGS

If a typical occurrence occupies six character positions in the input text, and if a 120-character line is allowed for each context line in a concordance, a complete concordance is twenty times as large as the input on which it is based. A concordance of the *Divine Comedy* runs to 1000 pages of 100 lines each; it is estimated that a concordance of a million words of input text will fill ten such volumes, and a concordance to the complete works St. Thomas Aquinas, 1,700,000 lines of input, will fill 100 such volumes. Publication of a concordance is therefore extremely expensive, and anyone who plans to produce a concordance should make arrangement in advance for publication, lest he discover that his work is to a degree in vain. There are many ways of publishing a concordance, for example on microfilm, and certain methods can reduce publication expense phenomenally.

Only in rare circumstances will one, or ten thousand, occurrences of a given item be useful. One occurrence is insufficient, and ten thousand are overwhelming. The information in a concordance can be limited to what is useful by many different plans. One way is to delay preparation of the concordance until an analytic notion comes to mind, and then to collect from a large amount of text only the occurrences that are relevant to the analysis, with as much context as the analysis requires, and to make the arrangement of the concordance appropriate to the immediate objective. This is in fact a plan that can be overruled only in special circumstances. Where the works of a particular author have literary merit, attracting a wide audience of scholars, giving the public access to a concordance is appropriate. But very often the scholar who thinks he would like to use a published concordance would do best to demand access through a computer.

The remarks in this chapter are made from a linguistic viewpoint; in documentation, concordances (as of abstracts) have served as bibliographic tools. If a text is annotated with psychological or sociological interpretations, concordances can serve the purposes of those sciences. Indeed, it is only by wearing the blinders of a devoted linguist that we are able to bring a chapter on the making of concordances to a close.

EXERCISES

1. Taking letters as unit occurrences and spaces as boundary marks, make a concordance of a text about 50 characters long. What practical value might such a concordance have, if made on a larger scale?

2. Suppose each word in a dictionary were cut into segments representing morphemes, and each segment replaced (or coupled) with a canonical representation. What are some possibilities for concordance making, and some reasonable purposes?

3. A student of literature is asked to discuss a character in a novel (e.g., a heroine). Design a concordance to assist him.

4. A linguist is analyzing the use of a noun case, and has a syntactically annotated text. What kind of concordance does he need?

5. A documentalist ·believes that certain technical terms are ambiguous; each is presumed to be used in several branches of knowledge. He has a collection of abstracts and wants to list, separately for each technical term, a list of all words occurring in the same abstracts with it. Design a program to help him.

REFERENCES

Concordances from Computers (Sydney M. Lamb and Laura Gould; Mechanolinguistics Project, University of California, Berkeley, 1964) describes a set of programs.

"An Inventory of Fifteen Million Words" (Roberto Busa, S.J.: *Proceedings of the Literary Data Processing Conference*, International Business Machines Corporation, 1964, pp. 64–78) describes the work of a large center devoted to the transcription of texts and the production of concordances.

Proceedings of the Literary Data Processing Conference (Jess B. Bessinger, Jr., Stephen M. Parrish, and Harry F. Arader, eds.; International Business Machines Corporation, 1964) contains papers on concordance making and studies of style, etc.

Chapter II

TECHNIQUES FOR LINGUISTIC RESEARCH

Computer programs for some linguistic purposes can be tailored to the special characteristics of particular languages, but when the purpose of the program is investigation of an unknown or only partially known language, such tailoring is clearly infeasible. As Paul Garvin has remarked, programs for linguistic research must be based exclusively on linguistic universals. Clearly the linguist must make some assumptions about the nature of language; when he deals with an unknown language, he faces the risk of assuming too much. He must be circumspect about computer-aided research.

Garvin distinguishes three degrees of computer participation in linguistic research. The lowest level uses the computer merely as a compiler of data; programs to make concordances or maintain dictionaries are effective, but merely clerical, aids. The middle degree is computer testing of information gained in other ways, as when a machine-translation program and table of translation equivalences is tried out on new text. The highest degree is reached when the computer program actually embodies the linguist's analytic ideas; a device that could be parachuted into a jungle to learn an unknown language without supervision would be participating in linguistic research to the highest degree. We may find many intermediate levels, but these three mark the design of computer programs in accordance with meta-linguistic principles, linguistic theory, and—on the lowest level—with practically no theory at all.

I. SEGMENTATION

Materials in an unknown language can come to the linguist with utterance boundaries marked, or without; with word boundaries (or morph boundaries) marked, or not. If the linguist has a collection of utterances, or words, with no marked boundaries for smaller units and no list of units to consult, he generally wants to begin by making cuts and listing the units he discovers. Two procedures are considered in this section. The first is designed for segmentation of utterances; the second is intended to isolate prefixes and suffixes of words.

I.I. Identification of morph boundaries

A procedure like the one described here was proposed by Zellig S. Harris as an explication of one kind of distributional analysis; his paper was written before the introduction of computers, but it calls for data manipulations on a scale that is hardly feasible without automatic aid.

The linguist is given a text transcribed phonemically, with utterance boundaries marked but with no indications of morph boundaries. The objective of the procedure is to establish them and make a list of the morphs occurring in the corpus. Harris's procedure is based on the reasonable supposition that the number of morphs of any given length, K, is very small compared to the number of strings of length K over the phonemic alphabet. The language analyzed must also permit relatively free combination of morphs. Of course, every language imposes certain restrictions on morph sequences; it is only required that sequences be relatively free, as compared with the restrictions that apply within a morph.

The corpus is a collection of utterances. We fix on one of them, beginning with a certain phoneme. Collecting all other utterances beginning with that phoneme, we compute the uncertainty at the next position, that is, we take a numerical measure of the freedom of choice of the second phoneme, given the first. Now, taking the subset of utterances beginning with the same two phonemes that appear at the beginning of the one we wish to segment, we compute the uncertainty of the next transition, and so on. What we expect to find is a steady decrease in uncertainty until we come to the end of the first morph, with a substantial increase at the boundary. If the uncertainty in predicting the $(n + 1)$-st phoneme from the first n is larger than the uncertainty in predicting the n-th from the first $n - 1$, there is a boundary between positions n and $n + 1$. Naturally, all sequences beginning with this specific substring of n phonemes must be segmented at this place, not just the sequence we began with.

Since it must be supposed that there are differences between initial morphs and second morphs in utterances, the proper order of operations is to make one cut in every utterance first, then submit the entire corpus of truncated strings to the whole procedure.

Problems can arise. In a language with derivational or inflectional suffixes, the restrictions encountered after the last phoneme of a stem morph may be as great as at the previous position. Hence, to be reasonably certain of making all appropriate cuts, the linguist must apply the procedure from left to right and also from right to left. Merely going from right to left would have no intrinsic merit, since a language with few suffixes can have prefixes which would make the procedure ineffective in that direction.

Another limitation on the effectiveness of the procedure is that it does not bring to light such phenomena as the formation of words in Arabic by intercollation of consonant sequences C–C–C with vowel sequences v–v: CvCvC. Another procedure could discover that phenomenon, but how many different procedures will be needed to untangle all the compositions of morphs into utterances in the natural languages of the world? The answer is probably that only a few procedures will be required, and that linguists would do well to get them programmed at once.

If word boundaries are marked, as in a written text, the procedure can take each word as an utterance; hence, if there is one, a dictionary of words can be used as the corpus for investigation.

The Harris procedure has been programmed several times, by students who made preliminary tests—generally satisfactory—and had no opportunity to continue by refining their methods and making subtler tests. Although a linguist would today want to define morph in terms of syntactic or psycholinguistic properties, he should not cavil at a statistical procedure able to furnish him a tentative list of items for inspection and study. The procedure will undoubtedly be tested again.

1.2. Stems and affixes

Without pretending that affixation is a universal characteristic of human language, we can nevertheless claim that many languages take stems that carry lexical meaning and affix to them at either end, elements of syntactic importance. The prefixes and suffixes are commonly few, the stems numerous. From this beginning, we can develop a procedure for the segmentation of words in a language of the appropriate type.

To begin the identification of suffixes, let us take a list of word forms in alphabetical order—that is, arranged lexicographically according to whatever plan we choose for the transcription we are using. If two word forms are identical, except that one is longer than the other; the added part is a possible suffix. The longer word may consist of the shorter word plus the suffix. Relying on this pseudo-rule, we produce a list of possible suffixes. Now we examine each word form in turn, testing whether one or more of the tentatively defined suffixes can be matched in it. In any given word form, we may find more than one suffix that could be cut from the end. We may also find that after some terminal suffix has been cut, another might be cut just before it. At this stage, it is hardly even interesting to speak of ambiguity. We want to consider all possibilities, and therefore make all possible single cuts on a word, all possible multiple cuts as well, and enter every remainder as a possible left part of the word.

Several procedures are now open to us. We can take possible left parts as sort key, but carry with each the list of one or more additional segments cut from it. With the new list, we can proceed exactly as before, since we may now find new pairs that differ only in that one is longer than the other. If we repeat this cycle many times, we certainly run the risk of going too far. Sooner or later, we will want to test our results against some criterion.

If we can establish any more logical regularities, they will serve as a check on the segmentation. For example, we can examine the set of items composed of a left part with one tentative suffix. Sorting these by suffix, we can feel confident about the status of any suffix that occurs with a great many left parts. On the contrary, we must feel uneasy about any suffix that occurs with only one or two items out of a long list of left parts. If we find that two suffixes occur with approximately the same set of left parts, we can feel reassured about both of them; they would appear to be systematically related. Perhaps—and this possibility must be checked eventually—they mark different syntactic roles for the composite item. If we find two suffixes that occur with nonoverlapping lists of left parts, we can look for phonological explanations. If we find, for example, that one occurs after consonants and the other after vowels, we can speculate—but eventually we must check this speculation—that they are syntactically equivalent suffixes, different morphs for a single morpheme.

Now, let us consider the set of composite forms that we tentatively regard as composed each of a left part with two suffixes. Sorting again by suffixes, we can check whether any of these composites are identical with one-suffix composites except for the introduction of an additional suffix at the end or between left part and single suffix. Any such pattern will be welcome as evidence that the suffixes identified so tentatively are linguistically real. The same kind of test can be applied here as before, and indeed similar tests can be applied to composites with any number of possible suffixes.

In principle, we are here engaged in doing several things: we are eliminating morphophonemic alternation, classifying stems, and establishing morphotactics.

Stem classification is a matter of determining classes of left parts that take a common set of suffixes or suffix sequences. It must be anticipated that some left parts will not be seen with all suffixes or suffix sequences allowed by the morphotactics. Statistical methods are called for, to determine when it is reasonable to class together left parts that have approximately but not identically the same suffixes according to the evidence available. Automatic classification procedures are perhaps needed here.

Morphophonemic alternations are sought by examining the phonemic properties of environments in which elements occur, examining with particular care pairs of items that occur in mutually exclusive environments.

The morphotactic rules come to light as restrictions on sequence are found. For example, some suffixes may appear only last among all the suffixes of a composite form. Others may occur only adjacent to the stem. Now, supposing that a stem-adjacent class has been established, consider the class of suffixes that occur either adjacent to the stem or following a single suffix of the first group. The linguist will inquire whether it occurs after all of the stem-adjacent suffixes, or only after a restricted set. He will also wonder whether, when it occurs, it appears with all the members of the previously established stem class, and never otherwise. Depending on whether the language has few or many stem classes, few or many suffixes, and short or long strings of them, the establishment of the morphotactics can be exceedingly simple or as complex as the development of a full syntax.

Considering how little investigation has been conducted to date, the best approach to this kind of morphological work seems to be the use of programs for relatively small parts of the complete job, so that the linguist can examine the results and choose the next procedure accordingly. Sooner or later, experience will be gained and linguists can decide whether it is worth organizing the programs for small elements into grand systems that carry out a large part of the work without the linguist's intervention.

2. SYNTAX

During 1961, Paul Garvin and Sidney Lamb independently conducted experiments with automatic procedures for tactic analysis. The problem posed by a text is that there are too many different types, each occurring too seldom, to make complete distributional analysis feasible. The linguist must somehow either begin establishing constructions for a few common types, or begin classifying the multitudinous types into a few categories on the basis of obvious properties. Lamb takes the former course (see Sec. 2.2); Garvin the latter.

2.1. Positional classification

A corpus consisting of utterances, each composed of identifiable morphs, has one very obvious marker in it, namely, the boundary between utterances. With respect to this boundary alone, three positions can be defined: the position at the beginning of an utterance, that at the end, and a position not adjacent to a boundary.

An occurrence of a morph is in one of these three positions; the occurrences of the morph throughout a corpus are collectively in one of seven categories. For one morph, occurrences may be found in all three positions; in any two (there are three pairs of positions); or in just one. It takes only a simple machine procedure to identify each occurrence as falling in one of the three positions, to determine for each morph type what category it belongs to, and then—by a kind of dictionary lookup—mark each occurrence of a morph according to the category to which its type belongs. Thus, Garvin's invention is a way of reducing myriad types of morphs to seven categories, the text from a transcription of morphs to a transcription of preliminary category symbols.

This invention puts the linguist over his initial hurdle. He can now, if he wishes, sort the utterances into lexicographic order by category symbol. He would thus bring together, somewhere in his list, all three-item occurrences composed of (1) an item that occurs only in initial position, (2) an item that occurs in all three positions, (3) an item that occurs only in middle and end positions. Many different procedures might be considered at this stage; among them, the one suggested by Lamb would be a possibility, but Harris's segmentation procedure could also be applied.

2.2. Identification of constructions

Although Lamb's procedure is intended to work without preliminary classification of morphs, it might well be used after Garvin's method had been applied. Let us consider it in the version originally proposed by Lamb.

For every morph type in a text, Lamb counts the number of times it occurs and the number of distinct types that appear on its left and on its right. He supposes that if the neighbors, on either side, are restricted to a small set, the likelihood is high that the item and its neighbors are partners in a construction. This supposition is not certain; one must allow, as Lamb does, for many different kinds of failure of the assumption.

Lamb proceeds by choosing one item, with enough occurrences for some hope of statistical reliability, with a very restricted set of neighbors on one side or the other. This item, wherever it occurs, is taken to be in construction with its neighbor on the selected side. Now, throughout the text, these two item sequences are replaced with a symbol for the newly established construction. (In fact, the new symbol is added; no information is discarded. It will be simplest, for our exposition, to think of the pair of items as replaced with a single symbol.) A replacement of this kind changes the count of neighbors for other items in text. Also, the construction symbol itself must be added to the list of types, and neighbor counts must be made for it.

The same process is repeated for another item with its neighbors. When a construction is formed with one partner itself a construction, the internal construction must consist of an item together with a list of neighbors. The items on the list are now said to belong to one class, and all their occurrences are replaced in the text with a class symbol. Again, this replacement changes neighbor counts.

Among the possible events in an analysis of this kind, there is the discovery that a construction was formed by mistake. For example, an English preposition might be associated with its right neighbor, which is sometimes a noun, sometimes an adjective, sometimes an article. When a class of nouns is formed, it may be recognized that an element of this class is practically the only neighbor available on the right for an article. Lamb's procedure allows for recognition of such a happening, and can replace the article in a previously established preposition-plus-right-neighbor construction with article-plus-noun as a new construction.

Lamb has experimented with his procedure but never on a very large scale. The results he has published have demonstrated a certain merit for the procedure, and further experimentation should be expected.

2.3. A self-correcting parser

When an imperfect parser is applied to a text, it makes mistakes. There is no infallible way to describe what a mistake is, since even informants may well differ about the proper analysis of a given sentence. Consultation of informants is indeed one way to establish, with a clear degree of certainty, what mistakes are being made. It is not the only way, however, since fairly weak assumptions about the nature of good parsing can lead to automatic error-detection schemes.

For example, if the parser finds no correct structure for a sentence (or if a parser with some measure of likelihood for its different results finds none with high enough probability) there is excellent reason to believe that something is wrong. If a parser capable of assigning more than one structure to a sentence actually does so, and certainly if it applies many different structures, there is again reason to suspect an error, since the naive view is that sentences in natural text are generally unambiguous. If a parser develops many partial structures, and eliminates most of them in the end, it may be suspected that there are mistakes in the part of the system that produced the unwanted analyses, although that is not so certain. Pendergraft has suggested a method based on principles like these.

Let us assume that we have available a large corpus of text, a dictionary, a grammar, and programs for dictionary lookup and parsing. Applying these systems to the text, we can obtain automatically partial, complete, or multiple analyses of the text. Next, applying an algorithm based on error detection principles like those just described, we can mark the sentences, and perhaps even points within sentences, where the parser probably made mistakes. The text, analyzed and marked, is then submitted to a program designed to produce revisions of the dictionary and the grammar. Applying these revisions, we can restart the entire system. Pendergraft's aim is to operate in cyclic fashion, occasionally adding new text, until an extremely satisfactory dictionary and grammar are produced.

One of the key elements in Pendergraft's research scheme is automatic classification; it has the purpose of assigning items that display similar properties to one class, excluding from that class items manifesting different properties in the same body of data. Thus, for example, a research algorithm might undertake to improve the classification of items reflected in a given dictionary by taking into account places where existing class assignments had allowed a parser to form structures that were subsequently deemed to be mistaken. Naturally, whenever such a change is made in a dictionary, corresponding changes must be made in the grammar to show that, for example, a rule formerly assumed to apply to all nouns is henceforth to be applied only to members of a noun subclass.

The methods of automatic tactic analysis that have been described are all based on assumptions about the statistical properties of item distributions in natural text. All recent theorization in linguistics requires that tactics on one level be related to the structure of the next higher level. Thus, syntactic structures are expected to correlate with semantic structures. Furthermore, psycholinguistic evidence is now regarded as relevant to decisions about syntax. What the informant considers correct is, *prima facie*, the right answer. Future extensions of research procedures will undoubtedly take these considerations into account more fully.

3. SEMANTICS

Tradition says that one linguist, who had heard enough of frequency counts, predicted ironically that when the counters had grown tired of tabulating single items they would begin to count words by pairs. He was, of course, exactly correct. He probably did not foresee, however, what purposes would be served.

One objective of word counting, rather recently recognized, is the classification of texts by subject matter. The problem may seem peculiar to the librarian, yet it is also a fitting one for linguists. The way an author or speaker uses words is conditioned by his professional dialect, the stylistic requirements of the setting in which he speaks or writes, and by the exigencies of his subject matter. It is therefore necessary, for some kinds of linguistic research, to conduct separate analyses of texts within single professional specialties, settings, and topics. The methods of automatic classification provide a means for sorting out texts into these categories, taking the individual text as an item to be classified and admitting as relevant properties of a text the occurrence counts for the vocabulary items it contains.

Such a method amounts implicitly to pairing each word in a text with the collectivity of all the others in it. For other purposes, it is more appropriate to pair an occurrence of a word or morpheme with one or a few other occurrences adjacent to it in the sense of lying within the same sentence, contiguous before or after, or syntactically related.

I conducted a very small experiment of this sort in 1958; its design is similar in spirit to the methods of Harris and Lamb outlined above. Taking one scientific paper, I cancelled all function words and reduced all other words to canonical forms. A typist then prepared index cards, placing on each card one pair of consecutive, normalized items. By sorting alphabetically, I obtained counts for all distinct pairs, and laid out a diagram showing the high-frequency pairings. The general result was that the network of interconnections was semantically comprehensible. The specific result was that almost all of the very high frequency pairings were lexically idiomatic; that is, the high frequency combinations were words coupled with a special meaning for the author of the paper.

One of the special advantages of dependency theory is that in studies of word co-occurrences it provides a syntactic definition of adjacency. A governor is adjacent to each of its dependents; each item in text is adjacent to its governor. An immediate constituent model, in which an item can be partner in construction with a complex entity, does not give an equally simple definition of item-item pairing. Frequency counts taken over governor-dependent pairs provide an opportunity to test the hypothesis that the meaning of an ambiguous item is by and large determined by its syntactic environment. When a text has been annotated syntactically and also marked to show, at each occurrence of an ambiguous item, what meaning it has, automatic routines can collect the occurrences of an item, each with its syntactic neighbors, and sort them by meaning. Thereafter, automatic classification methods can be applied to bring out whatever relationships exist between meaning and environment.

Information about meaning can be obtained through studies of paraphrase and of translation. One technique is to select a word for study and then choose a collection of sentences in which it appears. Next, submit each sentence to one or more informants and ask for a list of items that can replace it, without change of meaning, in the given sentence. This step establishes a list of possible replacements for the item over all the contexts initially tabulated. Now the informants must be asked to specify, for each sentence and each possible replacing word, whether the replacement is acceptable. This step systematically verifies that all allowable replacements have been considered in all contexts. The results of these data collection procedures can be arrayed in a matrix, each row being identified with one sentence and each column with one possible replacement. If there is a way to rearrange the rows and columns so that all of the replacements in one consecutive group of columns are acceptable in all of the contexts represented by one consecutive group of rows, and nowhere else, and so on for other blocks of rows and columns, it can be said that each block of words is a set of synonyms for one meaning of the original word, and each block of sentences a range of contexts in which the word takes on that meaning. Such a result is indeed gratifying, but must be regarded as a halfway point; the next problem is to establish correspondences between properties of the sentences and properties of the meanings the basic word has when it appears in them. Stefflre has experimented with several words in different languages, and has obtained strikingly clear results for the first part of the process.

A procedure like Stefflre's could be used in studies of translation; instead of replacements in the same language, the informants might be asked for translations into another. It is also possible sometimes to obtain original texts and translations prepared professionally, that is, for a customer whose purpose was not linguistic research but rather to understand the contents of the document originally written in a language unknown to him. Translation is an art of sufficient complexity and mystery to make the study of relationships between original text and professional translation a rewarding endeavor. Mersel has investigated techniques for automatic matching as a first step. Obviously, the investigator must not assume that a text and its translation contain the same number of sentences, and certainly not the same number of words.

Mersel's procedure begins with automatic dictionary lookup. Starting with one of the texts, he consults a dictionary in which one or more equivalents in the second language are given for each word in the first. Provision must indeed be made for the case where the dictionary contains no entry for some source language items. Now, the text in the source language has been replaced with a string of sets, some possibly null, of items in the second language. Take the first sentence in each text, and attempt to match each item in the target-language sentence with an element of one set in the representation of the source-language text. No two items in the target text can be matched with elements in one set of the source text. Matching will not be complete; professional translators are not so slavish as to translate every word into a single word. A numerical measure of completeness of matching is noted for the first pair of sentences, and the second pair of sentences is attacked. If the match on the second pair of sentences is not good enough, several possibilities must be considered: the second sentence in one text may match part of the first sentence in the other text; the second sentence in one text may match the second and third sentences in the other; or the translation may simply be very free. When matching has been completed as well as possible throughout both texts, the unmatched items can be submitted to a linguist for study.

It should by no means be assumed that, if two matching sentences contain each an unmatched item, one is a translation of the other. The translator may well have adopted a turn of expression that includes equivalents for all but one of the items in the source sentence, discards it, and introduces an entirely new element. Mersel reports instances of such pairs. The matching process can be made far more elaborate, if necessary. For example, dictionary lookup and automatic parsing can be performed in both languages, and the structures matched in accordance with a translation table (cf. Chap. 13, Sec. 2.1). As larger volumes of text in several of the languages of the world come to be available in computer-usable form, procedures like this will have great practical significance for the linguist interested in comparative and typological studies.

REFERENCES

"Research Methodology for Machine Translation." (H. P. Edmundson and David G. Hays; *Mechanical Translation*, Vol. 5, No. 1, July 1958, pp. 8–15; *also* RALP pp. 137–147) describes a way of combining machine procedures with human effort in the development of a language description.

Design for a Language Processing Laboratory (Robert F. Simmons; SP-1366, System Development Corporation, October 1963) sketches the elements of a facility for linguistic research.

"Computer Participation in Linguistic Research" (Paul L. Garvin; *Language*, Vol. 38, No. 4, October–December 1962, pp. 385–389) expounds the three degrees.

"From Phoneme to Morpheme" (Zellig S. Harris; *Language*, Vol. 31, 1955, pp. 190–222) explains the procedure mentioned in Sec. 1.1.

"Automatic Linguistic Analysis—A Heuristic Problem" (Paul L. Garvin; *1961 International Conference on Machine Translation of Languages and Applied Language Analysis*, H. M. Stationery Office, London, 1962, pp. 655–671) presents the method of Sec. 2.1.

"On the Mechanization of Syntactic Analysis" (Sydney M. Lamb; *1961 International Conference on Machine Translation of Languages and Applied Language Analysis*, pp. 673–684, H. M. Stationery Office, London, 1963; *also* RALP pp. 149–157) gives the method sketched in Sec. 2.2.

"Quarterly Progress Report, 1 May 1965–31 July 1965" (To the National Science Foundation; from the Linguistics Research Center, The University of Texas, Report No. LRC 65 NSF-25) contains a brief description of the methods attributed to Eugene D. Pendergraft in Sec. 2.3.

Some Eliciting and Computational Procedures for Descriptive Semantics (Volney Steffire, Peter Reich, and Marlys Wendell; manuscript) describes the method of rearranging word-sentence matrices.

A Manual for Automatic Dictionary Revision (Ramo-Wooldridge, Canoga Park, Calif., September 1960) describes the text-translation matching procedure ascribed to Mersel.

"Application of the Theory of Clumps" (Roger M. Needham; *Mechanical Translation*, Vol. 8, No 3/4, June–October 1965, pp. 113–127) is a general discussion of one method for automatic classification.

"Experiments in Semantic Classification" (Karen Sparck Jones; *Mechanical Translation*, Vol. 8, No. 3/4, June–October 1965, pp. 97–112) reports studies of synonymy.

Measurement of Similarity Between Nouns (K. E. Harper; RM-4532-PR, The RAND Corporation, May 1965) shows that synonyms, antonyms, etc. are similar in the sense that they govern the same adjectives and genitive nouns and depend on the same noun governors.

Some Combinatorial Properties of Russian Nouns (Kenneth E. Harper; RM-5077-PR, The RAND Corporation, September 1966) reports the varying tendencies of nouns to govern genitive dependents.

Dynamic Simulation of Historical Change in Language Using Monte Carlo Techniques (Sheldon Klein; SP-1908, System Development Corporation, December 1964) attacks one of the many kinds of problems not touched upon here.

"The Logic of Cognate Recognition in Historical Linguistics" (M. Kay, RM-4224-PR, The RAND Corporation, September 1964) lies in an area not examined here.

Chapter 12

DOCUMENTATION

An author sits alone producing a manuscript. He writes sometimes from an outline and sometimes from a full knowledge of his subject matter, with no more than a general idea of what he will say. He may know the earlier literature in full, or only what he has done himself. He may write for the most knowledgeable members of his speciality as most narrowly defined, or for as wide a portion of his discipline as he can reach, or for novices just beginning in the field. His manuscript when he completes it may give facts, one after another, or a description of experimental equipment and procedure followed by a statement of results, or a complex theoretical construction. Whatever he writes and whatever he writes about, if he contributes in some way to man's understanding of the universe, his product belongs to the vast domain of scientific documentation.

The document he produces must be made available, in many different senses of that term, to the audience that can use it. It probably must be reproduced in many copies. Someone must summarize it, someone must list it among references to documents similar in content or intention, and at least one copy must be preserved into the furthest future.

These are the elements of the documentation industry. The editors and publishers of scientific journals, abstracters and indexers, librarians and the operators of scientific information centers all belong to this industry. So for that matter do many secretaries and printers. If we omit the term "scientific" and think of documentation in its broadest sense, all forms of writing except those produced solely for the pleasure a reading gives to the customer belong within its domain. Thus, the law, analyses of art and literature, theology, philosphy, and most writing on engineering and the practical arts belong in this field.

I. FOUR DISTINCTIONS

The most important distinction to be made in analysis of documentation processes is between the content of documents and their linguistic expression. Only the most sophisticated system conceivable could make the separation in practice, analyze the text of a document and extract from it a representation of its content so that thereafter the expression could be neglected. Indeed, this alone would not be enough, for the form of expression has value in itself. The difference between a good textbook and a bad one is as often the way the author puts his ideas into words as the choice he makes of information to include. Hence until it is possible to construct elegant expressions of content it will not be desirable in some applications to store only content, for that would lose the stylistic contribution, the expository value of the work analyzed.

Granted then that expression is to be retained, there is still a sequence of distinguishable levels at which text can be transcribed. Is a graphic representation to be retained, as on the printed page or microfilm image? Is an encoded representation, including or excluding controls that can be used to remake a graphic image, the proper version? Should parsing be carried out and only enough information be retained to synthesize the same text? Should still more upward conversions be performed? We cannot be certain in advance that one level will be correct for every documentation center, or for every part of the international documentation system.

As long as the independent contributions of authors, published one by one, retain their identity, it is appropriate to make a second distinction, namely between presentation of the complete contribution and indication of its content. Indications may take such diverse forms as extracts, abstracts, or index entries. Some abstracts do no more than say where, in the whole field of science, the contribution lies; others undertake to summarize the actual contribution offered; if an abstract gives some expert's evaluation of the accuracy and importance of the original author's results, it is a review.

A third distinction that must be considered is between announcement and retrospective search. If contributions are made one at a time, many persons will want to know something about the new contributions of the day, the month, or the year. But from time to time a newcomer will want to scan backward in time, seeking out all of the contributions in the history of his subject. His subject may be narrow or broad; he may define it to include elements of several old topics. His field will be hard to separate from closely related ones, and the potentially relevant contributions from the past will be exceedingly numerous. Retrospective search sometimes calls for very powerful tools.

Finally, there is the customary distinction between the computer as clerk and the computer as higher-level linguistic processor. Even where the computer serves as no more than "reactive typewriter" it is useful because it eases the burden of perfecting the graphic image of the linguistic expression of a text. Simple programs can help prepare copy, justify lines of type, rearrange index entries and abstracts, and make up pages. Attempts have been made at automatic indexing, abstracting or extracting, and subject classification. One goal set for the future is a kind of automatic encyclopedia.

2. PUBLICATION SYSTEMS

The use of computers for insertion of controls into a stream of text, so that pages of print take on the size and appearance desired, began changing the publishing industry about 1964. Early experimental systems showed how the computer can be used to aid author and editor, but the whole process of copy preparation, from first typing to final typesetting, can be linked together by transfers of text on magnetic tape or over wires. The computer can link primary and secondary publications; abstract bulletins and other bibliographic periodicals can be produced from copy collected automatically during original publication. But the secondary materials can move directly to libraries on magnetic tape, ready to serve as input to the local catalog.

2.1. Copy preparation

The elementary problems of text acquisition are treated in Chap. 4; good solutions to them, supplemented with a file-management plan and a refined scheme for revision of stored text, give the author a powerful tool. Automatic copy-preparation systems enter text into machine storage the first time it is typed. Thereafter it can be altered or rearranged, but it is not retyped in full. If typewriters are linked directly to the computer, text is probably stored on discs. If the typewriter is linked only indirectly, tape storage is satisfactory. Whatever the physical medium, something like the catalog system is needed to organize the file. It must be assumed that many typists, each working over a period of weeks or months on several different texts, will have access to the same major file. It is necessary to identify each text—article in preparation, chapter of a book, letter or memorandum, etc.—and to identify subunits. Two or three levels of organization within the document are desirable, to simplify the making of alterations. These units can be pages, paragraphs, and lines; or they can be numbered main sections, numbered subsections, and sentences. In fact, the wise designer probably provides considerable freedom to the individual user of his system. If the catalog system is used, each line or sentence is the content of a datum; several classes of label data are provided so that the user can impose structure in his text.

The essential operations in a copy-preparation system are probably those of setting up a new text, inserting a line of text at any specifiable place, replacing a line, deleting a line, and transferring completed text to an output system. With just these operations, the typist can start a new text, and add to it line by line until the first draft is complete. Then, during the same session or after an editorial reading, the typist can delete, insert, and replace lines to produce a revised draft. Finally the text is passed to the next stage in the documentation sequence.

The typist's deskside machine may be conventional in the sense of using keyboard, mechanical printer, and paper, whether it is connected directly to the computer or merely punches a paper tape. If the machine is connected to a computer directly, it may use no paper at all, but instead display what is typed on a cathode ray tube. In either case, the typist must be able to introduce three kinds of information: text, instructions, and identifiers of location. The direct-coupled typewriter has the advantage of being able to return information immediately; when the typist needs to alter a line or make complex changes in the text, seeing the results of the alterations as soon as they are performed is a convenience.

Sometimes it seems wise to design a copy preparation system around a standard keyboard, not demanding installation of extra keys or operating features. In that case, the conventions that allow the typist to distinguish for the machine between the three kinds of information call for good human engineering. Many techniques are available. One character can be deleted from the set on the keyboard and used exclusively to indicate that instructions are to be entered. Thus in effect it is a shift key, giving a new interpretation to whatever is typed next. If locations are taken as part of the instruction shift, any convenient notational system can probably be used without difficulty. The instructions can be named with short, hopefully mnemonically efficient character sequences. Locations can be determined either relatively or absolutely, that is to say, relative to the beginning of the whole text or relative to current location. Both schemes may be useful at different times, therefore may well be included in the system. The typist who makes a mistake halfway across the line will be happy to have a way of getting into the instruction system without cancelling the half line already typed; thus, if instructions can be started only when the carriage is flush left the typist loses the advantage of being able to cancel that character. But then, perhaps the typist is well-served if only one or two special instructions can be given in mid-line. Or, for that matter, perhaps a backspace-typeover convention can be established, allowing the typist either to go back and delete or go back and retype within a single line.

If the typist is to receive information from the computer, the cathode ray tube has the advantage of presenting it much more swiftly than the typewriter mechanism. At least a paragraph can be displayed on a small screen, and it is to be expected that approximately as much as appears on a standard page will be displayed to tomorrow's typist. Alterations can be made when ordered and the result presented for inspection immediately. Location can be determined by some mechanism, whether key, light pen, or joy stick, that moves a pointer over the display tube.

The character set is a perpetual problem for the typist. Technical material uses more characters than any single typewriter can supply, and polyglot texts call for accents, digraphs, and even whole new alphabets. It is possible to provide cathode ray tube displays with infinite character sets; typewriters with interchangeable type faces can do the same thing. There remains the question of how to maintain the correlation between keys and characters. One answer is to have complete sets of characters and for each set an established correlation of character with key and shift; then the typist begins by informing the computer what character set is to be used. If the character set is to be changed, the typist must enter a new instruction mode and announce the change. Certainly with the cathode ray tube it would be possible to enter an instruction announcing that a certain key in a certain shift is to be treated temporarily as correlated with an arbitrary character needed for the job in work.

The cost of operating the system need not increase very much with a great expansion in the number of available operations, and many of them contribute to its effectiveness as a typist's aid. A curious example is the expansion of abbreviated input. For example, in typing the present textbook it might be convenient to define "cp" as a typist's abbreviation for "computer". Instead of typing out the eight-letter word in full, the typist could key just two characters whenever the author used the word; a program furnished with a dictionary of abbreviations peculiar to the given text would then make the expansion. In English and other natural languages, the universally common words are spelled with few letters each; frequency is inversely related to length. In individual texts, some frequent words are long, but the words that can usefully be abbreviated differ from one text to another. Hence each author must decide for himself what to abbreviate.

Programs for controlling the apparatus of citations are also useful. An author may want to list his citations in order of first mention in the text, or alphabetically; in either case, adding or deleting references is troublesome, since a single insertion or deletion can force renumbering throughout the text. If the typist can put an ambiguous mark in the text at each place where a citation is wanted, and then introduce the citations in random order but with identification corresponding to the marks put in text, the program that ultimately alphabetizes or serializes the citations and converts the arbitrary marks in text to their final form is earning its way.

Instead of adding or replacing whole lines, the typist can more conveniently work with single words. A program to open up the datum containing a full line, count off words, and operate with them is not too complex. The system could also include programs to find common spelling errors, point out repetitions of words, and so on. In fact, the whole range of mistakes listed by the investigators who wanted computers to evaluate the essays written by students seeking college admission can be brought to the author's attention if his secretary uses an automatic copy-preparation system.

The business of an author is to prepare a text that says what he wants to say, to mark it off into sections as he wishes, to show the places where footnotes and references are required, and transmit just that much to an editor. What he transmits is customarily a manuscript—typewritten sheets of paper. But the paper copy can go with a version on paper or magnetic tape. The editorial function is that of revising; to perform it, the editor needs only a computer system that permits alteration of a stored text, and presentation of the revised text for approval.

The task of a designer is to specify page size and layout, type faces and sizes, and other details of the presentation of a text. Up to this stage, it is unnecessary for the stored text to be marked off into lines or pages, nor should functions be indicated implicitly by features of presentation. The publisher's or typographer's computer system converts the internal representation of textual units and their functions into controls for a graphic presentation device. The designer gives parameters for translation of the function *subheading* into controls for typeface, size, and position. Likewise, such other functional categories as *footnote, abstract,* and so on must have their translations.

Up to this point, the catalog system could well be used, and the text could be stored in sentence data. The typographer's program must run sentences together, one after another, to make paragraphs; it must establish paragraph indentation, even out line lengths by putting blank spaces of appropriate width between words; and it may need to hyphenate words in order to satisfy the esthetic criteria of the publisher. In languages that determine hyphenation graphemically, these programs are trivial. English hyphenation is partly graphemic, but partly lexical; the places where a string of letters can be broken are sometimes determined not by what the letters are, but by what words they represent. English hyphenation must be done by dictionary lookup—or by trickery.

2.2. Secondary publications

Scholarship requires easy access to its literature. Secondary publications ease the scholar's path. Some, like *Current Contents*, furnish titles of articles as soon as possible after first publication, so that the scholar may be aware of new works. Abstract bulletins provide more detailed indication of content, and the publication requires more effort. Indexes are published for individual books, for volumes or extended runs of individual journals, and for abstract bulletins. Library catalogs furnish information about the library's holdings, and include indexes by author, subject, and title.

How and where the information contained in secondary publications is to be produced has been a matter of much dispute. In the past, librarians have produced their own catalog cards, relying in part—in some libraries—on the Library of Congress as a central producer. Abstract journals have been written by volunteers, but some primary journals require authors to write abstracts. Indexing has been done to a large extent by professional indexers.

There is a growing tendency for primary journals to require of authors all of the secondary information about each contribution. Thus, in addition to the basic manuscript, the author is asked to provide index headings, an abstract, and possibly other information. What the author submits is put through the complete editorial process, including judgment for adequacy.

If authors universally provide such information, and put it into the same copy-preparation system they use for their manuscript, or if it is acquired for automatic processing when it is first set in type, it can be transferred from the editorial computer used in primary publication to the one used in producing secondary publications. The only problem is how to select, in a flow of text, the information that properly belongs in secondary publications, and how to isolate such units as the last name of the first author. The most convenient technique is clearly to use functional coding as part of the input. This coding can be implicit; thus, if the title of the contribution is typed flush left, on the first line of the manuscript, or if it is made the content of a datum in catalog format, it can be identified without difficulty. The editors of secondary publications must of course screen what is submitted to them, since they cannot assume that every article published in certain journals, and no articles published in other journals, are to be included in their coverage. Except for this screening, secondary publications derived automatically from primary flows should appear about as soon as the primary contributions themselves.

Another kind of secondary publication, long familiar to lawyers and transferred to science, is the index by publications cited. A review paper discusses and cites the earlier literature; subsequent papers in the field reviewed are likely to cite it. A citation index makes it possible to find them. In some instances, virtually the whole literature of a new field can be located by consulting the citation-index entry for one paper of high originality.

Experiments suggest that the connection structures formed by citations can be simplified and rationalized. The user of a raw index can miss items he needs merely because they fail to cite any of the publications he looks up; he may have to look up many cited publications to find an adequate part of the literature he needs. In a simplified and rationalized index, he would get automatic help. He might, for example, look up a publication and find that it belonged to a certain cluster. Turning to the entry for the cluster, he would find listed both the members of the cluster and publications that cited any of them—or, perhaps, enough of them to confirm a substantive relationship.

With new methods for the preparation of index and abstract bulletins, the classic methods of distribution become obsolete. The declining cost of computation makes such operations as merging monthly indexes into cumulative bulletins economically feasible. Abstracts can be set in type for monthly publications, sorted by topic and cumulated at year's end, and reprinted in bibliographies for narrowly defined subject areas. Without computers, the high clerical costs of rearranging the copy, resetting the type, and remaking the indexes would be prohibitive. Even though these costs decline, those incurred in printing, binding, and shipment cannot but remain high.

But information can be disseminated in other ways. One is in microform. In principle, photocomposition could yield a microform master as readily as one of normal size; all subsequent operations would be less expensive. Another possibility is to distribute indexes and abstracts encoded digitally. In a large research center, files on magnetic tape or other media can be used for retrospective searches and also for current awareness services.

A plan with much to recommend it is the reduction of subscription lists; in the limit, an abstract bulletin can be published for a single user. This plan has been called selective dissemination of information. The interests of each client must be recorded in terms that correspond to the indexing or subject classification of new material. Were the plan to be followed on a very large scale, clusters of users would surely be identifiable. Each cluster would constitute the subscription list for an abstract bulletin that should remain small because it had to include only items of interest to a handful of specialists. A bulletin of this type could cover a specialty in depth, add related material from other specialties, and cover a much broader field by noting only surveys and contributions of very great novelty and significance. (Presumably abstracts of no interest to anyone would not be printed at all.)

Finally, there is the possibility of letting the user sit at a console through which he could reach all extant indexing and abstracting. The files required would be large, but not unthinkably so. One set of files could be linked to a large network of consoles, serving a huge population. Reproduction costs would be eliminated; when the costs of consoles, files, communications, and computing fall low enough, this plan will surely be adopted on a large scale, if not universally.

2.3. Libraries

In the traditional view, a library is a collection of books, periodicals, pamphlets, and—more recently—microforms, phonograph records, motion-picture films, and other objects of intellectual content. The catalogue of a library is a statement of its holdings. Customarily, library catalogues show what periodicals are held, but do not index the content of journals.

Copy-preparation systems can be used for construction of card catalogues. It is only necessary then that the material be presented in the format of the 3 × 5 card. Computer-printed sheets can be cut apart and collated with existing cards. However, it is not necessary that card cataloguing be continued permanently. Other physical forms, such as the book, are feasible.

If a library uses a card catalogue, new cards are produced, collated, and that is all. It would be almost twice as expensive to maintain duplicate card catalogues, where a library serves users scattered over such an area as to suggest such a plan. Renewal of old cards, as when they become illegible or obsolete on account of the information they present or the format they use, is also expensive.

If a bookform catalog is used, all of the information in it must be retained in computer storage—perhaps on magnetic tape—so that new entries, even if printed separately for immediate use, can be collated in the computer for production of an occasional cumulative index. Thus, a bookform catalogue might be reprinted in full once a year. The librarian must be prepared to pay for reprinting the whole catalogue at such times. However, producing multiple copies is economical—a university might have a complete catalogue of its library in every department. Or selection can be imposed: the physics department can have a complete catalogue of the physics collection.

When many secondary publications are produced by automatic systems, local librarians will be able to consider the use of entries prepared outside, selected from magnetic tapes provided by central producing agencies, and combined with similar flows from other centers. If a common format is not used for all such secondary flows, and if the indexing systems are not mutually compatible, the librarian's task will be difficult. Moreover, information from the library's order department must also be in the computer, to control the selection properly.

If a librarian can obtain and merge flows of information from many major centers, he may choose to neglect the difference between what he holds and what he does not; his catalogue may become rather a catalogue of what there is than one of what he has. In that case, it becomes extremely large. But at that stage, it is perhaps wiser to purchase the catalogue from a central agency than to produce it locally.

3. CONTENT PROCESSING

3.1. Abstracting

Abstracts can be written by the author of the article abstracted, by a volunteer, or by a professional abstracter. None of these plans is quite satisfactory, however, and many attempts have been made to produce abbreviated statements of the content of an article automatically. The techniques used most widely are based on selection of key sentences from the text of the article. Thus they are automatic extracting methods, rather than plans for abstracting and stating in more general terms than the author himself uses what his purpose and findings are.

H. P. Luhn was apparently responsible for the notion that words of intermediate frequency in a text mark sentences of high interest. The commonest words in a text are either grammatical words or general terms; rare words—from the point of view of a single text—presumably do not name concepts of much importance to the author. A sentence containing an unusual concentration of medium-frequency words might therefore be expected to state one of the author's major points. Experiments of this kind have been somewhat unsatisfactory. First, the connection between words and concepts is not so simple. Since an author may use different phrasings to express the same notion, he may in fact not express his main ideas with medium-frequency words. Furthermore, he may never express his main idea clearly in a single sentence. Again, it has not proved possible to select a few sentences from a long article; even reasonably understandable extracts have run 10 percent of the total length of the article. Extracts of this kind tend to be disjointed; following an author's ideas from a sentence taken here and another taken elsewhere is hard for the reader.

Other investigators have used word pairs, but Harper's discovery that a word pair used early in a text can be replaced by a representative of the combination later shows one reason why this system should not be expected to give much better results than the first. Another technique is to use first sentences of numbered sections, to take section headings, and so on. These are techniques that make use of superficial, or low stratum, characteristics. Great success could not have been predicted for them, but the evidence seems to be that they worked rather badly after all.

A plan exists for a better method, but there are still too many gaps in our knowledge of language to make it workable. A high-quality automatic abstracting system might begin by text input, dictionary lookup, syntactic parsing, and stratal conversion to obtain a representation of the text in the form of sememic networks for individual sentences. The next step would be to couple together the sememic networks of all the sentences in the text, obtaining one network covering the entire article. In this process, it would be necessary to establish the centrality of ideas. What sememes and relations among sememes convey the main point? There is little doubt that authors generally have techniques available for showing what is central to their papers, but these devices have not been tabulated and categorized. Another way of saying the same thing is to remark that intersentence connections are a new problem in linguistic research. Progress toward automatic abstracting seems to depend on the success of research into the structures of texts.

3.2. Indexing and classification

Automatic indexing has been attempted by schemes very similar to automatic abstracting. Words or word combinations of medium frequency in a given text, or of unusually high frequency in the text as compared with the whole language, have been taken as key terms.

Concordances of titles and of abstracts, usually with entries for common words suppressed, have been called indexes of key words in context, and have gained considerable popularity. The computing cost is extremely small, and they can be distributed rather rapidly after the input material is available.

Use of unstandardized terminology in an index imposes a great burden on the user. Different authors use different words to express the same idea, and the user of a KWIC index or any other kind based on the graphic shapes of items found in the texts indexed must think of all possible expression forms. Dictionaries of index terms, listing alternative expression forms but making one of them standard, have been constructed for several fields. They are often called thesauri. In addition to providing for computer listing of titles under standard terms, rather than the word the author chooses, a thesaurus can give the index user additional guidance by pointing to related terms, partial synonyms, and terms of narrower or broader significance. The establishment of a thesaurus, and maintenance thereafter, is a very difficult job. Computers are used for the purpose, and can be of more than clerical help.

One standard technique is to aid the indexer in controlling his vocabulary by application of automatic classification techniques. Words are the objects to be classified, and the documents in whose titles or abstracts they appear are their properties. Thus words are classed together if they co-occur in many abstracts. Each class can be presented to the designer of the index, who determines whether the class is useful, and if so provides a standard term to replace all its members in indexing.

Problems of homonomy arise when the author's language is to be replaced with standard terminology. The same word, used by different authors, may be replaceable by different index terms. Schemes for automatic elimination of homonomy in this application generally depend on examination of context. Thus, a word is assumed to refer to term A or term B depending on whether certain key words appear with it in the title or abstract of the document.

Some of these indexing techniques can also be applied to the task of subject indexing of books. Author indexing is a reasonably simple task, since the graphic shapes of names are generally distinctive. For example, there is capitalization, or the presence of initials. Topical indexing can be performed by making a selective concordance, consulting a dictionary for standardization of terms, and so on.

If fully automatic indexing is not satisfactory to some customer, aids to the indexer can be imagined. With cathode ray tube displays, an indexer can go through a file of abstracts or the text of a book using a light pen or other cursor to mark phrases that he wants to index. These phrases can be alphabetized for him, inverted if he wants to use noun rather than adjective as main key, and so on. This is simply another instance of replacement of human clerical efforts with computation.

We have seen that index terms can be classified according to the documents in which they appear; documents have also been classified according to the words that appear in them. This is essentially a standard application of clumping, factor analysis, or some other procedure. A few points are worth noting. The terms that serve as most powerful discriminators of major categories of documents may not be very useful in discriminating finer subcategories. Thus, the term *computer* might distinguish articles on computation from articles on psychology, but if *computer* was then used to subclassify psychological documents the results might prove less satisfactory to users than if other terms were chosen that could not distinguish psychology from computation because of their use with different meanings in the two fields. Again, word combinations may be more discriminating than single words, but once it has been established that a word combination is valid in a text it may be appropriate to count the frequency of the combination as equal to the frequency of one of the member words, unless the component words are also used in that text in other known combinations.

REFERENCES

Machine Recording of Textual Information During the Publication of Scientific Journals (Lawrence F. Buckland; Inforonics Inc., Maynard, Mass., May 1965) reports experiments in keyboarding of text for primary publication in such a way that data for secondary publications can be picked out.

Computer Typesetting: Experiments and Prospects (Michael P. Barnett; The M.I.T. Press, Cambridge, 1965).

"Comparison of the Results of Bibliographic Coupling and Analytic Subject Indexing" (M. M. Kessler; *American Documentation*, Vol. 16, No. 3, July 1965, pp. 223–233) gives statistics regarding two methods for grouping journal articles.

"UDI-5, An Advanced System for Selective Dissemination of Information" (A. B. Barnes, A. A. Briggs, J. Gauss, and A. Resnick; *Proceedings of the 19th ACM National Conference*, Association for Computing Machinery, New York, 1964, Paper L2.2).

Libraries of the Future (J. C. R. Licklider; The M.I.T. Press, Cambridge, 1965) surveys improvements that could be made, mostly by use of computers.

Intrex: Report of a Planning Conference on Information Transfer Experiments (Carl F. J. Overhage and R. Joyce Harman, eds.; The M.I.T. Press, Cambridge, 1965) sets forth a plan for experiments with a computer-based library.

"The Automatic Creation of Literature Abstracts" (H. P. Luhn; *IBM Journal of Research and Development*, Vol. 2, No. 2, April 1958, pp. 159–165) is another of the author's suggestions for use of vocabulary as a clue to meaning.

"Problems in Automatic Abstracting" (H. P. Edmundson; *Communications of the Association for Computing Machinery*, Vol. 7, No. 4, April 1964, pp. 259–263) sketches a variety of methods.

Keyword-in-Context Index for Technical Literature (KWIC Index) (H. P. Luhn; Report RC-127, Advanced Systems Development Division, International Business Machines Corporation, Yorktown Heights, New York, 1959; *also* RALP pp. 159–167) is the original publication on its subject.

"Progress in Automatic Information Retrieval" (Gerard Salton; *IEEE Spectrum*, Vol. 2, No. 8, August 1965, pp. 90–103) surveys the field and discusses the author's SMART system.

"The SMART Automatic Document Retrieval System—An Illustration" (Gerard Salton and Michael E. Lesk; *Communications of the Association for Computing Machinery*, Vol. 8, No. 6, June 1965, pp. 391–398) gives further details.

"Answering English Questions by Computer—A Survey" (Robert F. Simmons; *Communications of the Association for Computing Machinery*, Vol. 8, No. 1, January 1965, pp. 53–70) leads the reader into an area not treated here. The objective is that of a documentation system; the methods are like those of automatic translation (Chap. 13); but theories outside the domain of linguistics are needed.

Chapter 13

AUTOMATIC TRANSLATION

According to rumor, a short paragraph about machine translation appeared in *Popular Mechanics* around the turn of the century. In the world of tomorrow, it was predicted, any patron of the telephone system would be able to dial any point in the world through a central switchboard that would translate what he said into his target's tongue and translate what was said to him back into his own language. If the rumor is true, that may be the first recorded mention of automatic language processing. During the 1920's and 1930's, two inventors are reported to have attacked the problem, one in Russia and one in France. In the late 1940's, attempts to make the computer translate began in the United States, and work was soon under way throughout the world. Thus, machine translation was pursued as an end in itself before the more general field of computational linguistics was mapped and named.

From a later perspective, machine translation is only one application of the computer as a language processor, and a difficult one at that. There seems to be no limit to the amount of information about language that can be consumed by translating systems, but translation is wanted at a low price. The problem is clearly one of engineering: how can enough information to deliver satisfactory products be brought to bear at a cost the customer will pay?

I. A MODEL OF THE TRANSLATION PROCESS

According to Bar-Hillel, a good human translator should be equipped with fair knowledge of both source and target languages and also of the special subject matter of the documents to be translated. In addition, he should have general background knowledge and intelligence. It is unlikely that a computer will be equipped with all these faculties in the near future, yet Professor Bar-Hillel's statement is a recapitulation of the various models that have been proposed for automatic translation.

I.I. Monolingual and interlingual operations

Translation has been described as an unnatural task. Most human beings are probably able to speak and understand only their native languages, and that has probably been true since the race began to speak. Every person who talks is under constant pressure to make himself understood. In the long run, this constant pressure should force any single natural language into patterns that are comprehensible to a typical human speaker. Within one language, semantic patterns must be consistent, and their relationship to speech sounds must be reasonably simple. Relative to this standard, the amount of interlingual communication that goes on is so small that one might set at zero the pressure toward mutual comprehensibility of different languages. The fact that the human species is adapted to monolingual communication is prima-facie evidence that a machine might be constructable that would produce intelligible sentences and comprehend them. But there is scarcely any evidence to show that translating machines can be built at all.

What has to be translated is surely the content of the texts submitted. If a text is regarded as a string of words, as it surely can be, it must be true that the content of the text is represented by the words and their order. But this representation of content is highly indirect, according to contemporary linguistic theory, for several levels of analysis intervene between content and word. Transfer from one level to another in a given language, or monolingual processing of the kind we have examined in previous chapters, is surely natural. An attempt can be made to translate at any level; the designer of the translation scheme therefore faces a major decision: how much monolingual analysis and synthesis will yield value for money? It is probably true that translation is least unnatural at the highest level; the ideas in a text are probably so shaped by human nature, by the common culture of western civilization, and by other factors as to be approximately translatable. The words and word orders of one natural language are, by contrast, peculiar to it. The diagram in Fig. 50 displays some of the alternatives open to the designer.

The diagram in Fig. 50 is not identical to, but is based on, diagrams presented by Yngve, Pendergraft, and Lamb. In it we can see what several schools of linguistics would agree on, but not all of the special attributes that they would, individually, insist on. Instead, the details necessary for a concrete diagram have been established in a way that may be equally unacceptable to them all. Any linguist well versed in a particular theory will have no difficulty in translating the diagram into his own terms.

According to the diagram, there is a major distinction between processing in accordance with linguistic theories and data, and extra-linguistic processing. A place is granted to consultation of an encyclopedia; if the author of a document relies on his reader's background to

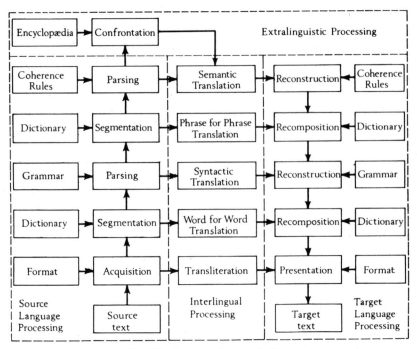

Fig. 50—Automatic translation

such an extent that definitive interpretation of his meaning is impossible without that factual knowledge, a translation system must fail if it has no body of facts available.

The linguistic processes are divided (vertically, in this diagram) into those based on knowledge of the source language, those relying on knowledge of the target language, and those linking the two. But in each column there are several processes, not just one, so that levels can be seen. Finally, each level of processing involves both an algorithm and a file of information.

1.2. Levels of translation

Let us follow some of the paths in this diagram. Except for a possibility that we shall consider later, and which is irrelevant to translation anyhow, all paths start with source text, in the lower lefthand corner of Fig. 50. The text is acquired for processing by a system like the one described in Chap. 4. Even an acquisition system, which deals only with the graphic shapes of characters and features of arrangement on the input page, requires information that can be supplied to it in the form of tables. Using these tables of code interpretations, it normalizes the source text and delivers it to one of two other processors. There are several of these choices, and in each case we assume that only one of them is followed.

To begin with, let us assume that the output of the acquisition processor goes to interlingual processing. On this level, interlingual processing can consist only of transliteration. Each character and feature of arrangement of the source language is replaced with a character or string of characters, or feature of arrangement, of the target language. After interlingual processing, there always follows a process peculiar to the target language. In this case, there is nothing to do but produce a text, following the format instructions supplied which take into account the characteristics of the presentation device. In short, the path we have traced does nothing but make a copy of the source text, using the characters and arrangement of the target language.

If the source text, once acquired, is relayed to the next higher level of source-language processing, it is matched against a dictionary, by one of the techniques described in Chap. 5. The text, taken as a string of characters, is segmented into substrings, for each of which some arbitrary label is substituted. Each segment can be the representation of a word or morpheme, and the segmentation can be done with or without recognition of ambiguity. We describe translation on this level generically as word for word, even if the units translated are not words. The translation substitutes the arbitrary labels of one language for those of the other. Note that even if the segmentation leaves no ambiguity, a given unit of the source language may be translatable with any one of several target-language units. The translation process determines, as far as possible, which one of those units to use in a given context. The target language recomposition process replaces each arbitrary label with a string of characters; for a given label, there may be alternative spellings, among which choice is to be made according to the context.

If higher level processing is performed, it proceeds in the manner we have already discussed. Parsing is carried out by an algorithm of one of the kinds discussed in Chaps. 6, 7, and 8; the result of parsing can be submitted to another dictionary lookup, as described in Chap. 9, and the results analyzed for consistency and interrelationships by another parser. After the highest level of source-language processing, translation takes place, and a sequence of target-language processors develops the output. Different schemes of translation are characterized by the level to which they go in the diagram.

According to the diagram, five levels of source language processing are possible, and only the highest yields an output that can be confronted with encyclopedic knowledge. In principle, it would be possible to add more levels, to write algorithms that did the work of two or more of those shown in the diagram, or to design an encyclopedia for confrontation with the results of lower-level processing. Indeed, many of these alternatives have been tried. The diagram is an idealization, and should not be adopted without further thought as a plan for action, much less taken as denying the workability of any other approach.

The intelligence of Bar-Hillel's translator presumably is applied in the confrontation of a new source text with an encyclopedic store of factual and theoretical knowledge. It takes but little intelligence to determine whether an encyclopedia contains a fact stored in the same terms as are used in a text. But what if the encyclopedia contains a generalization, of which the textual assertion is a particular instance? The truth of the instance follows from the generalization, provided the algorithm for confrontation has a way of matching general and particular statements. Or what if two or more statements in the encyclopedia can be combined, by some rule of argumentation, to yield some textual assertion? The making of such deductions, and in particular the selection of those facts from the encyclopedia that lead to the statement submitted for testing, is a complicated business. For the present, let us return to linguistic processes, and examine this model of translation from sememic and transformational points of view.

2. THE TRANSFORMATIONAL MODEL

This section does little more than hint at the work a linguist must do if he proposes to design a translating machine in accordance with the principles of transformational grammar. At the lowest level, there is little to be said; let us begin at the level of grammar and parsing.

The single processor devoted to parsing in Fig. 50 would, for the transformationalist, be divided into several smaller elements. As recounted in Chap. 8, the grammar would include a covering surface grammar, used by one element of the parser to produce at least those surface structures needed for a given input string. The grammar would also include transformation rules, stored in reverse form. The parser would therefore submit, to a higher level source-language processor or to a translator, base P-markers—constituency diagrams with all transformations undone.

2.1. Syntactic translation

The best way to conceive of base P-markers, in the context of syntactic translation, is probably to assume that they contain specific identification of lexical items, clear indications of what rules of the base grammar were applied, and at what position, and possibly indications of some transformations (in particular, those that would be optional if such special markers were not included). The work of syntactic translation then consists of finding, for each element of a base P-marker, a set of possible translations. Note that this includes translation of lexical items as well as translations of rules and transformation markers. The translation of lexical items is not the same as if word-for-word translation were being performed, since any "word" is a carrier of both lexical and grammatical information; the process of parsing can be assumed to reduce two words that differ only syntactically to a single lexical item.

At this level, reconstruction consists of finding choices from among the alternative translations of individual items that fit together to make a complete base P-marker, on which transformations can be performed to produce a surface marker. For example, reconstruction might begin with consideration of the various rules offered as translations of the original rule in the source-language base P-marker. Each of these rules expands a starting symbol into a string of symbols, some of which may be optional. It need not be the case that the same elements are optional in the source-language rule and in each of its translations; if in the source language rule there is an optional item, there can be two different rules for translating it, one providing translations of all the obligatory elements in the expansion, the other providing translations of those and also the optional item as an obligatory member of the expansion. Another possibility is that one of the category symbols in the expansion of the source-language starting symbol can be translated with any one of several category symbols in the target language. The source language element is expanded, by means of a rule that has its own translation. The illustration in Fig. 51 shows how this kind of problem can be treated. Figure 51a shows a base P-marker in the source language; two rules are involved, those listed in the source-language column of Fig. 51c. Each has a translation, as shown in the second column; the translation of the first rule, however, allows either Y2 or Y3. Furthermore, the symbol-translation table (Fig. 51b) allows for the translation of X0 by Y0, of X1 by Y1, and of X2 by either Y2 or Y3. But when the reconstruction program comes to translate the second rule, it finds that there is no corresponding target-language rule expanding Y3; hence Y2 must be chosen, and the only complete translation of Fig. 51a is the target-language P-marker shown in Fig. 51d. Note that the order of categories need not be retained from one language to the other. The target language equivalent of X3 is Y5,

XO
X1   X2
X3   X4

(a) Source-language P-marker

Source	Target
X0	Y0
X1	Y1
X2	Y2, Y3
X3	Y5
X4	Y4

(b) Symbol translation

Source	Target
X0 → X1 — X2	Y0 → Y1 — {Y2, Y3}
X2 → X3 — X4	Y2 → Y4 — Y5

(c) Rule translation

YO
Y1   Y2
Y4   Y5

(d) Target-language P-marker

Fig. 51—Syntactic translation

and that of X4 is Y4, according to Fig. 51b. If X3 is expanded by another rule, the translation of that rule must expand Y5; if X3 is a terminal node, the lexical item there must be translated at Y5.

Another problem is that a rule may have to be translated by a complex of rules. For example, suppose that the source language has a rule expanding some element into a string of three category symbols. The translation of that rule might do the same, but it might equally well establish that the original symbol is expanded into a string of two category symbols, one of which is further expanded into two.

Another case that might arise is the appearance in a translation of a category symbol that is not the translation of any single category symbol in the source-language P-marker. For example, suppose that an adjectival element in English is translated into French by a rule that expands adjectival element into adjective base plus gender element plus number element. In the simplest instance, such elements are mere dummies, causing transformations to be applied subsequently in target-language reconstruction. This is not necessarily the case however, since such an element may be chosen freely, in so far as syntactic consider-ations apply, from some set of alternatives. In translation from English to Russian, for example, any aspect might be equally grammatical, so that no Russian transformation could be expected to determine aspects. The choice of aspect, however, is undoubtedly meaningful. It has been pointed out repeatedly, for example by Mel'chuk, that every language has its own specifications of certain meanings that must always be expressed. The problem arises in slightly different terms when we reach semantic translation; for the present, we can only say that some special devices may permit valid decisions in certain instances. For example, the choice of aspect may condition certain selections, as of adverbs, in Russian. The choice of adverbs, however, is determined in translation by the content of the source-language sentence. Thus, if the wrong aspect is chosen, reconstruction fails when the grammaticality of the adverb is tested.

In general, reconstruction proceeds by the development of a number of P-markers, some of them blocked before completion, and others developed completely. If the base grammar of the target language is taken to be context sensitive, these context sensitivities are checked at this stage. Reconstruction continues with the application of transformations. It ends with submission of a surface P-marker to the recomposition program.

As in word-for-word translation, recomposition fits together lexical items. This time, however, it does so under the control of a surface P-marker. Lexical items have been carried forward from the translation stage, and tested during reconstruction for consistency with the syntactic context in which they appear. The dictionary now is used to obtain spellings for them, and selections from among alternative spellings are made in accordance with the syntactic context as well as the linear context of the terminal string. The problems of presentation are no different in the transformational model from what they were in word-for-word translation.

2.2. Semantic translation

In the transformational model, a base P-marker can be submitted for further processing prior to translation. The dictionary shown at this high level in Fig. 50 consists of partial specifications of P-markers, including specifications of lexical items. It can do two things. One is to replace combinations of lexical items, as developed in the base P-marker, with single items, or with different complexes; this stage deals with idioms. The other thing the dictionary does is to provide the information necessary for semantic parsing. What happens on the highest level is a consideration of whether the semantic features associated with the various lexical items in a base P-marker are compatible, in view of the syntactic relations assumed among them. It also seems likely that the transformational view will eventually distinguish semantic relations from syntactic. Semantic translation replaces the features and relationships of the source language with those of the target language. Again, coherence must be checked. There is, however, a possibility that must be remembered. If the universal features of human language are of the right kind, the coherence rules of the source and target languages in any translation scheme will be identical, and the semantic features will be the same. In that case, the result of semantic parsing in the source language is identical to the input to recomposition in the target language.

If semantic parsing can be performed at all, it will provide a version of the content of a text that is independent of the source-language grammar. It may not be quite independent of monolingual charac- teristics, but it would certainly have this property: any meaning that is contained in it will be contained explicitly. Thus, if the information needed to determine aspect of a Russian verb is present, it is findable. There remains the possibility that such information is altogether absent. We will consider later what good engineering practice would be in such a situation.

3. THE SEMEMIC MODEL

It would not be to the point to go through the translation model a second time in so much detail, since many of the problems that must be dealt with are the same regardless of theoretical orientation. Further- more, the stratificational view of translation is very close to its general view of linguistic theory, as presented in Chap. 9.

The output of a parser is, in one version of stratification theory, a dependency tree. Each node is labeled with lexical and syntactic information; the lexical information identifies an item, but the items are distinguished from one another only to the degree necessary given what the dependency tree altogether tells about the syntactic position of the item. As in the transformational model, lexical items need not be distinguished from one another at this stage merely because their syntactic possibilities are different. Syntactic translation translates the grammatical and lexical information, node by node, separately. Recon- struction then attempts to produce a coherent dependency tree in the target language. In this case, it is perhaps not so reasonable to talk about rule-for-rule translation. The individual items are translated individually, and the grammar of the target language provides the rules by which they must be related. For example, a Russian sentence might include a noun serving subjective function for a verb and simultaneously governing a participial modifier. In Russian, the modi- fier might fall before the noun. The Russian subjective function can sometimes be translated into English with the subjective function, and participial modification can be translated by participial or clausal modification. The reconstruction program would determine whether a lexical item, translating the Russian noun, could be found capable of serving the subjective function and simultaneously governing either the participial or clausal function. It might turn out that the participial modifier could only follow its governor in English. Given possible translations of functions, the grammar of English would be called on to provide a rule for each node allowing the complex of functions surrounding the node, leaving an acceptable order for the elements with different functions, and specifying grammatical forms for the individual items.

In the stratificational model, the higher level dictionary lookup called for is one pairing sememes with their lexemic representations. The dependency tree is segmented into partial trees each representing a sememe, and translation at this level replaces the sememes of the first language with corresponding sememes in the target language. If parsing is performed after this dictionary lookup, its object is to determine semotactic well-formedness, and to establish the sememic relations that obtain in the source-language text. The translation supplies for each sememe and each sememic relation a list of equivalent sememes or relations, or of complexes of sememes in relation to one another. Reconstruction produces a well-formed sememic network in the target language and thereafter the operations are those of Fig. 49, as discussed in Chap. 9.

In fact, the stratificational model of translation consists precisely of a sequence of upward conversions in the source language followed by translation of the highest stratum and downward conversions in the target language.

According to stratification theory, an encyclopedia would best be stored as a sememic network. In that case, confrontation of text with encyclopedic store is a matter of matching or in some manner comparing textual sememic networks with those stored as an encyclopedia. Furthermore, the source text can be used to introduce new information into the encyclopedia by the upward conversions shown on the left in Fig. 50, and the encyclopedia can be reduced to textual form by starting at the top of the diagram and going down through the processes on the right.

4. ENGINEERING

The general model displayed in Fig. 50 can be understood in several ways. It provides a framework in which linguistic theory can be brought to bear on problems of translation, and it also suggests to the engineer charged with the development of an operating system what components he must have. The engineer must deal with three kinds of information. First, he must know his market: what is wanted, and how much of it. Second, he must know what the field of linguistics can provide at the moment: what dictionaries, grammars, semantic analyses, and so on exist, and what more can be obtained for what cost. Finally, he must know what hardware can be obtained and what relative costs are associated with internal processing, transfers among various kinds of storage, input and output operations of different kinds, and so on. His task is to put these intellectual and mechanical components together in a way that will satisfy his customers. Confronted with such a task, a good engineer becomes an inventor, adding many special tricks in an attempt to get more than a pure scientist would deem possible.

4.1. General considerations

Clearly, any machine translation system must include components for the acquisition of source-language text, the presentation of target-language products, storage of files, and some logical processing. The designer must determine how much capacity and power he requires, and devise an arrangement of equipment to suit.

For extrinsic reasons, he may be forced to purchase all the equipment he will need and assemble it in a single room. Or perhaps he can share some of his machines with other users; for example, the acquisition and presentation equipment might be shared between the translation facility and a publishing operation. If his storage and processing equipment can be used part of the time for other work, he may be able to afford a much larger, more powerful machine than his own work would justify. A big computer has a large capacity, perhaps more than needed for translation, but it has a larger range of instructions, larger storage for programs and data, and other advantages that may make its use highly profitable if it can be occupied for enough hours per day.

The choice of computer is linked with decisions about how processing will be batched, and how storage will be handled. The size of the complete translation program depends on how many levels of monolingual analysis are to be performed; the size of the files that will have to be consulted also depends on the number of levels, but in addition on diversity of languages and of subject fields. The designer can choose between putting more programs or more files into high-speed storage; he certainly needs magnetic tapes, disc files, or some other form of supporting storage. If he must work with a small processor, he has little freedom in making this choice, but if the processor is large he may have enough freedom to make the decision important and difficult.

If he can store programs for the entire translation process in high-speed memory, the designer can plan on sentence-by-sentence translation. Then when dictionary lookup yields ambiguous results, parsing—following just behind—can eliminate some of them as they appear.

Likewise, the ambiguities left by parsing the first few words of a sentence can be reduced by higher level processing and therefore be prevented from increasing the complexity and processing time in the latter part of the sentence. A system that works in this manner must include a way of consulting files—dictionary, grammar, and so on—without excessive loss of time, since there must be repeated consultations during the processing of each sentence.

The designer's other alternative is to batch the text, bring one file at a time into high-speed storage, and at each stage process one batch of text against one linguistic file. Thus, he performs dictionary lookup in one step, parsing in another, and so on. As long as transfers between secondary storage and high-speed memory are expensive, this plan is likely to be advantageous, even though it does not permit immediate elimination of ambiguity and does require reading and writing text on magnetic tape between successive processes.

No matter how large or small his computer, the engineer may be forced to adopt one plan rather than another to satisfy his market. For example, if the translation system is intended for the support of face-to-face communication, so that text is acquired sentence by sentence from conversations as they go forward, and each participant depends on computer output to understand what the other party is saying, the processing can only be done sentence by sentence. Reliance on human intervention for help in translation can force the design in either direction (see Sec. 4.2).

The acquisition system can consist of an automatic reading machine, or of typists operating paper-tape typewriters or consoles directly coupled to the computer. The more powerful and sophisticated systems are attractive, but they are not economical unless their capacity can be used either by the translation system or a group of users including it. In some situations, the designer may choose to contract for acquisition of text by a service bureau, which can accept the responsibility of finding other users for its equipment.

The presentation system wanted for translation output is just the kind needed in any publishing operation. In translation, there may be the special problem of reassembling illustrations taken from the original text with translation of the source-language copy, but this is only a minor variation on insertion of illustrations in original publications. The designer may choose to include an editing console, where the reinsertion of illustrations can be controlled by a human operator.

When the engineer has considered the requirements of his customers, and knows what degrees of promptness and accuracy they require; when he has examined the state of linguistics, and decided what level of linguistic processing is possible and necessary; when he has decided where the translation will be performed, and what hardware will be required; then at last he can design a translation system and begin to assemble the parts. Before reaching a final decision, he will probably develop several alternative designs and estimate the cost and effectiveness of each. Before the academic linguist decides that his own situation is more comfortable than that of the engineer, let him remember that similar decisions must be made, on similar grounds, when a laboratory for computational linguistics is established in a university. In the university laboratory, the range of work to be performed is presumably so much broader than the single task of machine translation that the decision is inevitably more difficult.

4.2. Use of human operators

Unless overriding extrinsic considerations force him to do without them, the designer can consider the use of human operators at any place in the translation system. He can make the entire automatic processing system an aid to a human translator, he can produce a complete translation automatically but submit it for human editing, or he can rely on human operators only to supply new information when the system requires it.

If the system is conceived as an aid to human translators, it is little more than a copy-preparation system with dictionary lookup as a supplementary feature. The translator sits at a console reading a source-language text and typing its translation. What he types is translated as draft copy, which can be printed for inventory or review, revised, and ultimately printed on publication masters. On finding a word or phrase of which he is unsure, the translator types a control character and then the item for which he requires assistance. When the program receives the control character, it initiates dictionary lookup; the entry found is typed on the console. The entry need not be a unique and exact translation; presumably what the translator wants is a range of choices, perhaps with some suggestions about how to choose among them. The translator indicates his choice, and goes on with typing the translation. This kind of system is most advantageous when well-qualified translators are available, but the flow of material to be translated is so technical and so diverse in content that the translators cannot be expected to know the vocabulary thoroughly.

In general, the work of a human translator is subject to review by editors; the product of an automatic translation system will similarly call for review until the art is very highly developed. The draft translation can be presented at cathode ray tube consoles, where the editor can make revisions directly into the computer. Or they can be printed as proof copy, on which the editor can mark the revisions he wants to make; the revisions must be typed in as corrections to the draft stored in the computer, and merged with it before final printout.

Because any natural language is a very large and complex object to describe, and because languages change with time, translation systems will always require improvement and revision. Even if a translation system is designed to operate automatically from acquisition of source-language texts to presentation of its product in a form suitable for direct publication, it must have provision for asking the help of a translator when difficulties arise. The human expert can sit before a cathode-ray tube, or examine printed interrogation sheets. The system can ask him to choose among alternative P-markers or dependency trees; it can offer him source-language sentences with translations varying in some word or phrase; it can ask him for grammatical or semantical characterization of unknown items; or it can request grammatical explanations for sentences it cannot parse. His answers become part of the permanent file of the system. Such collaboration will raise many serious problems which as yet remain to be enumerated; whether they will be solvable is still unknown.

4.3. Linguistic engineering

Machine translation is on the one hand a way of putting together all of the systems we have seen in previous chapters; Fig. 50 gives a place to virtually everything we have seen how to do. There is more to it than that, however. The object of assembling a machine translation system is to produce translations, no more and no less. Given such an objective, the engineer wants to do as good a job as possible, at reasonable cost. To devise a system that produces the best possible result for the investment calls for the implementation of as many special tricks as possible.

Suppose, for example, that the investment allowable permits only word-for-word translation. To achieve complete syntactic translation might produce a substantially better product, but at a far greater cost. If only a little extra money is available, the engineer will use it in attempts to improve word-for-word translation without demanding of his system that it obtain a complete parsing of every input sentence.

One of his tricks is to store some idioms in the dictionary. The idioms that can be stored are those that occur in fixed order in text; if order is variable, or if the elements of the idiom are inflected, the matching will be too complicated. On the other hand, some sequences that would not be considered idiomatic if parsing were carried out may well be taken as idiomatic in this kind of system. With parsing, translation of individual items is controlled by syntactic context. Without parsing, an item must be considered idiomatic if its translation, variable with context, can be controlled by taking note of its neighbors.

Depending on the details of the system, it may be possible to make some slight changes in word order. Thus, the case endings of an inflected language may be translated by prepositions, unless there is a preposition in the immediate neighborhood in the source text; the preposition may be placed in front of the noun, or in front of items nearby that clearly are associated with the noun, even if complete parsing is not undertaken.

To continue, suppose parsing is feasible but nothing beyond that except what can be done at low cost. Perhaps the designer is convinced that something like transformational theory is the proper approach to analysis of language, but cannot do translation on the basis of transformational parsing because the information required is not at hand and cannot be obtained with the money available and in the time allotted. In that case, the parser may be somewhat superficial, and the grammar designed to make translation as satisfactory as possible—in contrast, if transformational parsing is intended, the surface parser and grammar used with it will be designed to simplify transformational analysis. An engineer accustomed to thinking in such terms may come to believe that the truth about language is nebulous and unattainable; he may even come to doubt the good faith of those who say that his surface parser, although it produces reasonably good translations, is not a true description of the source language. If he does adopt such a position, he is losing sight of his own purpose and of the difference between practical and pure science. On the other hand, if linguists, devoted to the pursuit of truth, denigrate the engineer's work, they too are missing the difference in objectives. It would be vain to design a parser with exactly the structure necessary for semantic analysis when there was no time or money to produce a semantic description of the source and target languages, and the output of the parser would be used for a long time only for syntactic translation.

Some of the other tricks that the engineer must consider involve statistical regularities. For example, if the translation of an input unit is more often one thing than another, the engineer is wise if he cannot do better to supply the more common translation in every occurrence. Naturally, if the two translations are almost equally frequent, it would be foolish to adopt a plan that leads to error half the time. On the other hand, if the difference in frequency is great (for example, if the word is given one translation correctly 90 percent of the time, and another translation only 10 percent of the time) it would be foolish to insist on giving both translations in every instance. Even better, the designer may be able to find a translation that is quite satisfactory in the more frequent context, and not very unsatisfactory in the rarer situation. Such considerations apply not merely to the translation of lexical items, but to decisions that must be made during parsing, and to the translations of syntactic rules.

At the highest level shown within the region of linguistic processing in Fig. 50, there is still room for engineering. That is, semantic translation as represented there calls for application of whatever tricks the linguist has at his command to avoid the necessity of going to an encyclopedia unless an encyclopedia, and a system for confronting text with the knowledge it contains, is physically available. A pure linguistic semantics may well exclude certain regularities that are entirely explainable on the basis of facts about the real world, on the grounds that the encyclopedia is the proper place for explanation of such patterns. But a semantic system to be used in utilitarian processing may constrain its analyses by demanding that they fit certain real-world conditions that can, with high probability, be taken for granted in interpreting source text. Beyond that, the engineer may choose to store a moderate amount of encyclopedic information, and to use a relatively simple technique for applying it in processing, rather than do without any at all. He would of course prefer to guarantee absolute perfection, but it will surely be a long time before computers, or human operators, can guarantee absolutely perfect translations. In the meantime, there are many customers whose needs are urgent and who can be satisfied reasonably well with the best that good engineering can make of existing linguistic knowledge.

REFERENCES

Machine Translation of Languages (William N. Locke and A. Donald Booth, eds.; John Wiley & Sons, Inc. New York, 1955) contains several papers of historical interest.

"La Machine à Traduire Française Aura Bientôt Trente Ans" (Michael Corbé; *Automatisme*, Vol. 5, No. 3, March 1960, pp. 87–91) describes a machine built by Artsrouni for the 1937 World's Fair.

Perevodnaya Mashina P. P. Troyanskogo (D. Yu. Panov, ed.; Academy of Sciences, Moscow, 1959) describes a machine built by Troyanskij late in the 1930's—and the difficulties put in his way by hard-headed engineers who disagreed with his linguistic theories.

Language and Information (Yehoshua Bar-Hillel; Addison-Wesley Publishing Company, Inc., Reading, Mass., 1964) contains, on p. 212, the author's list of qualifications for a good translator.

"The Nature of the Machine Translation Problem" (Sydney M. Lamb; *Journal of Verbal Learning and Verbal Behavior*, Vol. 4, No. 3, June 1965, pp. 296–311) develops the stratificational model.

"A Framework for Syntactic Translation" (Victor H. Yngve; *Mechanical Translation*, Vol. 4, No. 3, December 1957, pp. 59–65; *also* RALP pp. 189–198) proposes a model with recognition and construction routines for source and target languages, a structural transfer routine, and specifiers as the items transferred from one routine to another.

LIST OF COMPUTER INSTRUCTIONS

Let a, b, c, and d denote the contents of cells A, B, C, and D respectively.

Instruction	Page	Description
ADD (A)	10	Add a to the content of the working register.
AND (A)	81	Put 0's in the working register wherever cell A contains 0's. Leave the other positions unaffected.
GOTO (A)	10	Transfer control to location A.
INDEX (A, B, C, D)	77	Transfer control to location D if $a + b \leq c$, and to the next instruction otherwise. Replace a with $a + b$.
MULT (A)	25	Multiply the content of the working register by a. Place the result in the working register.
OR (A)	81	Put 1's in the working register wherever cell A contains 1's. Leave the other positions unaffected.
READ (A, B, C)	47	Read tape from unit a into storage beginning at cell B. There are c cells available.
SLC (A)	21	Shift the content of the working register to the left a characters.
SORT (A, B)	11	Hypothetical subroutine.
SRC (A)	21	Shift the content of the working register to the right a characters.
STORE (A)	7	Store the content of the working register in cell A.
STORE (A/B)	20	Store the righthand 6 bits of the content of the working register in the b-th 6-bit segment of cell A. Leave the other positions of cell A unaffected.
SUB (A)	25	Subtract a from the content of the working register.

SWR (A)	7	Set the working register to the content of cell A.
SWR (A/B)	20	Set the righthand 6-bit segment of the working register to the content of the b-th 6-bit segment of cell A. Leave the other positions of the working register unaffected.
TRANS (A, B, C)	7	Transfer control to location B if a is smaller than the content of the working register, to c if larger, and to the next instruction if equal.
WRITE (A, B, C)	47	Write the content of c cells, beginning at cell B, on unit a.

Relative addressing

When an address is given as A(B), the address used is obtained by adding b to the numerical address of cell A.

INDEX

Following a page number, f means figure, r means reference, and e means exercise. Thus, 131 (e 2) refers to Ex. 2 on p. 131.